The
IMPLICATIONS
of INERRANCY
for the
GLOBAL CHURCH

*The truthfulness of God's Word defended,
explained, and extolled by authors from
17 countries across the globe*

12-19-16

Faculty and Graduates of
THE MASTER'S ACADEMY INTERNATIONAL

General Editor Mark Tatlock

The Implications of Inerrancy for the Global Church
The truthfulness of God's Word defended, explained, and extolled
by authors from 17 countries across the globe
by The Master's Academy International

Printed in the United States of America

ISBN 9781498425834

Cover by Xulon Press

www.xulonpress.com

TABLE OF CONTENTS

FOREWORD

By John MacArthur

I n 1978, the Chicago Statement on Inerrancy was issued. Signed
by three hundred evangelical scholars, it led to the formation
of the International Council on Biblical Inerrancy. The intentions
of the Council were to stay off the increasing influences of skepticism and liberalism which had successfully and broadly infiltrated
America's mainline denominations and their seminaries. While the
nomenclature of the council was billed as international in scope,
the reality was a small number of signers to the Chicago Statement
represented church leaders from Europe, Asia, Central/South
America, or Africa.

In the intervening years, a gradual abandonment of inerrancy
by historically conservative and evangelical seminaries has
produced a missionary force which, tragically, has undermined
this great doctrine. Such a disservice, done in the name of contemporary missions, now reigns as the dominant influence upon
the international church. The irony of this reality poses a critical
challenge to the strength of both theological education and pastoral
ministry abroad. Never has there been a greater need than today
for addressing the doctrine of inerrancy and its implications for
the global church.

Since founding The Master's Seminary in 1986, my abiding
interest has been to produce graduates who can overcome this
betrayal. Our purpose has been to equip a new generation of pastors
and church leaders, who then will confidently base their ministries

on a high view of Scripture and the great doctrine of inerrancy. The profound implications which flow from this will result in pastors and denominational leaders basing their convictions in biblical truth instead of tradition or an exaggerated contextualization.

This long-awaited resource introduces you to the ministry of The Master's Academy International. TMAI is committed to these historic and fundamental doctrines, training pastors to be biblically literate, able to implement a philosophy of ministry not governed by the dominant influences of sociology and pragmatism. We aim to produce men of biblical conviction and spiritual courage.

The men who have authored the chapters in this volume are such men. Both missionaries and national church leaders trained by The Master's Seminary, they now serve as seminary deans and faculty around the world. Here, they address matters facing churches within their national context which stem from the affirmation or denial of biblical inerrancy, matters their students must accurately understand and teach.

These men share my conviction that the most strategic focus in missions should be equipping pastors to preach with confidence the authoritative, sufficient, and inerrant Word of God. Only this will lead to mature and effective churches, able to fulfill our Lord's commission to "make disciples of all nations. . . teaching them to observe all that I have commanded you." I praise God for both our missionary and national faculty members who understand the particular cultural threats to a national church's understanding of the Truth.

Considering the implications of inerrancy is long overdue within the missionary community. I trust these articles will assist those serious about advancing God's church and making disciples of the nations by illustrating how God's Word is reliable, authoritative, and sufficient for His global church.

John MacArthur
President, The Master's Seminary and College

INTRODUCTION

By Mark Tatlock
President, The Master's Academy International

B iblical inerrancy is an essential missiological issue. While its importance is not often recognized, the implications of either embracing or rejecting this doctrine are global. The essays contained in this book—written by TMAI faculty around the world—seek to illustrate from a first-hand perspective the profound implications of the doctrine of inerrancy for the global church. Careful consideration of one's view of Scripture reveals that much of today's ecclesiological confusion within international settings can be derived from the intentional or unintentional neglect of this truth among missionaries, especially those engaged in theological education, Bible translation, and publishing of theological resources. More often than not, neglect of this truth leads to an eventual minimizing of biblical authority within the church.

One's view on inerrancy will influence one's view on the doctrines of inspiration, authority, and sufficiency of the Holy Scriptures, as well as one's view on Theology Proper, Christology, Anthropology, and Soteriology. These doctrines lie at the heart of evangelism and missions—true gospel work. In addition, one's position on these great matters will inform their approach to biblical interpretation or hermeneutics, and from one's hermeneutic, an approach to preaching is derived. When a hesitation of conviction exists regarding an orthodox Bibliology, the outcome of knowing, proclaiming, and obeying God's Word becomes uncertainty. A chasm of confidence between God's people and God's Word is further widened when voices untethered to Scripture, but claiming to speak for God, are affirmed within the church.

Nowhere is this great divide more realized than on the mission field. Even where sound theology was introduced by historical missionary influence, the church's ability to mature and reproduce itself is stunted when it is dependent upon oral or church tradition rather than skilled study and interpretation of Scripture. This situation breeds doctrinal confusion when contemporary views of biblical authority are shaped by religious tolerance, syncretism, or relativistic contextualization. It will be illustrated by the authors of this collection of articles that these challenges stem from a doubt regarding the inerrancy of the Bible, and can lead to a redefining of the gospel itself. The great cause of missions is to win people to Christ and not to masquerading gospels. In the end, the original mission of extending the Kingdom by proclaiming the good news of the gospel, is ultimately endangered.

This trend in missions can be attributed to the decline of seminaries and Bible colleges in the West who abandoned their allegiance to their own historic doctrinal statements on inerrancy, and more specifically failed to provide accountability assuring faculty agreement with this doctrine. Coupled with an increasing commitment to enroll international students as part of their missions strategy, schools in the West have graduated generations of national church leaders who share no clear conviction on the matter. This result has led to national seminaries and denominational pastoral training programs which fail to uphold inerrancy. Plainly said, indigenous church leaders trained by many North American seminaries are characterized by uncertainty as to the veracity of the Scriptures, and rely on pragmatic approaches to ministry. Our missiological legacy in too many places has been the successful export of the increasing skepticism of the American theological community. We have witnessed the fulfillment of Kevin Vanhoozer's prophecy:

> It may be only a matter of time, given globalization and patterns of higher education, until the rest of the world is faced with similar challenges to biblical authority posed by biblical criticism, naturalistic

scientism, and skeptical historicism." (Kevin J. Vanhoozer, "Response to Michael F. Bird," in *Five Views on Biblical Inerrancy*, 190.)

In developing countries, both economics and ecumenism can present obstacles to a pastor receiving the necessary training to accurately handle the Word of God. In addition, denominational leaders, seeking to overcome abuses associated with colonialism, have inadvertently led their people into even greater spiritual poverty and biblical illiteracy, having no watermark by which to judge the Truth. Under such circumstances, false gospels abound. Lack of biblical discernment by pastors produces churches susceptible to error.

In-vogue contextualizing trends—currently embraced among Western missionaries and now accepted in large part by conservative mission agencies—are making higher criticism and its derivatives mainstream within missiology. Ironically, missionaries who were sent out to redeem men and women from false religions have now become advocates of practices which keep potential converts enslaved to false churches. Whether it is the extremes of the Insider Movement, the exploitations of the Prosperity Gospel, the radicalized influences of Liberation Theology, or accommodating philosophies of Bible translation, Western missiology increasingly has been guilty of perpetuating spiritual injustices against the global church. Tolerance is unloving when it masks error.

The recovery of a genuinely sound missiology begins with resolving the issue of whether God's Word is true and without error. If it is, then it presents a challenge to much which is heralded within the contemporary missions movement. Realities such as pragmatism in church growth methodology, lack of doctrinal conviction or agreement among faculty of international seminaries and Bible colleges, and the production of much-needed but misinformed theological resources by national church leaders can be corrected.

There is great hope that a renewal among indigenous churches is taking shape. Many national pastors now have direct access to resources espousing the historic doctrines of the Reformation. With greater exposure to faithful expositional preaching, a groundswell of interest in biblically sound teaching and theological education is occurring. It is here The Master's Academy International has focused its mission. With a concentration on equipping and training indigenous church leaders in essential doctrines, such as the inerrancy of God's Word, the greatest opportunity for reforming missions and serving the international church will be realized.

The Lord has employed graduates of The Master's Seminary to establish training centers and seminaries in seventeen different countries, with as many as thirty-four teaching locations. These schools have as their singular ambition to help the indigenous church train its own pastors and church leaders in biblical integrity. Each training center is committed to preparing gifted men to lead churches in the context of their own country and culture. These men are trained to evangelize (Matthew 28:18-20), equip others for local church service (Ephesians 4:12), and entrust this ministry to the next generation of faithful men (2 Timothy 2:2).

In this inaugural edition of the TMAI Imprint, you will engage with faculty and even select graduates from our training centers around the world. All are church leaders who understand the state of the church in their nations and recognize the positive and negative effects of Western mission efforts. These capable men will provide the reader with specific implications of inerrancy within their cultural setting. For example, in Albania where the evangelical church was preceded by Islam, or in the Czech Republic where an Atheistic regime eclipsed the church, confidence in God's revelation can cut through competing worldviews, enabling evangelical churches to have a bold witness.

You will learn of the importance of this doctrine as it relates to the evangelical church in European and Latin American Catholic contexts. In Italy, Spain, Mexico, and Honduras, a latent dependence upon tradition will be shown to create unsound and unbiblical practices by church leaders. This same dependency on the authority of tradition will be examined as it relates to the Orthodox Church in Ukraine, Russia, and Croatia. The dominant practices of contextualization and syncretism in India and the Philippines will provide a lens on the needed recovery of inerrancy.

The state of affairs facing churches in Western European settings such as Germany and Switzerland—where rationalism birthed higher criticism leading to the eventual decline of mainline denominations' high view of Scripture—will also be covered. Practical issues such as church polity, church growth, and the role of women within the church will be examined in contexts where leading denominational voices have been long disenfranchised from scriptural authority, such as in South Africa and Malawi. Also in this survey, the supplanting of Scripture's authority by personal experience will be considered in contexts where derivatives of liberalism have become the dominant influence upon the church in places such as New Zealand and China.

I invite you to take advantage of this collection of essays, written by faithful churchmen whose conviction is that God's Word stands inerrant, shining brightly and capable of guiding men out of darkness into the Light.

Mark Tatlock
President, The Master's Academy International

BIBLICAL INERRANCY AND MUSLIM EVANGELISM IN ALBANIA

By Florenc Mene (Albania)

An American missionary was once trying to convince a young Albanian Muslim that Christ is the only way to salvation. Confronted with the young man's belief that the Bible is full of contradictions, the missionary replied, "The Bible is a human book. As such, it may contain historical errors, but not theological ones. It is God's Word because it tells the truth about God's salvation. In that sense, it is inerrant."

With this reply, the issue was settled in this young Muslim's mind. The Bible is not completely inerrant. If it contains errors in other matters, how can it be trusted on such an important matter as the salvation of souls? Later, in God's providence, that young Muslim became a Christian. He trusted Christ when he met other Christians who believe that the Bible tells the truth in everything it says. That young Albanian Muslim is the writer of these words.

In Christian-Muslim dialogues, Muslims focus on challenging the reliability of the Bible. They want to prove that it is not reliable so that no one will trust it. Christians in Albania must not be oblivious to this Muslim way. In order to effectively evangelize in such a setting, they must realize that the Bible's inerrancy is a pivotal point with their Muslim friends. Once Christians became fully aware of

17

this, evangelism will be more effective as the Muslim is confronted with the Bible's claims to total truthfulness in everything.

The first section of the paper will survey the Muslim position on inerrancy of the holy books. In the second section, their position on the Bible will be explained. Finally, the proper Christian approach to biblical inerrancy will be explained. This same section will also show why belief in biblical inerrancy is important in raising the effectiveness of Muslim evangelism in Albania and beyond.

Inerrancy and Inspiration in Islam

Muslims have a well-defined view on the nature of a book that has been revealed by God. They believe that a book that is inspired by God is inerrant. By inerrant they would mean completely free from fraud, deceit, or contradictions of any kind. A holy book tells the truth on all matters, spiritual or otherwise.[1] The rationale of this view is simple and straightforward. If a book that claims to be from God does not tell the truth—even if inadvertently—that book cannot really be trusted. No contradictions of any kind can exist in a holy book.[2] God cannot contradict Himself.

This position on inerrancy is also maintained in the Muslims' holy book, the Qur'an. Claims to complete truthfulness and perfection abound in its pages.[3] As a result, it alone can be trusted in matters of salvation. Thus, Muslims would not even fathom believing in partial inerrancy of their holy Qur'an or any other holy book. Partial inerrancy to them is only partial truth.

The Muslim Position on the Bible

This study now considers what Muslims believe concerning the Bible, its origins, later corruption, and its present errant state.

---

[1] The lofty terms Muslims use about the Qur'an and the contradictions they attribute to the Bible illustrate this point. See, for example, Yusuf Estes and Gary Miller, "Bible Islam: Bible Compared to Quran," http://www.bibleislam.com/bible_vs_quran.php (07Apr. 2008).

[2] Ahmad Deedad. "Is the Bible God's Word?" http://www.jamaat.net/bible/Bible7-9.html (08 Apr. 2008). This sentiment is also echoed in the Quran (4:82).

[3] To mention just a few, Surahs 6:115-116; 10:65.

It will be seen that many Muslims have come to the conclusion that the Bible cannot be trusted because of its many purported contradictions in doctrine and other areas.

The Bible: Its Initial Inspiration

Unlike followers of many other world religions, Muslims freely accept that the Bible is a holy book. It is part of their basic tenets of faith.[4] The Qur'an bears testimony to the fact that the Bible is a holy book from God. It says to Muslims, "Believe in all the Scripture" (3:119).[5] Moreover, Muhammad says to the people of the Book (i.e., the Christians and the Jews), "I believe in whatever book Allah has sent. . .Let there be no argument between us" (42:15). The Qur'an encompasses both Old and New Testament with the term "Scriptures," and it commands Muslims to declare that they believe them to be revelations from God (2:136, 285; 3:79, 84, 119; 4:136). Based on their most holy source, the Qur'an, Muslims believe that the Bible was a book originally revealed and inspired by God.

The Bible: Its Later Inaccuracies

According to Muslims, the Bible is no longer a holy book. It was changed through the centuries for various reasons. According to Muslims, the Qur'an seems to intimate that this began in Muhammad's time. As to the reasons for these changes, Muslims believe that the Bible was intentionally twisted by Christians and/ or Jews in order to hide prophecies that predicted Muhammad's coming as the last and greatest prophet from God. Qur'anic verses are cited in support of this kind of change.[6] The Bible, the book

---

4   Daniel Wickwire, *101 Questions about the Bible and the Qur'an* (Ankara: ABC Matbaacilik, 2002), 1-10.

5   All Qur'anic citations in this paper are taken from Mohammed Marmaduke Pickthall, *The Meaning of the Glorious Koran: An Explanatory Translation* (New York: Mentor and Penguin Books, n.d.).

6   The Qur'an, 3:71, 4:46 are two such samples. Nevertheless, the Qur'an is not accusing the Jews and Christians of textual corruption of the Bible, but just verbal corruption with their mouths. For a fine response to this Muslim claim, the reader is referred to John Gilchrist, *The Christian Witness to the Muslim, The World of Islam: Resources for Understanding*, 2.0 [CD-ROM] (CO: Global Mapping International, 2006)

that was originally from God, thus lost its authority as the result of numerous changes in history.

The Bible: Its Lost Inerrancy

Muslims do not simply go to the Qur'an or their traditions to support their position for a changed Bible. They bring forth so-called historical arguments that claim that the Bible, in its present state, contains numerous changes of a diverse nature. These purported changes are then taken as proof that the Bible is no longer inerrant.[7] Some types of purported errors in the Bible are listed below.

Difficulties in manuscripts

Muslims have been quick to pick up on an ongoing assault against the Bible's integrity by the critical community of liberal scholars. They point out figures that show that there are thousands of variants—and, as a result, errors—in the numerous biblical manuscripts.[8] Such cases also include interpolated verses like 1 John 5:6. The addition of this verse is a classic case of willful corruption of the Bible on the part of Christians to provide a scriptural basis for the doctrine of the Trinity.[9]

Discrepancies in the Bible

Other classic arguments against the Bible include purported contradictions within its own contents. These contradictions are of a diverse nature and involve discrepancies in numbers, contradictions

---

[7]   For a sample of such arguments see "Contradictions and Proofs of Historical Corruptions in the Bible," http://www.quransearch.com/contra.htm (23 Feb. 2008).

[8]   Ahmet Deedad. "Is the Bible God's Word?" in *The Last Great Frontier: Essays on Evangelism*, comp. Phil Parshall (Philippines: Open Doors with Brother Andrew, 2000), 398-99. Deedat quotes the figure of 50,000 mistakes in the Bible as showing that it is corrupt beyond redemption. He claims to have gotten that figure from Christian sources. A good site that answers many Muslim claims against the Bible is "Answering Islam – a Christian-Muslim Dialog and Apologetic," http://www.answering-islam.org/ (23 Feb. 2008).

[9]   "The Lie of 1 John 5:7," accessed April 1 2008, http://www.answering-christianity. com/1john5_7.htm

in biblical genealogies[10], and disagreements in doctrine.[11] Again, these attacks are neither new nor Muslim in origin. They are part of the liberal European heritage with its barbed attacks on the Bible. Nevertheless, the Muslim mind especially rejoices over such perceived discrepancies because these shatter the Bible's credibility.

Muslims strongly believe that only an inerrant holy book is considered authoritative and binding. Also, Muslims consider the Bible to have been God's Word in its original form, but they assert that it has since been corrupted beyond remedy, containing numerous contradictions and errors.

Inerrancy According to Scripture: Strong Basis of Evangelism

It is important to now examine the proper Christian position on the Bible and its inerrancy. First, inerrancy will be viewed from a biblical context, allowing the Bible to speak for itself. Muslims and Christians hold some common ground on the matter of inerrancy, when inerrancy is viewed from a biblical perspective. Second, the Bible's preservation will be considered. God has caused the preservation of His Word, and human history concurs with this fact. Christians can be confident that the Lord who inspired His Word has also made it available to our generation. Finally, it will be seen why belief in biblical inerrancy is so important in raising the effectiveness of Muslim evangelism in Albania.

The Bible and Its Inerrancy

The Bible should be allowed to have its own voice in the matter of inerrancy. A key verse to be considered here is 2 Timothy 3:16. This verse claims that all Scripture was breathed out by God Himself.[12] Inspiration presupposes inerrancy. As inspiration

---

[10] "The Bible: What They Didn't Tell You," accessed April 8, 2008, http://www.islamnewsroom.com/content/view/292/52/

[11] "Glorious Islam: Ask yourself," http://www.muslimtents.com/gloriousislam/english.htm (09 Apr. 2008).

[12] Gordon R. Lewis and Bruce Demarest., *Integrative Theology*, v.1 (Grand Rapids, MI: Zondervan, 1996), 143.

applies to all of Scripture, so does inerrancy. When God speaks, He tells the truth about all matters, whether religious or historical. The historical aspect of Scripture cannot be separated from its theological aspect.[13]

The Scripture's authority hinges on its complete truthfulness (i.e., inerrancy). Two passages stand out as proof. The first passage is Matthew 5:17-20. Jesus is speaking about the continuing author- itative nature of the law. The Scriptures are thus totally inerrant, even to their smallest letter. As John MacArthur puts it, "No other statement made by our Lord more clearly states His absolute contention that Scripture is verbally inerrant, totally without error in the original form in which God gave it."[14]

Similarly, the way Scripture quotes other Scripture is signifi- cant. It shows the Bible's absolute authority confirmed in its own pages. In Matthew 22:43-45, Jesus's entire argument hinges on the word "Lord." Jesus is quoting from Psalm 110, where David calls the Messiah his Lord, though he would be His descendant. This single word, "Lord," is the basis for Jesus declaring that David implied that the coming Messiah would be a divine person as well as human.[15]

The Bible is adamant about its truthfulness in all matters. The Scriptures, in their original form, always tell the truth about everything. This is the Christian's common ground with Muslims. Christians who believe in inerrancy may be disbelieved, but their testimony will be heard and possibly respected.

The Bible and Its Preservation

Muslims would not object if they were told that the Bible was inerrant in its original form. The relevant question to be answered is

---

[13] Norman L. Geisler, ed. *Inerrancy*. (Grand Rapids, MI: Zondervan, 1980), 143.

[14] Louis A. Barbieri Jr. "Matthew," in *The Bible Knowledge Commentary: An Exposition of the Scriptures by Dallas Seminary Faculty, New Testament,* ed, John F. Walvoord and Roy B. Zuck (Wheaton, IL: Victor Books, 1985), 30. See also John MacArthur Jr., *The MacArthur New Testament Commentary: Matthew* (Chicago: Moody Press, 1989), 262.

[15] Craig L. Blomberg put it this way: "[Jesus] bases his argument on Ps 110:1, assuming the accuracy of the Davidic superscription, and the inspiration of the actual text itself, which would therefore imply its truthfulness." Craig L. Blomberg, *Matthew*, vol. 22 in *The New American Commentary*, David S. Dockery , ed. (Nashville, TN: Broadman,1992), 336.

how well the Bible has been preserved until now. If it has not been preserved well, it cannot be regarded as authoritative and inerrant in the matter of salvation. Inerrancy becomes a moot point if the copies of the Scriptures are not faithful to the originals. So the question arises: how well has God preserved the Bible until today?

This section will show that the Bible has been faithfully preserved in its entirety until the present day. First, the importance of preservation will be considered in order to show that God has preserved His Word only through secondary causation. Second, the Bible's preservation down to our time will be examined from a historical perspective. Here, the nature of the so-called errors will also be examined by showing evidence for the accuracy of transmission of the Old and New Testaments. Variants in the manuscripts do not amount to doctrinal contradictions.

Preservation: its importance

Preservation is closely related to God's providence. God must have a hand in the preservation of His Word in order to make it actively available to men at all times.[16] William Combs defines preservation by saying, "God preserves his Word forever, unchanged, and primarily in heaven (Ps 119:89). . . . On the other hand, on earth it is God's people who are responsible for preserving and transmitting His Word."[17] Nevertheless, divine providence can be clearly attested by the fact that God has made it possible for the Scriptures to have been faithfully transmitted throughout the centuries.[18]

In order to hear and obey God's Word, one must possess it. Therefore, preservation is more than a historical fact. Evangelicals assert that "the preservation of Scripture was always assured even though God carried out His will to preserve the Scriptures primarily

---

[16] William D. Barrick. "Ancient Manuscripts and Biblical Exposition," *The Master's Seminary Journal* 9/1 (Spring 1998): 27.

[17] William W Combs. "The Preservation of Scripture," *Detroit Baptist Seminary Journal* 5 (Fall 2000): 28.

[18] Merrill F. Unger, "The Inspiration of the Old Testament," *Bibliotheca Sacra* 107 (October 1950): 445.

through the actions of human wills."[19] In other words, preservation was the work of God's providence by means of secondary causation.

What about human responsibility in preserving God's Word? That is attested to by the Scriptures. God expects man to be responsible for faithfully preserving and transmitting His Word to the other generations (Deut 4:2; 12:32; Rev 22:18-19, etc.).[20] While man has often failed to do so, God has still found a way to make His Word available for all generations.

Preservation attested by history

Evangelical tradition as a whole holds to a providential kind of preservation through secondary causation. As to the extent of preservation, the manuscript evidence shows that preservation has not been perfect, but God has allowed human errors to enter the copies as an inevitable result of non-miraculous providential restoration. Therefore, preservation is not related to one single manuscript, but to the manuscript in its totality. Nevertheless, this preservation, under divine care and providence, has proven to be remarkable in both the Old and New Testament texts.

Proving that the Scriptures have been preserved with great accuracy is not a hard task in view of the present evidence. In the case of evangelizing one's Muslim friends, this task gets immensely easier. As already explained, Muslims believe that the Bible still existed in an uncorrupted state before Muhammad, and that it was only corrupted during his lifetime or later. However, the Bible in Muhammad's time is the same in its contents as the Bible today. The following external evidence will concentrate on showing that the Bible has not been corrupted, either before or after the life of Muhammad.

---

[19] William W. Combs. "The Preservation of Scripture," 10.

[20] William D. Barrick. "Ancient Manuscripts and Biblical Exposition," 27.

Evidence of the accuracy of transmission of the Old Testament

The Hebrew Bible comes to us mainly in the following manuscripts: 1) The Aleppo Codex (ca. tenth century). It contained almost all of the Pentateuch and all of a number of other books. 2) The Leningrad Codex (ca. 1010). Both of these codices represent the famous Ben Asher tradition of scribes, otherwise known as the Masoretic Text. The famous Dead Sea Scrolls, found in 1948 in the vicinity of the Dead Sea, testify to the accuracy of the transmission of the Old Testament text.[21] The scrolls found there date roughly between the second century B.C. and first century A.D. Their text substantiates the fact that the Old Testament text has been passed down through the centuries in a very faithful way by the scribes.[22]

The meticulousness of the ancient scribes is something that should be stressed at this juncture. The scribes had an intricate procedure for copying the manuscripts because they considered even the omission or addition of a single letter as sin. They calculated the number of letters in a book, the middle letter, and the middle verse of a book to check for accuracy. God providentially used the meticulousness of the scribes to preserve the text of the Old Testament with outstanding accuracy.[23]

We can thus conclude that the thousands of Hebrew manuscripts "provide overwhelming support for the reliability of the Old Testament Text".[24] The case is thus settled for the historical preservation of the Old Testament. By Muhammad's time this was the text used by the Jews. It has remained virtually unchanged down to this day as shown by the examples of the Aleppo and the Leningrad Codices.

---

[21] Josh McDowell. *Evidence that Demands a Verdict: Historical Evidences for the Christian Faith,* vol. 1 (San Bernardino, CA: Here's Life Publishers, 1979), 57.

[22] Neil R. Lightfoot. *How We Got the Bible,* 3d ed., rev. and exp. (Grand Rapids, MI: Baker Books, 2003), 138-139. Also, Henry Morris declares, "There is no reasonable doubt that our present Old Testament. . . is practically identical with the text in use several centuries before Christ." See Henry M. Morris, *Many Infallible Proofs: Practical and Useful Evidences of Christianity* (El Cajon, CA: Master Books, 1974), 41.

[23] Ibid., 131-33.

[24] Norman L. Geisler. and William E. Nix, *A General Introduction to the Bible,* rev. and exp. (Chicago: Moody, 1986), 382.

Evidence of the accuracy of transmission of the New Testament

The integrity of the Old Testament text is largely an outcome of the meticulous care of the scribes and scholars in the transmission process. The fidelity of the New Testament text, on the other hand, rests on the multitude of manuscript evidence. There are approximately 5,366 partial and complete manuscripts that date from the second to the fifteenth centuries.[25] The most important ones are Codex Sinaiticus, Codex Vaticanus, and Codex Alexandrinus. These manuscripts come from diverse locations and time periods—a strong indicator that there was no plot on the part of Christians to corrupt the Scriptures.[26] It would have been an impossible feat to corrupt every single Bible text over such a large geographical area, during such a great period of time, by all Christians in the world. Furthermore, the above-mentioned three codices predate Muhammad by centuries.

Can we arrive at the original text despite these variants? The answer lies in text criticism, which "attempts to seek and eliminate errors by using plausible explanations for emendations that have crept into the text".[27] Text criticism is an objective science with clear rules. It has contributed greatly to the restoration of the original text of the New Testament. Its answer is a resounding yes. Thus the text of the originals can be established beyond reasonable doubt.

What are some doctrinal consequences of the variations in the text? Most of them are trivial, with no consequence at all to the text. Others are substantial, consisting not of a single word, but of a verse, and sometimes several verses, but still having no bearing on the text as such. Finally, a few others have a certain bearing on the text (such as John 7:53-8:11).[28] The important thing is to note that no single Christian doctrine is endangered by any kind of variants in the text.[29]

---

[25] Ibid., 385.

[26] Norman L. Geisler, *Christian Apologetics* (Grand Rapids, MI: Baker Book House, 1976), 306. Geisler lists the most important evidences of NT manuscripts.

[27] Ibid., 435.

[28] Neil R. Lightfoot. *How We Got the Bible*, 96-103.

[29] Morris, *Many Infallible Proofs*, 23.

To what degree can the original New Testament text be established? Through the meticulous work of the textual critics, like Westcott and Hort, the text of the New Testament has been restored with great accuracy. According to Westcott and Hort, only a thousandth part of the NT represents substantial variation![30] This would mean that the text we now possess is at least 98.33 percent pure whether the critic adopts the Textus Receptus, Majority Text, or Nestle-Aland![31] According to Ezra Abbot, the figure is more likely 99.75 percent![32]

This section revealed some important points. First, the Bible teaches its own inerrancy. Second, it can be historically shown that the same Bible that existed before and during Muhammad's day also exists today. Moreover, removing the barriers of textual variants, Christians can sincerely point out these facts to their Muslim friends. The same Christ and gospel message appeared in the Bible of Muhammad's day as in our own day.

Benefits of Biblical Inerrancy in Albanian Muslim Evangelism

The Bible claims total inerrancy for its contents. It is also clear that the Bible has been preserved through the centuries with great faithfulness on the part of God through secondary causation. Christians, therefore, must believe both in the Bible's original inerrancy and its present inerrancy. How does belief in biblical inerrancy bear on a Christian's effectiveness in Muslim evangelism? This question finds a twofold answer.

First, the Bible demands total inerrancy. Those who call themselves Christians are to put the Bible above their personal opinions. It must be their only standard of authority. Belief in a partly inerrant Bible is not spiritually healthy, nor is it self-consistent. If Christians

---

[30]   Neil R. Lightfoot. *How We Got the Bible,* 126. (For sake of clarification, the Textus Receptus, the Majority Text, and the Nestle-Aland text are critical texts of the Greek New Testament. Their minute differences stem from the fact that they have made different choices on which manuscript to accept as more authoritative at different points in the New Testament text.)

[31]   Geisler and Nix, *A General Introduction to the Bible*, 475.

[32]   Ibid.

deny the Bible's inerrancy, a great problem arises. Christians make their human minds a higher standard for judging truth than God Himself. They become the ones who decide which sections of the Word are inerrant and which are not.[33] This unhealthy attitude toward the reliability of the Scriptures cannot produce effectiveness in evangelism. A Christian who is not certain on the truthfulness of the Word will be a poor witness to the world. He will proclaim a gospel that rests on a very shaky foundation.

Second, Muslims themselves believe in total inerrancy. While differences in the concepts of holy books between Muslims and Christians exist, inerrancy is a common ground between the Bible's claims and the Muslims' beliefs. A Christian who only partly believes the Bible's contents will not be an effective witness to Muslims. The Muslims will shut their minds to Christian evangelism immediately, once they recognize that they do not believe in the total reliability of their own holy book.

Christian witness and belief in biblical inerrancy must go hand in hand. Belief in lesser degrees of inerrancy is not uncommon in Christian circles, even in Albania.[34] This may not seem dangerous to a post-modern Western culture. Nevertheless, to Muslim evangelism this is detrimental. If Christians do not believe in an inerrant Bible, Muslims cannot be expected to accept its message. On the other hand, Christians who fully trust the Bible's contents are ready to be used as vehicles through which God will proclaim His message to the lost sons of Ishmael. Christians who believe in inerrancy are able to preach the Word in boldness and in power. They alone give the Word the credit and authority it deserves. This, in turn, will give God free reign to work through His Word.

Conclusion

The spiritual sons of Ishmael in Albania are lost. Brave Christian men and women are needed who are ready to confront their lost compatriots with the gospel claims. For that to happen,

---

[33] Wayne Grudem. *Systematic Theology*, 100.

[34] It is only inevitable that the beliefs of founding missionaries will subject their churches to deplorable consequences in the area of evangelism and Christian life.

the sword of the Spirit, God's own Word (Eph 6:17), must be kept ready at hand. It must not be ignored, nor half-heartedly trusted. Unless the wielder completely trusts this sword, he will not use it with conviction. It takes courage to trust the power of God's Word above all human devices and arguments. Nevertheless, full belief in its total inerrancy and reliability is necessary. It alone shows that the Lord of the Word can be really trusted in everything. It alone opens the way for the Holy Spirit to use His people to evangelize Albanian Muslims and the entire Islamic world with effectiveness.

INERRANCY AND THE CRISIS IN THE CHURCH IN CROATIA

by Misko Horvatek (Croatia)

There is a crisis in the church in Croatia. Many national leaders as well as missionaries have set aside inerrancy and a high view of Scripture. They are in pursuit of theological views that lower Scripture and raise cultural relevance. But what certainty do such missionaries and leaders offer God's people if they believe that their task is to identify the constantly changing topics relevant to a particular culture? What kind of spiritual influence can we possibly hope to exert upon church members and theology students if all we have to offer the spiritually needy are our own uncertain conclusions?

In this essay we will see the crisis in the Croatian churches, the origins of the crisis, and how that crisis is evident in the pulpit and the pews. In the final sections, we appeal to fellow leaders in Croatia to uphold inerrancy and a high view of the Scriptures and to build up and lead their congregations to greater Christ-likeness. No matter what part we have in this crisis, no matter how directly or indirectly we are affected, we all should renew our commitment to the Scriptures and our calling to shepherd God's flock in Croatia with the inerrant Word.

Seeds of the Crisis

The first discernible seeds were planted as a result of the Pietistic movement in Europe two centuries ago. Pietism had a wide influence throughout Europe. It had a destructive impact on Christians in the pulpit as well as the pew.[1] It left pastors unprepared to recognize and even unwilling to combat the dangers and challenges of nineteenth-century rational liberalism and then, later, the inherently existential theologies of Pentecostalism and the Charismatic movements in the twentieth century.

More seeds were planted as the Pentecostal and Charismatic movements grew in influence. These groups emphasized the role of spiritual gifts and taught believers to connect with the supernatural through various spiritual experiences. Such experiences became the measure of spiritual life for many. This theology resulted in near total confusion among believers in many Croatian churches. Pastors who did not hold these views of spiritual gifts were told that these new congregations possessed a vibrancy missing from their own congregations. Being ungrounded in sound doctrine and ill-equipped to discern the theological threat that these movements presented, many pastors and congregations were lured away from the truth.

Over the last twenty-five years, there has been an invasion of missionaries who do not hold to inerrancy. Although well-intentioned men and women, they are steeped in theological liberalism. They have caused great theological damage to congregations and denominations, both within Croatia and in the countries that surround her. Europe has long suffered from this virus. In the past hundred years or so, pastors and theologians who have abandoned the doctrine of biblical inerrancy have brought about the spiritual death of many evangelical churches throughout Europe. They have robbed other churches of their spiritual effectiveness for the Lord. The number of evangelical churches in Croatia is declining, and a great number of those whose doors remain open are spiritually dead and biblically disconnected. Those who have abandoned inerrancy have planted more seeds. We are now reaping the harvest. We now have a crisis in the pulpit and in the pews.

---

[1] "Pietism" by M. A. Noll in *Evangelical Dictionary of Theology*, ed. Walter Elwell (Grand Rapids, MI: Baker Academic, 2006), 926. "Pietistic tendencies can lead to inordinate subjectivism and emotionalism; it can discourage careful scholarship; it can fragment the church through enthusiastic separatism; it can establish new codes of almost legalistic morality and it can undertake the value of Christian traditions."

Crisis in the Pulpit

Considering the church in Croatia, it is evident that there is a crisis in the pulpit.[2] Although there are many issues facing the church, there are two especially troubling problems that plague our churches. As more and more leaders abandon a high view of Scripture and a biblical understanding of inerrancy, the leadership of the Church becomes less and less qualified to lead God's people. Furthermore, as the leadership loses faith in Scripture's trustworthiness, passionate preaching of the Word of God gives way to superficial and man-centered teaching.

The crisis in the pulpit begins with the lack of qualified leaders. Europe is a spiritual wilderness largely because so many of its pastors and theologians have been trained in liberal universities and seminaries, the vast majority of which have abandoned the doctrine of biblical inerrancy. Pastors who are poorly trained or learn ineffective doctrine often produce spiritually weak churches. Such churches do not play an important role in their societies and are making no spiritual impact in their countries. Reformation has died out. Revivals are long gone. Some would say that Europe has become a graveyard of missionaries and evangelical churches.

In order to prepare pastors to do "God's business in God's way,"[3] churches need to have men in leadership who have mastered the entire counsel of God and accept the Bible as the inerrant Word of God. Only then can they provide mature biblical guidance for their congregations. This is the way the Lord Jesus went about preparing His church leaders. It took Him three-and-a-half years to train and mold His men for the most important ministry under the sun. One pastor commented, "The strength of any given church is measured by the consistency with which the theology, preaching, and morality of its leadership correspond to the revelation of Scripture . . ." The Word of God has not, however, been accepted as the final authority for faith and practice in many churches in Croatia. The result has proved devastating, especially

---

[2]   Walter C. Kaiser. *Preaching and Teaching from the Old Testament* (Baker Academic: Grand Rapids, Michigan), 196.

[3]   George J. Zemek. *Doing God's Business God's Way* (Grand Rapids: Michigan, 2003)

in the election of improperly trained, immature, and spiritually unqualified leaders.

In addition to the crisis in leadership, the Church in Croatia is facing a lack of faithful preaching and teaching. It is increasingly the case that churches led by biblically unqualified leaders are not concerned with moral qualifications and theological convictions. They allow their preachers to walk into the pulpits and preach whatever they want. They allow friends into the pulpit who misinterpret biblical texts and do not seem concerned. It appears, at times, that everybody is welcome to the pulpit and nearly anybody is accommodated.

In the churches in Croatia it is not uncommon for pastors to contact the more well-known preacher in their area and say, "I do not know what else to preach. I have already exhausted all the texts and have preached on almost every issue." It is not unheard of for a pastor to call another in order to ask, "Could you send me a sermon you have already prepared so that I might have something to preach on Sunday?" For a number of years, the author of this paper himself was also guilty of these kinds of practices as he sought to minister to God's people. He simply lacked the opportunity for proper theological training.

Too many pastors are not adequately trained for the glorious ministry of teaching the eternal, infallible, and inerrant Word of God. Although well-meaning, such men are guilty of starving the flock of God over which they have oversight. They serve their congregations an unending stream of "fast food" sermons wrapped in thin tissue paper and kept under the heat lamp of "relevance." While often satisfied by the experience, God's people are malnourished by such ministries. Apart from sovereign grace, this type of pulpit ministry can only produce nominal Christians.

Crisis in the Pews

In view of the crisis in the pulpit, we should not be shocked to find a crisis in the pews. God's people in Croatia often live between the hammer and anvil of shallow sermons. This does not edify the church or equip the saints. Such a pulpit ministry systematically eradicates any enthusiasm and hunger for a greater knowledge of the Word of God by billing itself as quick and "relevant." So many are caught in a never-ending cycle of sermons, conferences, and seminars, *always learning but never coming to a true knowledge of the truth* (2 Tim 3:7). Some pastors impose a host of extra-biblical rules and expectations upon God's people which has the effect of sending them on never-ending guilt trips. It is little wonder that the church seems stagnant and that believers are losing their appetite for the Word. They simply do not understand it, and their diet of moralistic preaching has blinded them to their biblical obligation to understand it. This, in turn, saps their desire and power to evangelize the lost for the Lord. Too many churches in Croatia are full of nominal evangelical believers who fail to rise above the often superficial and moralistic preaching of their poorly-trained or liberal pastors – men who either merely pay lip service to the doctrine of inerrancy or who have abandoned the doctrine altogether.

An Appeal to Uphold the Inerrant Word

Fellow leaders, fellow pastors, brothers and sisters in Christ, we need to reaffirm our commitment to the inerrant Word of God. Do we not read in 2 Timothy 3:16 that all Scripture is *given by God* (θεοπνευστος)? God 'breathed' Scripture by His breath of Spirit *(pneuma)*, the Holy Spirit? The apostle Peter wrote in 2 Peter 1:21 that "men moved by the Holy Spirit spoke from God."[4] Both of these men were divinely authorized to deliver these words, and neither would dare to communicate something other than what God wanted them to write. They were *carried*, *moved*, *led* and *directed* by God Himself. In connection with this, Maier has written: "Inspiration did not render the biblical writers sinless, but it rendered their doctrine inerrant."[5] We can, therefore, depend upon the eternal Word of our eternal God – that upon which we can implicitly trust to decide all matters of faith and practice.

Just as the apostles were sinners saved by grace, chosen and enabled to speak for God, so also were the prophets of the Old

---

[4]   All Bible quotations are taken from the NASB unless otherwise stated.

[5]   Gerhard Maier, *Biblical Hermeneutics*, (Crossway Books, 1994), 140.

Testament. When the prophets wrote Scripture, their writings were free from any errors. Rolland McCune writes:

> In Psalm 19:7-9, David lists six statements about God's special revelation in words, each containing a special name, an attribute and an effect of that Word. All the adjectives of vv. 7-9 lead to the ideas of absolute truth–perfect, sure, right, pure, clean and true–all synonyms for inerrant.[6]

Why should God's people lack confidence in the Bible, which guarantees us victorious living and promises us theological triumph over the false teaching if applied faithfully? Steven Lawson reminds us that the Bible possesses "power to convict human hearts, exposing sin and revealing one's true need for God and grace." He goes on to say that the Word also has the "power to convert" for "no one can be saved apart from hearing and heeding God's Word." Moreover, Lawson points out that the Word also has the "power to conform a believer into the image of Jesus Christ."[7] The Christian preacher and teacher should bear in mind that, aside from the Holy Spirit, the best companion he has in the ministry is the inerrant Word of God. R. Albert Mohler makes the point that inerrancy "must be understood as necessary and integral to the life of the church, the authority of preaching, and the integrity of Christian life."[8] Men of God who have the opportunity and privilege of being trained in healthy theological institutions are biblically obliged to entrust these same convictions to other church leaders. They must commit themselves to teaching and cultivating these same convictions in the next generation of pastors, teachers, and preachers. A commitment to the biblical doctrine of inerrancy is an invaluable asset in the effort to protect God's people and God's churches from the kinds of theological chaos and moral crises that inevitably result from those who abandon this doctrine.

---

[6]   Rolland McCune, *A Systematic Theology of Biblical Christianity*, Vol. I (Biblical Studies Press, 2008), 91-92.

[7]   Steven J. Lawson. "The Sufficiency of Scripture in Expository Preaching," *Expositor*, vol. 1, 7-9.

[8]   R. Albert Mohler, Jr., "The Bible and the Believer," *Expositor Magazine*, 21.

An Appeal to Transform Lives with the Inerrant Word

Fellow leaders, fellow pastors, brothers and sisters in Christ, reaffirm your commitment to transform lives with the inerrant Word of God. It is heartbreaking to hear about members of evangelical churches who have grown little since their conversion and baptism. We need to emphasize the biblical and practical doctrines involved with sanctification in our teaching and preaching. We need to recognize that the main biblical goal of all believers is to resemble their Savior, Jesus Christ. The apostle Paul wrote to the saints in Galatia, "My children, with whom I am again in labor until Christ is formed in you" (Gal. 4:19). In order to help believers become like Christ, Paul taught and exhorted them through his epistles. He also commanded the Corinthian believers to be imitators of him just as he was imitating Christ (1 Cor. 4:16; 11:1). It is a lifelong process as explained by Daniel R. Hyde:

> We are his "workmanship," as Paul says (Eph. 2:10). Sanctification, then, is the process by which God sets apart His people from the rest of the world that they might serve Him and love Him. By it, we become less and less conformed to the pattern of the world (Rom 12:2) and more and more conformed to the pattern of Jesus Christ, the image of God par excellence (Rom 8:29).[9]

We need to commit ourselves anew to a high view of the Scriptures which flows into teaching and preaching that leads our congregations closer to Christ.

Conclusion

The crisis in the church in Croatia is severe. It is time for pastors, missionaries, and leaders at every level to respond in faith. We must restate our commitment to the Scriptures as the inerrant

---

[9] Daniel R. Hyde, *God in Our Midst: The Tabernacle and Our Relationship with God* (Ann Arbor, MI: Reformation Trust, 2012), 156.

Word, sufficient and authoritative in the life of the church. We must recommit ourselves to teaching and preaching that brings about transformed lives. As those entrusted to shepherd the flock in Croatia, we need to train up the next generation to carry on the work of our Lord. Let us draw together around our Lord Jesus Christ and His Word to turn back this crisis in our churches.

Inerrancy, Atheism, Church, and the Czech Republic

By Lance Roberts and Anthony Vahala (Czech Republic)

The authority and inerrancy of Scripture continues to be a hotly-debated issue. In the Czech Republic, the conviction about the Bible, God's perfect self-revelation, finds itself in a very peculiar context, namely that of atheism. The secular Czech culture, which prides itself in the enormous value it places on science, exerts considerable pressure on the church and its commitment to the key doctrines of the Christian faith. One of the greatest temptations to which churches may succumb concerns the doctrine of the inerrancy of Scripture.

In both missions and secular circles, the Czech Republic is often regarded as one of the most atheistic countries in Europe, if not in the whole world.[1] One recent study, which helped contribute to this notion, even called for the eventual termination of religion in Czech altogether.[2] These projections are largely based on census studies and general mainline religious categories. A census comparison indeed

---

[1] Hans Georg, Ziebert and Ulrich Riegel, "How Teachers in Europe Teach Religion," in *Is the Czech Republic and Atheistic Nation?* Petr Rattay (Munster: LIT Verlag, 2009), 45

[2] In March 2011, BBC News headlined an article that revealed a recent study done under the auspices of the American Physical Society and reported at their meeting in Dallas, TX. The study, based on census information, which was then plugged into a mathematical equation, calculated that Czech Republic had the highest level of religiously-unaffiliated people (60%). The scientists concluded that at such a high level of religiously-unaffiliated people in the country, religion as such is inescapably heading for extinction. http://www.bbc.com/news/science-environment-12811197.

shows a drastic decline of affiliation for the mainline denominations in the Czech Republic during the period from 1991 to 2011.[3]

Atheists ridicule the "simplistic convictions" of believers who still "naively" confess and defend the inerrancy of an ancient document. Christians are the recipients of all manner of insult and derision because of their convictions about Scripture, and they must be prepared to defend those beliefs to their critics (1 Pet 3:15). The aim of the first part of this article is to help believers understand the intricacies of atheism in the Czech Republic and help them recognize the kinds of atheism that believers encounter in the Czech society.[4] One's convictions about the inerrancy of the Scripture and good grasp on the cultural milieu will enable believers to confidently engage and counter the (Czech) atheistic culture. Further attention will also be given to the effects of the secular atheist culture on the local church in view of the fundamental doctrine of biblical inerrancy.

Understanding Czech Atheism

How atheistic is the Czech Republic? While the above-mentioned findings suggest that the Czech Republic is overwhelmingly atheist, there are some obvious limitations to a census-based study. The results are limited to the categories used in these studies and may not speak to the various nuances that characterize the Czech mindset. The religious sections in Czech bookstores, or the beliefs that one may encounter among Czechs themselves, are not as clear-cut. People are interested in religious, mystical, supernatural, and even magical phenomena. They buy books on dream interpretations, tarot readings, and eastern meditations; they

---

[3] The Catholic Church went from 4,523,734 affiliated members in 1991 to 1,467,438 in 2011, a decline of over three million members. Prominent Czech Protestant denominations recorded a similar decline. The Czechoslovak Hussite Church reduced their numbers within the same timeframe from 178,036 to 39,276, and The Evangelic Church of Czech Brethren declined by over 150,000 members, from 203,996 to 51,936. "Population by religious belief and by municipality," last modified in 2011. http://www. czso.cz/sldb2011/eng/redakce.nsf/i/tab_7_1_population_by_religious_belief_and_by_ municipality_size_groups/$File/PVCR071_ENG.pdf, (Accessed November 11, 2014).

[4] It is very likely that some of the traits of the Czech atheist culture will resemble other heavily secular and atheistic societies around the world. Therefore, the readers may find that some of the principles shared in this article apply also in their particular context.

knock on wood, make crosses when an ambulance is passing by, and avoid black cats.[5] The census study reveals a general disinterest in organized religion, but this does not mean people are apathetic towards religious experiences.

Atheism is often considered to be an inseparable part of the Czech national identity, one that has been developing over the past two centuries. Understanding the issues of biblical inerrancy and atheism in the Czech context requires a useful definition of atheism.[6] Atheism is generally defined as a belief in the non-existence of deities, but one cannot oversimplify the definition or the context in which it occurs. Although the term atheism itself suggests a worldview that distinguishes itself by a denial of any supreme beings, in the Czech Republic, atheism is not a monolithic idea.[7]

It may be more helpful to think of Czech atheism in terms of a spectrum. On the one end, there are the informed atheists, those who align themselves with what is currently known as the New Atheism, anchored by men such as Richard Dawkins, Sam Harris, Daniel Dennett, or Christopher Hitchens.[8] According to Albert Mohler, this movement is defined by eight characteristics: 1) unprecedented anti-theist boldness; 2) specific rejection of the Christian God and the Bible; 3) specific rejection of Jesus Christ; 4) confidence in the scientific argument; 5) refusal to tolerate even a moderate form of belief; 6) an attack on tolerance of various religious beliefs; 7) a questioning of the parental right to raise one's children in the faith; and 8) seeking to eliminate religion in order to

---

[5]   There are literally hundreds of Czech superstitions available on the Internet that speak to even the smallest details of human existence. For example, "If a pregnant woman passes under a clothes line, her baby will be born with the umbilical cord tied around its neck."

[6]   Zdeněk Nespor, *Religious Processes in Contemporary Czech Society* (Prague: Institute of Sociology, 2004)

[7]   This is even attested by a recent documentary done by the main Czech TV station (Česká Televize) that explored the notion of atheism in the Czech Republic. "Ta naše povaha česká: Ateismus po Česku," last modified in 2008, accessed November 11, 2014, http://www.ceskatelevize.cz/porady/1100627928-ta-nase-povaha-ceska/308295350270004-ateismus-po-cesku.

[8]   For more on the New Atheism see Albert Mohler, *Atheism Remix: A Christian Confronts the New Atheists* (Wheaton: Crossway, 2008)

preserve human freedom.[9] In the wider Czech context these ideas are propagated by blogs such as Osar.cz (Ateisté ČR), or Facebook pages (https://www.facebook.com/nesvatyhumor). The latter attempts to communicate an atheistic worldview in a humorous manner, although its approach is by no means subtle. The website unashamedly supplies a feed of atheistic quotes and cartoons that in their content and fervency illustrate Mohler's summary.

Moving from this end of the spectrum to the other, one finds a smorgasbord of ideas and convictions that exhibit the more-or-less anti-religious sentiment of atheism. One cannot overlook the element of superstition and spirituality that is, to various extents, mixed into this quasi-atheism.[10] What accounts for such a splintered worldview? How can such a diverse mix of skepticism and spirituality retain the label atheism?

The answer is most likely found within the concept of anti-clericalism; a historical movement that principally opposed religious establishments that often exerted great power and (social, religious, and political) influence on its subjects.[11] Historically, in the Czech context the religious establishment was the Catholic Church. Consequently, "anti-clerical" often meant "anti-Catholic." In the middle of the last century, the incoming Communist regime exploited this attitude toward the established church in order to spread its anti-theist (Marxist) propaganda. The resulting cocktail was rather effective and its potency only grew as time went on, especially with the passing of the Communist era (more than twenty years ago) when the religious floodgates were reopened. To the mix of pre-Communist anti-clericalism and Communist materialism and atheism, popular folklore superstitions, ideas from Eastern religions, and various other cults were also added. The end result was and is an ideological concoction that at times still labels itself as atheist, though in reality the *theos* that it predominantly denies is that of the Catholic Church, or perhaps some other institutionalized

---

9   Ibid., 54–63.

10 It is not unusual to have a medical doctor, atheistic in his or her beliefs, who knocks on wood, think that number 7 brings luck, or expects bad news because he or she had a dream about a deceased loved one.

11 José Mariano Sánchez, *Anticlericalism: A Brief History* (University of Notre Dame Press, 1972).

religious group. In such a context it is not viewed as contradictory, at least on the popular level, to say that a person is an atheist (i.e. not affiliated with any established religious organization) and also has some level of spirituality.

Therefore, what should one make of this self-proclaimed atheist society that also appears to be deeply religious? Where does the authority and inerrancy of Scripture fit within this conflicting context? What lessons are there for the church as a whole?

Countering Czech Atheism

It is difficult to engage a "silver bullet" approach to such a broad spectrum of atheism, one that ranges from New Atheism to more of a nominal version of atheism. On the one hand, the arguments one encounters with New Atheists will be along the more philosophical lines outlined by Mohler. On the other hand, the arguments one hears from the nominal atheists are more existential, such as, "If there is a good God, then why did he let my mother die of cancer?"[12]

One way to begin to engage the atheists is to graciously challenge their position. Those behind the vehement mockery directed towards Christians committed to the inerrancy of the Bible must answer an important question: "On what basis can someone criticize the Bible?"[13] The inerrancy and authority of Scripture offer

---

[12] Although the answers offered by atheists may vary greatly, it can be argued that all of the answers they supply can be reduced to a very basic source. The human nature fears authority, exposure, and the holiness of God. All of these factors reveal man's depravity and his utter inability to be righteous before God. Becoming an atheist is then a feeble attempt to suppress the notion of a God-created universe and "free" oneself, apart from Christ, from the guilt imbedded in one's soul. R. C. Sproul discusses this idea in his book, *If There's a God Why Are There Atheists?* (Orlando: Ligonier Ministries, 1997).

[13] A clear example of such mockery can be found on the above mentioned Facebook website. On one of the images one finds a picture of a Bible, next to which one finds the following descriptions:
Number of angry gods, breaking their own commandments: 1
Number of angry gods, breaking their own commandments: 1
Number of commandments: 10
Share of nonsense contained in the book: 100%
Share of original nonsense: 15%
Share of nonsense adopted from other cultures: 85%
Sacredness of the book: 0%
Moral value: 5%
Number of people murdered by God: 2,476,633
Number killed by Satan: 10.

a unique approach to engaging atheists of all sorts of convictions (i.e. New, Nominal, or in-between). They do so by revealing an underlying reality that is true of all human beings. It is a simple but profound truth that by the grace of God and the power of the Holy Spirit, believers can crack open the door for a meaningful and life-changing discussion with Czech atheists. Doug Wilson, a protestant theologian, demonstrated this reality in a dialogue with one of the pillars of the New Atheism, the late Christopher Hitchens. While engaging in a back and forth debate with Hitchens, Wilson said:

> Your book and your installments in this debate thus far are filled with fierce denunciations of various man-ifestations of immorality. You are playing Savonarola here, and I simply want to know the basis of your florid denunciations. You preach like some hot gospeler— with a floppy leather-bound book and all. I know the book is not the Bible and so all I want to know is what book it is, and why it has anything to do with me.[14]

The reality is that everyone lives by a book. Wilson pointed out a very simple reality, which he followed with a question: why should anyone submit to the authority of any particular book?

Objections might mount from atheists or the like, that they do not live by a book, but the concept here is more metaphorical than literal. The statement that everyone lives by a book simply means that everyone has a worldview, so while they might not have an actual printed corpus to which they adhere, everyone has a set of beliefs and convictions by which they operate in this world. For (conservative) Christians, this book is the Bible; for Muslims, it is the Qur'an; for the Jews, the Old Testament; and so on. For atheists and others who do not adhere to a specific written document, their "book" consists of personal beliefs, opinions, and convictions they hold to and by means of which they understand and justify their existence. Reminding the atheist of this plain reality begins to level

---

[14] Christopher Hitchens and Doug Wilson, *Is Christianity Good for the World?* (Moscow, ID: Canon Press, 2008), 43–46.

the field, which in a secular culture often seems to disadvantage the Christians.[15] Both atheists and Christians live by a book.

This book, whether physical or conceptual, is the source of one's worldview and consists of five major elements. It shows what one believes about God, ultimate reality, knowledge, morality, and humankind.[16] These are very basic categories, but they reveal much about a person. The most elemental point is what one believes about God. This truth is foundational even to the atheist, who claims that he does not believe God exists (Romans 1). One's beliefs about God subsequently inform all the other categories. If, for instance, one denies the existence of God, then ultimate reality cannot be God-created, but perhaps self-created (evolution) or eternal. One of the tasks of a Christian is then to explore each of these categories in the atheist's worldview in order to gain an understanding of the book by which he or she lives.[17]

This exploration will of course require that the Christian listens well. Eventually, Lord willing, after listening and conversing with an atheist, the conversation can be reduced to this fundamental question: "Which book is right?" Posing this question provides an opportunity to contrast the inerrant Word of God with the fallible word of man. Philosopher and theologian Ronald Nash suggests three basic tests by which one can gauge the veracity of one's book (worldview). First, one begins with the test of reason, which explores and evaluates whether one's view (book) can withstand the scrutiny of the laws of logic. Second is the test of experience.

---

[15]   There is a considerable bias against Christians in the Czech culture. As noted earlier they are considered simple, devoted to ancient myths, and not in touch with reality.

[16]   Ronald Nash, *Worldviews in Conflict: Choosing Christianity in the World of Ideas*, (Grand Rapids: Zondervan, 1992), 26–53. The limited space of this work does not allow for an extensive discussion of every element of atheistic worldview or a detailed exploration of the potential points of apologetics to use with atheists.

[17]   The Bible gives some general categories that define the mindset of unbelievers (atheists), Romans 1:21–23 describes them as those who, "even though they knew God, they did not honor Him as God or give thanks, but became futile in their speculations, and their foolish heart was darkened. Professing to be wise, they became fools, and exchanged the glory of the incorruptible God for an image in the form of corruptible man. . . ." 1 Corinthians 2:14 reminds us that an unbeliever (man in a natural state), "does not accept the things of the Spirit of God, for they are foolishness to him; and he cannot understand them, because they are spiritually appraised." Paul, author of both of these epistles, was aware of these fundamental truths about the lost, nevertheless, he still observed the culture they lived in and used his observations to engage them with the gospel (Acts 17:16–34).

Here one seeks to determine whether or not one's view corresponds to reality. Third is the test of practice, which evaluates whether or not one can consistently live out his or her worldview.[18]

The Christian comes to such an evaluation from a very specific angle. He operates under the conviction that the perfect God and creator of the universe does everything flawlessly and impeccably, and in turn, this conviction informs his view of Scripture. The perfect God, who never errs, cannot but produce a perfect and inerrant word. Therefore, a believer can remain confident in Scripture, knowing that only a book inspired by God can accurately explain and define the reality which the very same God created. This confidence should be accompanied by humility, knowing that this great and sovereign God condescended to us and revealed Himself to us in an act of pure grace. Armed with the infallible word of God and the presence of the Holy Spirit, the Christian has more than enough at his disposal to meaningfully engage the atheist worldview. The inerrant Word of God is thus the bulwark of his ministry in an atheistic culture; it alone can stand the tests mentioned above, because its author (God) is the one who created reason, reality, and truth. Christians can boldly assume the inerrant

---

[18] Nash, *Worldviews in Conflict*. The basic outline of these tests is on pages 53–63. The aim of this article is not to articulate or defend biblical inerrancy; that notion is assumed here. For example, when applying the test of reason, not long ago I met a man in a parking lot at a local supermarket. He belonged to the cult of Lightseekers, a New Age cult group. In the midst of our conversation, after I shared that Jesus is the truth, the way, and the life, he informed me that he believed that "all truth was relative." I asked him, "So you believe that there is no absolute truth?" He was absolutely certain about that. Here is a clear logical fallacy, where the very foundational statement of someone's faith is a self-contradiction (self-referentially incoherent). This man was absolutely sure that there are no absolutes. Sadly, he was too blinded to see the plain logical contradiction of his belief. His view (his book) did not pass the test of reason. Second, the test of experience, I remember talking with a lost couple who at the time had no children. As we talked about kids they suggested that the reason children disobey is because the parents teach them so. Rather than getting offended that they are suggesting that I intentionally teach my children to do evil, I tried to explain to them that children disobey by nature. Sinfulness is in our DNA (Ps. 51:5). It is obedience that the parents have to cultivate. The couple's belief (their book) was naïve and did not correspond to reality. If by now they have kids, I am sure they have learned the truth firsthand. Finally, when it comes to the practical test, one can make an example of the famous postmodern movement. One of its fundamental points was the idea of multiple interpretations (deconstructionism). The idea was simply this, a text does not necessarily have a single true meaning and interpretation. In fact, the readers have the right to interpret (deconstruct) and supply their own meaning that can even contradict the original meaning of the text.

nature of the Bible; what they adhere to is perfect. Having the divine truth in their hands and hearts and with the aid of the Holy Spirit, Christians have all that is necessary to challenge atheists' errors and, by God's grace, their eyes will be opened to see the most excellent ways of Christ, the Savior of the world.

Inerrancy Inside of the Church

Because inerrancy lies at the heart of the Christian faith and life, the church cannot allow any compromise. The importance of this fundamental doctrine to the church is stated clearly in Article XIX of the Chicago Statement on Inerrancy,

> **We affirm** that a confession of the full authority, infallibility, and inerrancy of Scripture is vital to a sound understanding of the whole of the Christian faith. We further affirm that such confession should lead to increasing conformity to the image of Christ. **We deny** that such confession is necessary for salvation. However, we further deny that inerrancy can be rejected without grave consequences, both to the individual and to the church. (emphasis added)[19]

Before getting into the truthfulness of this declaration in the Czech context, it is important to grasp the church's cultural background that underlies the situation. This will help set the context for understanding any attacks on inerrancy within the church.

Cultural Background within the Church

In the United States there are multitudes of seminaries, Bible colleges and universities, theological journals, and even theological societies (i.e. the Evangelical Theological Society [ETS]). Organizations such as ETS naturally involve theological discussion and controversies, which is not out of the ordinary in America, but

---

[19] "The Chicago Statement on Biblical Inerrancy," accessed November 11, 2014, http://library.dts.edu/Pages/TL/Special/ICBI_1.pdf, 4.

is expected and often welcomed. In the Czech Republic, however, the church culture dictates something to the contrary.

Czech believers are not numbered in the millions, but thousands.[20] The number of professing Christians in the United States vastly outnumbers the inhabitants of the entire Czech nation. Consequently, for one to enter into theological debate in America, you become just one of the many tens of thousands or millions expressing his or her opinion. In the Czech Republic there are only tens of thousands of evangelical Christians, and believers are very mindful of this. In fact, it affects how they do ministry, how they preach the Scriptures, and how they approach controversial issues.

When reviewing the history of the Czech nation you find wars and conflicts all done in the name of Christianity. For centuries Catholics slaughtered the Protestants and the Protestants warred against the Catholics.[21] In modern times, the Communists came in with their atheist ideology and offered a "better" way — no religion. As a result, it seems that in most people's minds no religion means no conflict.

Recognizing the social context of avoiding conflict at all costs, and its influence upon the church, one understands how difficult it is to argue for the truth. In fact, Czechs are known for finding the "golden middle way," a popular Czech idiom to express a synthesis of two opposing views. With this background we come to the discussion on inerrancy in the church.

Inerrancy Under Attack

After living and ministering for over thirteen years in the Czech Republic, I cannot recall a native Czech initiating a conversation, discussion, sermon, or lecture on the subject of inerrancy. When recently questioning various pastors about the doctrine of inerrancy, they had no answer as to what others believe on the subject, even

---

[20] Research provided by Project Zet in 2000 listed 17,272 members of evangelical denominations and churches in the country, http://projektzet.cz/en/resources/research/research/Research.pdf, (Accessed November 13, 2014).

[21] The Hussite Wars of the fifteenth century, the Hapsburg takeover, the reinstatement of Catholicism in the sixteenth century, the war between the Protestants and Catholics at the Battle of White Mountain in the seventeenth century, and the subsequent Catholicization, have left a bitter taste in the mouths of believers today.

within their own denomination. Their response was that no one is talking about it, and no one desires to find out what others believe.

The reason for the lack of discussion on the subject is not because inerrancy is assumed, but because it is ignored. Due to the small Christian population and the vast number of atheists in the country, Christians seem to avoid controversy at all costs. Their greatest objective is to present a show of love and unity, and let the world know that they are Christ's disciples because of their love for one another.[22] Therefore, controversy and disagreement are avoided so as to make a statement to the unbelieving world, which vastly outnumbers people of faith.

The hesitancy to start a discussion on inerrancy within a denomination stems from a fear it would present division and add fuel to the argument that religion is divisive.[23] This is added to the reality that men are studying in liberal Bible schools in Europe where inerrancy is attacked, doubted, and rejected. These men then return to pastor churches and strip the church of its spiritual vigor by preaching without authority, avoiding controversial themes, and delivering philosophical musings.[24]

The result of this approach to inerrancy is that a silent attack on Scripture is waged without a shot fired or a warning trumpet blown. Such a covert assault on the truth, birthed in the classrooms of liberal seminaries, continually strikes at the heart of the life of the church. It is not militant in its approach; it is actually a war unknown by most. However, this attack manifests itself in those preaching without authority and labeling those who do as fundamentalists with a simple faith.

The fruit of this approach is preaching that is minimized and replaced with a variety of "spiritual" alternatives.[25] One pastor

---

[22] "Ekumena mezi protestanty a katolíky – nejde to!", accessed November 11, 2104, http://www.reformace.cz/zod/ekumena-mezi-protestanty-katoliky-nejde-cislo-121

[23] The memories of the previous religious battles are embedded in the mind of the culture, similar to how the Civil War is still in the minds of many in the southern United States today.

[24] The president of one denomination said that, in his view, people do not go to church for preaching, but for atmosphere.

[25] An example of one pastor comes to mind. He does not view preaching as vital. He once said he would not be upset in the least if a brother who was scheduled to preach one Sunday came and did not have a message. He said they would simply not have a

recently said, "You preach, I preach, and nothing happens. Don't make such a big deal out of preaching." In the past year another pastor stated in a denominational meeting, "You ask if the Bible is the Word of God. I say yes, but it causes me to ask about ten more questions."[26] Such expressions, as from these pastors, fly in the face of a sound view of the inerrancy, authority, and power of the Word of God, yet they go completely unchallenged.

When another Christian minister was questioned about his view on the lack of discussion on inerrancy, he suggested that there is a different, more critical failure in Christian circles. He said, "The greatest sin in our country is to criticize someone who professes to be a Christian." To criticize a man's theology is considered taboo in our post-modern age. "How judgmental" is the cry. Consequently, inerrancy and the authority of Scripture are left without a defense against the silent attacks taking place within the church.

The Practice of an Atheistic Perspective

The Czech evangelical church today finds itself in a position not much different from the world. The atheistic society denies inerrancy outright, while the church largely overlooks the subject altogether. Its defense of the truth is often no defense at all. There is a silent neglect and an unwillingness to allow the possibility of controversy within the church.

The result is that the church is little different from the world in its application of the Scriptures and in its defense of the truth. The controversial texts are overlooked, the theme of love is continually proclaimed, and the purity of the church is of little to no concern. Such a perspective is not difficult to find in the secular world.

The perceived unity of the church is given preference over the purity of the church, and ecumenism (the sacred cow of Czech evangelicalism[27]) is the result. Anyone rejecting ecumenism is

---

message, but fill the time with other things. His low view of preaching is a result of his view of Scripture. If he viewed it as inerrant, authoritative, and the very words of God, then no one would be able to keep him away from the pulpit on a Sunday morning.

26 Stated in a denominational meeting, fall of 2013.

27 David Novák, "Ekumena mezi protestanty a katolíky", accessed November 11, 2014. http://www.krestandnes.cz/article/

labeled a fundamentalist and marginalized within the evangelical church. Any attempt to bring the weight of Scripture into the conversation is rejected, thus showing the lack of conviction in an authoritative and inerrant text of Holy Scripture.

An outright rejection and a passive avoidance of an authoritative, inerrant text have grave consequences for the church, as the Chicago statement warned. Unfortunately, the evangelical church in the Czech Republic has allowed itself to be stripped of its authoritative message and replaced with a man-centered, results-focused approach to ministry and evangelism. Its mission is not to contend for the truth once delivered to the saints, but to present a façade of unity to an unbelieving world.

Denominational conflicts are carried on without any reference to Scripture, because no level of conviction exists that would support the thought that problems can be resolved by turning to an inerrant, authoritative text. Such a theology is the fruit of the three hermeneutical principals employed by the Czech evangelical church: 1) You cannot know if your interpretation is correct (post-modernism); 2) the Scriptures may say one thing, but practically it works differently (pragmatism); and 3) the golden middle way is the safest for the church. When one does not have a firm grasp of the authority, infallibility and inerrancy of the Scriptures, as the Chicago statement makes clear, then the whole of the Christian faith is compromised and manifests itself in a practical atheism that mimics the world.

Lack of a serious conviction regarding the doctrine of inerrancy proves to impede the spiritual growth of the church. Where there is no conviction there is no passion. Where there is no passion there is no pursuit, and where there is no pursuit there is no spiritual fruit. Truth falls by the wayside in order to create unity and present a façade of love and peace to appease an unbelieving world. And as the Chicago statements states, a rejection of inerrancy cannot take place without grave consequence to the individual and the church. The fruit of this truth is evident in every way. Churches are without sound preaching, have little to no evangelism, are without

david-novak-ekumena-mezi-protestanty-a-katoliky-jdeto/22924.htm.

spiritually strong and doctrinally sound leaders, and fail to equip and pass on the truth to the next generation (2 Tim 2:2).

In Defense of the Truth

Considering the devastating effects of rejecting or neglecting the doctrine of inerrancy, the church of Jesus Christ must take a stand. The health, vitality, and unity of the church is at stake. The spiritual growth of God's people requires nourishment only provided in the storehouse of God's truth, which is the Word of God.

The doctrine of biblical inerrancy is important because inerrancy is interwoven with the character and nature of God. A perfect God can only produce a perfect record. Considering that God chose to deliver to mankind such a written record, by implication man must need God's perfect message.[28] The church that teaches, defends, and proclaims the truthfulness and accuracy of God's revelation affirms the character and nature of God in its proclamation. To make known the inerrant Word of God is to make known the inerrant God of the Word.

The most significant contribution the church can make to the world is to make known what God has written. The God ordained method of this expression is called preaching (1 Cor 1-2), which is to proclaim what God has said. This type of preaching is known as expository preaching—preaching that reveals the meaning of a text of Scripture in its original context and applies it to the hearers. To declare what God has revealed is the greatest expression of love of the church to the world, and the greatest expression of a pastor to his sheep.

The church that embraces, defends, and preaches the inerrant Word of God is one with its roots sunk deep into the heart of God. It stands as a pillar of truth upon the sure foundation of God's Word, and draws its strength and vigor from the life-giving stream of God's revelation.

---

[28]   Dr. John MacArthur makes the point that because the Bible is inerrant, it demands exposition. John MacArthur, "Preaching the Book God Wrote, part 1, accessed November 28, 2014, http://www.gty.org/Resources/Print/articles/4825

The Czech Bible Institute (CBI) is committed to assisting local churches in the important work of teaching and preaching God's written revelation. CBI teaches that the Bible is the inspired, inerrant, infallible, authoritative, and all-sufficient Word of God. The first article translated and published in the Czech language by CBI was John MacArthur's "Inerrancy Demands Exposition." The battle for truth starts with understanding the nature of biblical inerrancy and is driven home with preaching of the Word of God.

The passion of CBI is to help equip the next generation of leaders to be men of conviction who will stand for truth no matter the cost. This begins with CBI's foundational Bible survey program and extends to the pastoral training program where men are taught how to rightly divide the Word of truth (2 Tim 2:15) and preach it in season and out of season (2 Tim 4:2). To preach the wisdom of men or the "felt needs" of the congregation is to silence the Spirit and quench His power. CBI's passion is for the Lord to raise up a new generation of men with the conviction to preach what God has revealed and earnestly contend for the faith once for all delivered to the saints.

Historical Critical Method
Biblical Criticism or Higher Criticism

THE POISONOUS FRUIT OF HIGHER CRITICISM

By Martin Manten (Germany)

Introduction

The task of every believer—pastors and leaders in the church in particular—is to rightly divide the Word of God. From Ezra's reigning desire to Paul's final instructions to Timothy, the common-thread conviction throughout Holy Writ is that the Scriptures must be diligently studied, personally applied, and faithfully taught to others. It can be overwhelming, however, even for the most mature believers, to find their way through the jungle of interpretive tools and modern methodologies that assail us from every angle. Each divergent approach claims to help Christians understand the Bible and find its true meaning, yet some of these are built upon dangerous presuppositions that have crept into modern scholarship. Consequently, the validity of such tools must be questioned.

One such tool is the Historical Critical Method (HCM)—sometimes known as Biblical Criticism or Higher Criticism. It is widely accepted today—and occasionally without much critical thought. This article endeavors to define the method, to shed light on its roots, development, and implications, and to warn fellow believers of its danger. It is the responsibility of a shepherd of God's flock to help the sheep find green pastures and to make sure that they are protected from wolves. This is a high calling that cannot be taken lightly, and it is the motivation behind the writing of this article.

A Brief Definition

In contrast to traditional approaches that emphasize the Bible's *divine* origin, the HCM emphasizes the Bible's *human* origin. Whereas conservative Bible scholars implicitly *trust* the Bible's historicity and *submit* to its claims, the HCM proponents implicitly *question* the Bible's historicity and seek to *arbitrate* its claims. The HCM does not begin with the traditionally foundational suppositions that the Bible is the Word of God and that its every statement is inerrant and binding; rather, it analyzes the books of the Bible from a secular starting point, employing the tools of historical science and the consensus of scholarly opinion to try to determine the human factors concerning authorship, dating, and underlying sources.[1] At the very outset, then, it is evident that the HCM marks a fundamentally different perspective than that which was clear to the early Thessalonian believers who accepted apostolic teaching "not as the word of men, but for what it really is, the word of God" (1 Thess 2:13).[2]

The Roots of the Historical Critical Method

There are many passages in the Bible that stress the importance and connection between the roots of a tree and the fruit it bears, or between the foundation of a structure and its stability. Consequently, it is reasonable to take a close look at the roots sustaining the HCM. Larry L. Walker provides a brief and informative summary portraying the main influences of the HCM and how they are interwoven:

> The primary influence on the formulators of higher criticism and its bearing on the origin and development of the religion of Israel was the philosophy of the age, which was dominated by evolutionary thought—unilinear progress from the simple to the complex. Such evolutionary thinking was applied by C. Darwin to

---

[1] Paul Enns, *The Moody Handbook of Theology* (Chicago: Moody Press, 1989), 552.

[2] All Scripture citations are from the ESV unless otherwise stated.

biology and by K. Marx to economics. Wellhausen, following the approach of J. K. W. Vatke, applied this scheme to Israel and ended up with three basic periods of history of development: pre-prophetic—prophetic—ethical-monotheism. The end result of this was that we have in the Bible not God's thoughts about man but man's thoughts about God, not a revealed religion but an invented religion.[3]

Other key concepts with formative character can be identified as the enlightenment and humanism. The common denominator of these three (evolutionary thought, the enlightenment, and humanism) is that they all elevate autonomous human reason as the final judge over truth. Eta Linnemann, a renowned former proponent of the HCM who rejected the approach after experiencing genuine conversion, cuts right to the heart of the matter:

> Research is conducted *ut si Deus non daretur* ("as if there were no God"). This means the reality of God is excluded from consideration from the start, even if the researcher acknowledges that God could bear witness of himself in his Word. The standard by which all is assessed is not God's Word but scientific principle. Statements in Scripture regarding place, time, sequences of events, and persons are accepted only insofar as they fit in with established assumptions and theories. Scientific principle has come to have the status of an idol.[4]

The consequences of applying the HCM are unavoidable: the Bible is humanized, the concept of divine authorship is downgraded, if not eliminated, and the traditional understanding of biblical truth is radically changed such that the message is relegated to mythology, legend, or spiritual coaching.

---

[3] Larry L Walker, "Some Results and Reversals of the Higher Criticism of the Old Testament.," *Criswell Theological Review* 1 (Spring 1987): 282.

[4] Eta Linnemann, *Historical Criticism of the Bible: Methodology or Ideology?* (Grand Rapids: Baker Book House, 1990), 84.

The Development of the Historical Critical Method

A change of paradigm usually does not occur suddenly. This is certainly true in the case of historical criticism. Charles Darwin, along with Enlightenment and Rationalist thinkers such as Locke, Hume, Kant, and Hegel, provided the general mindset which men like F. C. Baur, David Strauss, and Julius Wellhausen applied in constructing the HCM. Once the groundbreaking book *Prolegomena zur Geschichte Israels (Prolegomena to the History of Israel)* was published, there was no stopping the HCM as it ran like a wildfire devouring seminaries and denominations alike.

In the mid-19th century, F. C. Baur rejected the historic Christian doctrines and developed a historical-critical method by applying Hegel's philosophical grid to the Scriptures. He contended there was a conflict between the Jewish theology of Peter and the Gentile theology of Paul, and applied this critical lens to the whole of the New Testament. His student, David Strauss, reinterpreted the New Testament as embellished mythology and denied the historicity of its claims.[5]

Old Testament scholars presented unique historical-critical theories throughout the 18th and 19th centuries, as well, which eventually developed into an evolutionary pattern—sometimes called the documentary hypothesis or Wellhausen hypothesis—to account for the composition of the Pentateuch. This evolutionary scheme was applied to religious development in the Bible so that instead of acknowledging Israel's religion as divinely revealed, it was simply viewed as a human development of religion.[6]

Consequences of the Historical Critical Method

It is no exaggeration to say that the introduction of the HCM triggered a new era of Christianity. Starting with the few scholars briefly surveyed above, it slowly conquered the seminaries and then made inroads into the church. While the method pretends to "lend assistance to the proclamation of the gospel through

---

[5]   Enns, *Moody Handbook of Theology*, 551.

[6]   Ibid., 552.

an interpretation of the Bible that is scientifically reliable and objective,"[7] it accomplishes exactly the opposite. As Linnemann states, "It should be patently obvious that the manner in which historical-critical theology handles the Bible does not further the proclamation of the Gospel, but rather hinders it—it even prevents it."[8]

Liberalism

First of all, the HCM has served as a door-opener for liberalism in all its various forms. Rolland D. McCune comments:

> The influence of biblical criticism or higher criticism on the formation of liberal theology was significant because it delivered a hermeneutic or a method of interpretation of what was thought to be a culture-bound book, the Bible. Lower criticism dealt with the text of Scripture, but higher criticism went beyond and dealt with authorship, date of composition, purpose in writing, parallels to other forms of literature, and the like. In itself this was legitimate scholarship, but with the post-Enlightenment presuppositions, principally the ultimate autonomy of human reason, the discipline was devastating to the Bible through the development of the historical-critical methodology. Dillenberger and Welch note correctly: 'The decisive issue was not the specific interpretations of historical criticism, but lay at a deeper level—viz, at the level of the significance and authority of the Bible as a whole, i.e., precisely in the giving up of traditional conceptions of biblical revelation. The acceptance of biblical criticism meant the abandonment of the belief that the Bible is an infallible record of divine revelation.'
>
> An important plank was thus laid in liberalism's platform. The Bible came to be regarded as a record

---

7   Linnemann, *Historical Criticism of the Bible*, 89.

8   Ibid., 89.

⌈ of the religious experiences of men and not as the⌉
⌊ infallible, verbally inerrant revelation of God.[9] ⌋

The HCM is happily at home both within liberalism of doctrine, which denies the traditional doctrines of the Christian faith, and within liberalism of biblical scholarship, which challenges the authenticity, inspiration, and inerrancy of the Bible.

Permeating Every Aspect of Christianity

One might be inclined to think that a method that seems to be rather complex and philosophical would only garner the attention of the academy. Unfortunately, it has made its way even into the Sunday schools, as the following quote shows:

> This idea of the lateness of Mosaic law has not remained within scholarly critical circles, but filters down into the every-day area of Sunday school lessons. In the Sunday school lesson help called 'Workers with Youth', a lesson on 'God and Israel Make a Covenant' deals with the life of Moses and adds: 'The Bible attributes to him a great many laws which modern scholars believe came from later times, and many legends have arisen about the person of Moses' (published by the General Board of Education of the Methodist Church, lesson of April 11, 1955, p. 31).[10]

Eta Linnemann leaves no doubt that, "Anyone who studies scientific theology will inevitably be pushed in the direction of accepting this false assumption." She further remarks in regard to theological education, "The historical-critical method is not just the foundation for the exegetical disciplines. It also decides what the systematician can say and whether one accepts his

---

[9]   Rolland D. McCune, "The Formation of the New Evangelicalism: Historical and Theological Antecedents," *Detroit Baptist Seminary* 3 (Fall 1998): 11.

[10] Joseph P Free, "Archeology and Biblical Criticism. Archeology and Liberalism," *Bibliotheca Sacra* 113, no. 452 (October 1956): 337.

claims. It determines procedure in Christian education, homiletics, and ethics."[11]

Theology and Preaching Redefined

Furthermore, Tom Ascol correctly detects and describes the eroding effects of the HCM in theology and preaching:

> The near extinction of doctrinal preaching today strictly correlates to the modern disenchantment with systematic theology—the discipline, which seeks to arrange in an orderly and coherent (i.e. 'systematic') fashion the revealed truth concerning God in His various relationships. Quite obviously such an attempt is valid only if there is an inherent unity in the Scriptures. If there is no overall unity in the Bible, no coherence in all its parts, then the systematic theologian is on a fool's errand. This is precisely the conclusion of much of the modern theological world. By accepting the 'assumptions of the literary and historical criticism which rejects the Bible's own representations' many contemporary theologians are compelled to find genuine inconsistencies, contradictions, and errors in the text of the Scriptures. Once such discrepancies are assumed, any notion of theological unity within the Bible must fall. An error-ridden Bible cannot be expected to teach a system of truth. One would be foolish, therefore, to attempt a systematization of its teachings. Further, instead of talking about biblical theology, one should now speak of biblical theologies (plural).[12]

It is painfully obvious that preaching from an errant, evolved, man-made set of doctrines lacks any gospel-laden grace, transformative power, or semblance of hope. The HCM kills preaching

---

[11] Linnemann, *Historical Criticism of the Bible*, 83-84.

[12] Tom Ascol, "Systematic Theology and Preaching," *The Founders Journal* 4 (Spring 1991): 5.

from the start because it doubts the word of Christ—the only source whereby comes faith (Rom 10:17).

A Caution Regarding Intellectual Pride

Although there may be pressure to be recognized in academic circles, Christians need not adopt the HCM as a whole, nor any modified form of it. The grammatical-historical method, which assumes biblical inerrancy as a corollary of divine inspiration, and which seeks to understand Scripture on its own grammatical and historical terms, is absolutely sufficient as an exegetical and herme-neutical tool when it comes to determining the text's meaning.[13] The following observations and conclusions by Walker are as insightful as they are alarming. He quotes J. J. Reeve and comments:

> One professor who switched views, not just because of archaeology but because he saw the mindset involved in higher criticism, was J. J. Reeve of Southwestern Baptist Theological Seminary. In a word of personal testimony, he described first his experience at "one of the great universities" where he was overwhelmed with the scholarship of the critical approach and accepted it. He wrote, "This world-view *is* wonderfully fascinating and almost compelling." But he went on to describe two reasons for his rejection of the system: 1) the methods, and 2) the spirit of the movement. Some of his statements are worth noting verbatim:
>
>> It became more and more obvious to me that the movement was entirely intellectual, an attempt in reality to intellectualize all religious phenomena. I saw also that it was a partial and one-sided intellec-tualism with a strong bias against the fundamental tenets of Biblical Christianity. Such a movement is responsible for a vast amount of intellectual pride,

---

[13] Mal Couch, ed., *An Introduction to Classical Evangelical Hemeneutics: A Guide to the History and Practice of Biblical Interpretation* (Grand Rapids: Kregel Publications, 2000), 62-64.

an aristocracy of intellect with all the snobbery, which usually accompanies that term.

Although such reasoning may not sound very academic, Reeve seems to have sensed an element missed by many other scholars. He continued:

> I have seen the Unitarian, the Jew, the free-thinker and the Christian who has imbibed critical views, in thorough agreement on the Old Testament and its teaching. They can readily hobnob together, for the religious element becomes a lost quantity; the Bible itself becomes a plaything for the intellect, a merry-go-round for the mind partially intoxicated with its theory.[14]

These observations helpfully demonstrate another area of concern regarding the HCM and its current sway over biblical scholarship at the highest echelons of secular achievement. And while these concerns are expressed in academic circles, the ideas and attitudes that accompany them inevitably make their way to the pew. It is crucial, therefore, to expose this error and stand firm upon the foundation of biblical inerrancy and approach Scripture not as the intellectual plaything of man, but as the infallible Word of God. Only in this way is God's Word lifted up and man's pride laid low.

Final Comments about the Historical-Critical Method

The HCM has hit the evangelical world like a bombshell. Its implications are far-reaching and variegated. Below are just a few examples.

Regarding Inspiration and HCM

R. C. Sproul comments:

---

[14] Walker, "Some Results and Reversals of the Higher Criticism of the Old Testament," 284-85.

In the second half of the nineteenth century the pervasiveness of evolutionary ideas and the rise of higher criticism in biblical studies led certain theologians to question the historic concept of verbal inspiration. Attempts were made to modify the concept or to replace it altogether with a new doctrine of inspiration allowing for a theory of religious development and a patchwork Old Testament. Some theologians shifted the local of inspiration from the objective word to subjective experience.[15]

Regarding Inerrancy and HCM

Mal Couch writes:

Many of the major denominations that for centuries have held to full inerrancy of the Scripture have already or are now abandoning their position. Many Schools, the founders of which valiantly defended inerrancy, have caved in under academic pressure and now allow their professors to teach the ideas of higher and historical criticism. Although many Bible teachers and professors attempt to preserve belief in the doctrine, they find themselves up against not only a culture that is hostile to such a belief, but also growing disbelief from their own congregations and students.[16]

Regarding Hermeneutics and HCM

Couch points out:

The bottom line is, if Scripture cannot be trusted in some areas, it cannot be trusted in any area. Once full inspiration is denied, man determines what is inspired and what is not. Once there is a "crack in the dam" in

---

[15] David Horton, ed., *The Portable Seminary* (Minneapolis, MN: Bethany House, 2006), 30.

[16] Couch, *An Introduction to Classical Evangelical Hemeneutics*, 15, 58.

our belief in full inspiration, the flood is imminent. Dr. Schaeffer understood that once the flood begins, there is no end. . .The Bible is made to say only that which echoes the surrounding culture at our moment of history.[17]

Conclusion

It is hoped that the information presented in this short article will stimulate the reader's thinking and help him reach a personal conclusion on how to deal with the issue at hand. Much is at stake and a stand must be taken. The oldest deception the Bible reports is found in Genesis 3:1 and starts out with the question, "Indeed, has God said. . .?" From that point in history, sowing doubt in the Word of God still proves to be an efficient and robust deception. The historical-critical method is nothing less than a sophisticated and recycled form of Genesis 3:1, clothed in piety, seasoned with theologically-twisted terminology (or confusion of meanings, as Linnemann puts it[18]), and sweetened with the tempting reward of academic recognition. The HCM threatens everything from biblical inspiration and biblical inerrancy to Sunday school lessons and the efficacy of preaching. We who receive the apostolic teaching not as man's word but as God's must defend what has been entrusted to us to keep (1 Tim. 6:20-21).

---

[17]   Ibid., 16.

[18]   Linnemann, *Historical Criticism of the Bible*, 100.

How Egalitarianism Attacks Inerrancy in the Latin American Church

By Carlos Montoya (Honduras)

D enominational loyalty runs deep in the Latin American evangelical community. To some degree this loyalty is beneficial for the health of the church because fraternal camaraderie develops among the brothers and sisters across different local assemblies. Efforts to extend the kingdom of Christ are enhanced as there is a greater unified representation of churches. No doubt, denominationalism has played a great part in propagating Christ's church.

However, potential dangers loom over an unhealthy and at times blind denominational loyalty. Many churches have "sold their souls" to the whims of spiritually undiscerning denominational leadership, paving a way to the slow death of orthodoxy. Unfortunately, such a plight is not uncommon among the Latin American churches. Examples abound of the many local assemblies of a rather "conservative" line that have given way to unbiblical teachings and practices.[1]

---

[1] One such example is the proliferation of the charismatic movement in conservative denominations such as the Baptist, Central American, and Reformed Churches in Honduras.

Many of these teachings go unchallenged because of the lack of biblical discernment at both the local and denominational level.

Perhaps one of the most unsuspecting issues that has infected the Latin American evangelical church is the infiltration of egalitarianism regarding the role of women in the church.[2] This position has found many supporters because of the great lack of male leadership, a very common problem in the church. Some contend that since men are not "stepping up" to fulfill their leadership role, they must resort to gifted women to fill this void. The primary problem with this thinking is that it contradicts clear biblical teaching. Consequently, many have tried to soothe their consciences by the manner in which they interpret key passages.[3] The spectrum ranges from attributing dubious meanings to their interpretation to flat out rejecting the clear teaching. Such was the case in a denominational convention meeting a few years ago in Honduras.

Annually, this denomination gathers representatives from all the local assemblies to discuss various ecclesiastical issues as well as to provide a forum for encouragement and spiritual growth. In this particular year, a group of about two hundred pastors assembled to hear an invited speaker focus on various pastoral ministry issues.[4] As he was developing his message, he remarked that he saw no problem with women in church leadership positions. He expressed it with much enthusiasm, claiming this to be a "great advancement" in his own pastoral ministry. The majority of those attending received this comment with a round of applause. Later during a time of recess, a pastor approached the speaker to express concern about his comment regarding women in church leadership. The speaker explained that he believed that the term "pastor" is a generic term that can include both men and women. Disturbed by his response, this pastor asked him how he would interpret 1 Timothy 2:11-14:

---

[2] Egalitarianism is the view that states that man and woman are equal both in personhood and in their roles in marriage and the church.

[3] The three key passages are 1 Corinthians 11:3-16; 1 Corinthians 14:34-35; and 1 Timothy 2:11-14.

[4] This account was given by a MEDA seminary professor who attended the meeting.

A woman must quietly receive instruction with entire submissiveness. But I do not allow a woman to teach or exercise authority over a man, but to remain quiet. For it was Adam who was first created, *and* then Eve. And *it was* not Adam *who* was deceived, but the woman being deceived, fell into transgression.

The speaker proceeded to explain that after much study he had concluded that Paul was simply asserting his personal position on the matter, influenced by the chauvinistic culture of his day.[5]

Is this a legitimate conclusion? The implications are far-reaching. It directly undermines the authority of the clear directive of the passage. It is a direct attack on the inerrancy of Scripture because it implies that Paul's "personal position" is in conflict with what God approves for the church. Influenced by chauvinistic society, according to the speaker, Paul was misled. In other words, Paul was wrong. He wrote error. His personal position was in conflict with God's ideal church leadership profile. Consequently, thus begins the slow death of orthodoxy!

The purpose of this article is to expose the attack by those who deny inerrancy by undermining the authority of Paul's instruction regarding the role of women in the church, thereby disregarding inspiration and rejecting the superintendence of the Holy Spirit. Additionally, the article will define the damaging implications of this attack in theological study and ecclesiastical practice. A brief look at the argumentation by leading egalitarian, evangelical voices and the biblical response will be set forth. Furthermore, the article will offer a concise exegetical insight of 1 Timothy 2:11-14, the most definitive text of Scripture that clarifies the woman's role in the church.

---

[5] This pastor informed me that the conversation went from bad to worse. He was surprised by the speaker's response and immediately questioned how he could believe this, considering the inspiration of the Word of God. The speaker mockingly retorted, "Do you really believe that the entire Bible is inspired?"

Explaining the Attack

Questioning the veracity of God's Word has been the focus of modern liberalism for more than a century and has been a primary assault of Satan since the Garden of Eden. Challenging Paul's position on women's role in the church is no exception. However, not until the middle of the nineteen-seventies did *evangelicals* begin proposing the same kind of argumentation in regards to the ecclesiastical role of women.[6] Paul Jewett, former professor of systematic theology at Fuller Seminary, in his 1975 landmark publication, *Man as Male and Female,* claimed that Paul's teaching regarding women flowed from a mixture of his rabbinic background and his call for the gospel:

> The apostle Paul was the heir of this contrast between the old and the new. To understand his thought about the relation of the woman to the man, one must appreciate that he was both a Jew and a Christian. He was a rabbi of impeccable erudition who had become an ardent disciple of Jesus Christ. And his thinking about women. . .reflects both his Jewish and his Christian experience. . .So far as he thought in terms of his Jewish background, he thought of the woman as subordinate to the man for whose sake she was created (1 Cor. 11:9).[7]

For Jewett, these two perspectives of old and new are incompatible and "there is no satisfying way to harmonize the Pauline argument for female subordination with the larger Christian vision of which the great apostle to the Gentiles was himself the primary architect."[8] In reference to 1 Timothy 2:12-13, he believes Paul was wrong in his appeal to the Genesis 2 creation account:

---

[6] Wayne Grudem. *Evangelical Feminism: A New Path to Liberalism?* (Wheaton, IL: Crossway Books, 2006), 43-7. This author agrees with Grudem's concern that most if not all of egalitarian argumentation undermines the authority of Scripture and paves a new way to liberalism. Grudem defines liberalism as "a system of thinking that denies the complete truthfulness of the Bible as the Word of God and denies the unique and absolute authority of the Bible in our lives" 15.

[7] Paul K Jewett. *Man as Male and Female* (Grand Rapids: Eerdsman, 1975), 112.

[8] Ibid., 112-3.

. . . . Paul is not only basing his argument exclusively
on the second creation narrative, but is assuming the
traditional rabbinic understanding of that narrative
whereby the order of their creation is made to yield the
primacy of the man over the woman. Is this rabbinic
understanding of Genesis 2:18f, correct? *We do not
think that it is. . . .*[9]

Later in 1993, a pastor of the Christian Reformed Church,
Clarence Boomsma, voiced a similar position. Boomsma's contribution is especially alarming because of his conservative, Reformed
background. On the one hand, Boomsma affirms the priority of
inspiration for a proper understanding of 1 Timothy 2:11-14:

To propose that Paul was wrong in his application
of Scripture and therefore wrong to deny women the
opportunity to serve as teachers and authorities is to
call into question the inspiration and authority of the
apostle. Such a conclusion is not an option for the
believer committed to the Reformed confession of the
Scriptures as the Word of God. How can the difficulty
be resolved in keeping with our confession with the
Bible to be divinely inspired and our commitment to
the Scriptures as infallible in faith and practice?[10]

However, while his concern for a sound position on inspiration is commendable, his detailed argumentation of the passage
subtly undermines inspiration and, therefore, inerrancy. It is this
nuance that slowly poisons the springs of orthodoxy. In particular,
Boomsma states, "the singular importance of 1 Timothy 2:11-14
lies in its appeal to the authority of the Old Testament to undergird
the ordinance not to permit a woman to teach and have authority
over a man."[11] Diminishing the value of Paul's prohibition in

---

[9] Ibid., 119. Emphasis added.

[10] Clarence Boomsma. *Male and Female, One in Christ: New Testament Teaching on
Women in Office*, (Grand Rapids: Baker Books, 1993), 118, in the 2013 iBook edition
for iPhone.

[11] Ibid., 95.

this passage, he then posits that "practical instructions in the Bible that concern behavior and conduct must be understood and evaluated, and their permanent validity ascertained in the light of the doctrinal teaching of the Scriptures."[12] As a result, according to Boomsma, the doctrinal teaching of Galatians 3:28 is clearly non-restrictive regarding women serving in the church. Therefore, Paul's prohibition in 1 Timothy 2:12 must be interpreted in light of the non-restrictive nature of Galatians 3:28. He, thus, expresses his hypothesis:

> So unless it is clear that Paul is restricting the teaching of Galatians 3:28 in 1 Timothy 2:11-14 on the ground of other biblical truths, the biblical teaching of the unity and equality of men and women is the norm by which the church should be guided in its life and practice regarding women serving in the church's administrative offices, and practical prohibitions read in that light.[13]

Boomsma then launches into a lengthy treatise arguing for Paul's misuse of Genesis 2 when he prohibits women from teaching and exercising authority over men. His basic premise is expressed when he writes, "the fact that Adam was created before Eve in itself does not argue for man's priority over women."[14] He pointedly concludes, "the apostle's argument from Genesis 2 is *without support in the text*."[15] Making a qualification on the basis of Paul simply using the interpretation of the day, he adds the caveat, "This is not to say that Paul was in error when he adduces his argument from Genesis. . . ."[16] According to Boomsma, Paul's highly chauvinistic culture demanded that he restrict the ministry of women in order to remove any unnecessary obstacle for the advancement of the gospel, even if it meant undergirding this restriction with Scripture

---

[12] Ibid., 95-6.

[13] Ibid., 97.

[14] Ibid., 100.

[15] Ibid., 104. Emphasis added.

[16] Ibid., 104-6.

(Genesis 2) that does not give priority of man over woman, but was an acceptable interpretation of his day. Boomsma summarizes his conclusion:

> All students of the Bible are aware of how New Testament authors quote the Old Testament to substantiate a point they are making, and that such use of quotations was an effective argument for their readers in that time. *But such a method is no longer valid in our use of scriptural quotations.*[17]

How should we respond to this kind of reasoning? As mentioned, Boomsma's position on the priority of inspiration is to be commended. However, his subsequent reasoning undoubtedly undermines both the inspiration and inerrancy of Paul's prohibition in 1 Timothy 2:11-14. This disturbing subtlety permeates a seemingly sound exegesis of the passage. It is true that clearer passages on certain subjects can shed light on passages that are not as clear.[18] The problem with Boomsma's premise in placing Galatians 3:28 as a standard under which 1 Timothy 2:11-14 is judged is that the two passages deal with two distinct contexts. Though gender equality is heralded in the Galatian passage, that equality is defined by being "in Christ." As Johnson aptly states, "It does plainly teach an egalitarianism of privilege in the covenantal union of believers *in Christ.*"[19] Salvation and its blessings is the context of Galatians 3, whereas the 1 Timothy passage celebrates the privileges "in the church," giving emphasis to the distinction of male-female function as it pertains to leadership. One cannot view this comparison as one passage trumping another because they beautifully complement each other, highlighting one's union with Christ and one's function in the church. This becomes extremely important because Boomsma allowed a flawed interpretation of

---

[17] Ibid., 157-8. Emphasis added.

[18] Milton Terry. *Biblical Hermeneutics*, reprint (Eugene, OR: Wipf and Stock Publishers, 1999), 449.

[19] S. Lewis Johnson. "Role Distinctions in the Church: Galatians 3:28," in *Recovering Biblical Manhood and Womanhood*, ed. John Piper and Wayne Grudem (Wheaton, IL: Crossway Books, 1991), 164. Emphasis added.

his "standard" Galatian passage to trump 1 Timothy 2:11-14 to the extent of questioning Paul's legitimate appeal to Genesis 2.

In 1 Timothy 2, Boomsma acknowledges that Paul clearly gives a prohibition against women teaching or having authority over men in the church, and undergirds it with the Old Testament. He writes," "it is clear from verse 12 that the women in Ephesus were not allowed to engage in a form of teaching that gave them dominance over the men in the church."[20] He admits the plain understanding of this passage, that it undoubtedly prohibits women from teaching and exercising authority over men. Furthermore, Boomsma acknowledges that Paul bases such a prohibition on the authority of the Old Testament. Curiously, of all the egalitarian views for this passage, this one is grounded on sound exegetical principles applied to the immediate context. Lexically and syntactically speaking, it is flawless. In fact, all other egalitarian views fail in their exegetical analysis, being easily refuted by the exegetically skilled. Proponents of Boomsma's argumentation stand on solid grammatical principles and acknowledge that Paul meant just what he wrote. However, herein lies the poisonous and dangerous subtlety. Many are attracted to the interpretive soundness of the passage, but, because of their egalitarian presuppositions, they naively drink of the laced water, sacrificing the essential bedrock of biblical fidelity – inerrancy. Testimonies abound concerning how this argumentation has taken root in the Latin American church. This author has interacted with various pastors in Central America who testify to the ease with which leaders of denominations and para-church organizations advocate such reasoning.

Exposing the Attack

How can this be an attack on inerrancy when proponents like Boomsma claim to be committed to a conservative position on inspiration and inerrancy? Simply put, they soft pedal what Paul has done. They believe that Paul's misuse of an Old Testament passage such as Genesis 2 falls within the parameters of inspiration. How do they defend this? They assert that the social milieu of the

---

[20] Ibid., 138.

day accepted this incorrect interpretation, and therefore, Paul could legitimately use such inaccurate reasoning.[21] However, be that as it may, one must call a spade a spade! There is no other way to understand this but to acknowledge that Paul made a mistake or deliberately misled his readers. Either way, they are claiming that Paul does not accurately represent Genesis 2. From this perspective, this passage is obviously flawed; and if it is flawed, it is in error. If it is in error, it cannot be inspired; and if it is not inspired, it cannot be God's Word. If it is not God's Word, it has lost its authority over us. As Wayne Grudem warns, "To say that Paul made a mistake in writing 1 Timothy 2 is another step on the path toward liberalism."[22]

The Damage of the Attack

How serious is this attack? What are the far-reaching implications? Al Mohler expresses it well:

> Do we really believe that God breathed out and inspired every word of the Bible? Do we believe that the Bible, as the Word of God written, shares God's own perfection and truthfulness? Do we believe that when the Bible speaks, God speaks? If so, we affirm the inerrancy of Scripture without reservation or hesitation. If we do not make these affirmations, then we have set ourselves upon a project of determining which texts of the Bible share these perfections, if any. We will use a human criterion of judgment to decide which texts bear divine authority and which texts can be trusted. We will decide, one way or another, which texts we believe to be God speaking to us.[23]

---

21   Is it not curious that Paul feels pressured to use such reasoning in 1 Timothy and yet not in Galatians? Was the social milieu that much different in Galatia? This is an obvious inconsistency.

22   Grudem, *Evangelical Feminism*, 46.

23   R. Albert Mohler. "When the Bible Speaks, God Speaks: The Classic Doctrine of Biblical Inerrancy," in *Five Views on Biblical Inerrancy*, ed. J. Merrick, Stephen M. Garrett (Grand Rapids: Zondervan, 2013), 31.

Those who claim that Paul incorrectly uses the Old Testament are guilty of the error addressed by this warning. They place themselves above Scripture as the judges of the truthfulness of Paul's words. This kind of thinking makes *them* the ultimate authority rather than Scripture. They now can conveniently choose what to obey and what not to obey. What would restrain them from applying this same reasoning to other passages? The Scripture's authority is undermined and the Bible becomes nothing more than suggestive guidelines, a flat out rejection of historic Christianity!

Another unfortunate consequence is the insistence by denominational leaders to impose the egalitarian position on local assemblies. Having concluded that Paul's instruction is not normative for today, denominational leaders are not simply satisfied with allowing for differing views among the local churches but, instead, insist that all churches affirm an egalitarian position regarding women in church leadership. The Honduran church has experienced this firsthand, being practically bullied into conformance.

Additionally, we cannot ignore another serious potential ramification that flows directly from egalitarianism. Wayne Grudem issues an appropriate warning of how egalitarianism provides fertile ground for the current open-mindedness toward homosexuality. Though many evangelical egalitarians have refused to succumb to the pressures of the homosexual agenda, Grudem foresees the inevitable outcome,

> . . . . we would be foolish to ignore the trend set by a number of more liberal Protestant denominations, denominations that from the 1950s to the 1970s approved the ordination of women using many of the same arguments that evangelical egalitarians are using today. And those few prominent evangelicals who have endorsed homosexual conduct have already set a pattern of following evangelical feminist arguments.[24]

Is this what awaits the Latin American church?

---

[24] Grudem, *Evangelical Feminism*, 237.

The Defense Against the Attack

Built upon the foundation of the inerrancy of the Bible, applying proper exegetical principles proves that Paul's prohibition in 1 Timothy 2:11-14 is normative for today's church. A brief exposition of this definitive passage, highlighting exegetical insights pertinent to our discussion, will affirm its universal application for the church. [25] No doubt, submission is the overarching theme of these four verses. We can outline these verses in the following manner: *the expression of woman's submission (v. 11)*; *the explanation of woman's submission (V. 12)*; and *the reason for woman's submission (v. 13-14)*.

Chapter 2 verse 11 begins Paul's treatment of the woman's role in the church. Paul orders the woman to learn "in silence, in full submission." Here, he establishes the need for the woman to learn with a quiet attitude as an expression of a high standard of submission. He then moves on in verse 12 to explain what this high standard of submission entails: "But I do not permit a woman to teach or exercise authority over a man, but to be in silence."[26] Paul's use of the expression, "I do not permit" does not minimize the authoritativeness of this injunction. He speaks with the full apostolic authority given to him by Christ himself. Chapter 1 verse 1 establishes this authority, "Paul, an apostle of Christ Jesus according to the commandment of God our Savior, and of Christ Jesus. . . ." He speaks as an apostle of Christ under the commandment of God. There is no doubt that Paul's readers would have received this prohibition as the very words of God. The prohibition is clear: women are not to teach nor exercise authority over men in the context of the church. As mentioned previously, even egalitarian proponents such as Jewett and Boomsma acknowledge this. Yet, is it normative for today's church? The next verse answers this question.

---

[25] This brief exposition is not an exhaustive treatment that responds to the many different egalitarian arguments. It will simply highlight issues that pertain specifically to the egalitarian's attack on inspiration and inerrancy. For a detailed and exhaustive response to all the other egalitarian arguments, see Wayne Grudem, *Evangelical Feminism and Biblical Truth: An Analysis of More Than One Hundred Disputed Questions*, (Wheaton, IL: Crossway, 2012).

[26] Translation mine.

In verse 13, Paul gives the reason for this prohibition. He appeals to the Genesis 2 creation account to give an authoritative basis for the prohibition. The applicability of the prohibition through all cultures throughout history depends on the nature of the reason given for it. In other words, if the reason is universal, then the prohibition is universal. Paul states, "for Adam was formed first, then Eve."[27] Paul bases his prohibition on the order of creation as expressed in Genesis 2:18-23. Clearly, it is not an appeal based on culture or time sensitive circumstances. It is based on the unchanging reality of the creation priority of Adam over Eve, which remains true to this day. Thus, the prohibition of women to teach or exercise authority over men is applicable as much today as it was in Paul's time.

As previously mentioned, even Boomsma and like proponents cannot ignore this reality and equally acknowledge that Paul is appealing to the priority of man over woman based on the Genesis 2 creation account to undergird the applicability of the prohibition. However, their egalitarian presuppositions will not allow them to accept the universal nature of the prohibition. Hence, they attempt to dismantle Paul's entire argument, resorting to only one other option—the claim that Paul was mistaken in his appeal. This is a direct attack on inspiration and inerrancy. To attempt to prove Paul's misled appeal, they must argue that Genesis 2 offers no basis for man's headship over woman. However, it is no stretch of the imagination to fairly and legitimately conclude that various circumstances of the Genesis 2 creation account *do* lead one to affirm male headship. Moo rightly asserts, "The woman's being *created after man, as his helper*, shows the position of submission that God intended as inherent in the woman's relation to the man, a submission that is violated if a woman teaches doctrine or exercises authority over a man."[28]

Unlike advocates of egalitarianism, complementarianism upholds that Paul wrote under the inspiration of the Holy Spirit,

---

[27] Translation mine.

[28] Moo Douglas, "What Does It Mean Not to Teach or Have Authority Over Men," in *Recovering Biblical Manhood and Womanhood*, ed. John Piper and Wayne Grudem (Wheaton, IL: Crossway Books, 1991), 190. Emphasis added.

thereby securing the accuracy of his appeal.[29] This results in author-itative grounds to make the prohibition applicable to all times and cultures. Therefore, we affirm that the prohibition for women to teach and exercise authority over men is normative for today.

Al Mohler offers timely words: "The church must live by the Word of God, or it will depend upon some human authority as a substitute for God's Word."[30] A departure from the historical orthodox view of inspiration and inerrancy will only create a theology and practice that is right in one's own eyes. Many biblical injunctions go against the cultural grain and, sadly, many people succumb under the cultural pressure. A convenient solution is to "prove" the Scriptures wrong under the banner of evangelicalism. That is exactly what is happening in the Latin American church in regard to the woman's role in the church. Scholarship is highly esteemed in the Latin culture but hardly scrutinized. It is unfortunate that much of the church will surrender to this kind of teaching simply because it proceeds from international sources. With strong denominational loyalty among the churches, such teaching finds a seed bed for proliferation.

Thankfully, there exists a remnant of those who have maintained biblical fidelity amidst the pressure to do otherwise. One such example is a meek, quiet, elderly lady who attended a denominational women's retreat in a small Honduran town. Women leaders from the denomination, who knew that she came from a church that taught the biblical role of women, condescendingly asked her why she held that position. In a very humble but confident way she responded with the most profound and erudite answer: "Because the Bible says so."

As true ministers of the gospel of Christ, we have an urgent call to proclaim the truth. Our goal must be that men and women grow in the knowledge and love of Christ, founded upon the all-sufficient, inerrant Word of God. May God find us faithful in preaching Christ with power, passion and precision.

---

[29] Complementarianism is that "biblically derived view that men and women are complementary, possessing equal dignity and worth as the image of God, and called to different roles that each glorify him." "Our History", *The Council on Biblical Manhood and Womanhood*, http://cbmw.org/history (accessed on October 31, 2014).

[30] Mohler, "When the Bible Speaks," 42

Contextualization in Indian Missions and its Impact on Scriptural Authority

By Samuel Williams (India)

The purpose of this article is to analyze contextualization as a prevalent methodology in missions in India and consider its largely negative impact on our view of Scripture as inerrant and authoritative. Various methods arising from contextualization and their influence on man's view of Scripture will be discussed. We will survey how contextualization has impacted scriptural authority in the life of the church.

Contextualization – Birth in Asia

Contextualization is the adaptation of Scriptural truth to an audience-specific culture and people and has become a normative assumption in ministry today. As one author writes, "As soon as you express the gospel, you are unavoidably doing it in a way that is more understandable and accessible for people in some cultures and less so for others."[1] The frequency with which contextualization is used in ministry philosophy and practice lends to the

---

[1] Tim Keller, *Center Church* (Grand Rapids: Zondervan, 2012), 93.

assumption of its rightful place in historic and orthodox theology. The word itself is not emphasized in Scripture[2] but instead traces its historical roots to liberal theology. A branch of the World Council of Churches (WCC), named the Committee of World Evangelism and Missions,[3] first coined it. This body convened a conference in Bangkok (1972), where Shoki Coe, the General Director of the Theological Education Fund, a WCC agency, was credited with originating this term.[4] Their discussion of contextualization focused on how theology should adapt to indigenous cultures and societies.[5]

Much before contextualization became the mantra of the modern church, it was a term developed in missionary practice. In India, this was fueled by the natural syncretism[6] of Hindu Philosophy. Some of the first attempted bridges between Hindu Philosophy and Christianity were by an Indian Bengali, Keshab Chandra Sen (1838-1884),[7] who was influenced by Raja Ram Mohan Roy.[8] For instance, Keshab Chandra Sen, was drawn to the Christian doctrine of the Trinity and began to find parallels to it in Hindu concepts of the divine (*Brahman*).[9] These kinds of ecumenical tendencies became attractive to Indian missionaries and churchmen.[10] An analysis of contextualization in Indian missions can aid the present-day church in discerning its theological and practical outcomes.

---

[2] A distinction should be made between adaption of the truth versus transferring established truth into a new language and culture. The latter practice Scripture does encourage (1 Cor. 9:22).

[3] Founded in 1961 in New Delhi.

[4] Richard W. Engle. "Contextualization in Missions: A Biblical and Theological Appraisal." *Grace Theological Journal*, 4:1 (Spring 1983), 87.

[5] Ibid., 87.

[6] An attempt to combine different religions and belief systems, based on the assumption that there is truth to be found in all religions.

[7] Chan, *Grassroots Asian Theology*, 53.

[8] Raja Ram Mohan Roy founded the *Brahmo Samaj*, a monotheistic Indian movement functioning even today, integrating Hinduism with Christ's morality.

[9] Simon Chan, *Grassroots Asian Theology: Thinking the Faith from the Ground Up* (IL: Intervarsity Press, 2014), 53.

[10] Robin Boyd. *Indian Christian Theology*, Delhi: ISPCK, 1969, 38. Boyd states, "the interpretation which they [Ram Mohan and Keshab Chandra] provided were later to be taken up by others, both Christian and non-Christian.

Mission Contextualization and the Doctrine of Scripture

The development of contextualization in India began in comparisons between "western" and "Asian" theology.[11] Transformation was proposed against a colonial mentality that made western faith normative for the eastern believer. As one writer says, "they [Western theologies] perpetuate a Western world-view, Western values and Western theological presuppositions . . . they unconsciously perpetuate an unacceptable theological imperialism."[12]

This attitude allowed missions practitioners to evaluate and even seek to adapt and change parts of theology. Sadhu Sundhar Singh (1889-1929), an influential Indian Christian mystic and missionary, famously said, "Indians do need the water of life, but not in a European cup. They should sit down on the floor in church: they should take off their shoes instead of their turbans. Indian music should be sung. Long informal addresses should take the place of sermons."[13] Sundhar Singh's philosophy influenced much of the landscape of the Indian ministry of the gospel. Two methodological trends are observed here:

1. Reductionism in Systematic Theology

Systematic theology, with its classical subdivision of scriptural teaching is seen as an outflow of western thought.[14] Theology from the Indian standpoint cannot be considered as "dogmatic" but as "mysterious."[15] True theology cannot be derived from an official creed; it must be written through a direct experience of Christ.[16] While there are no unified records of this kind of "theologizing,"

---

[11] Lee, Moonjang. *Identifying an Asian Theology: A Methodological Quest*, Common Ground Journal (Spring 2009), 60.

[12] John R. Davis, *Poles Apart? Contextualizing the Gospel* (Bangalore: Theological Book Trust, 1993), 14.

[13] V.K. Bawa, *Christianity is Indian: The Emergence of an Indigenous Community*, ed.Roger E. Hedlund, (Delhi: ISPCK for MIIS, 2000), 130.

[14] Commonly outlined as, Bibliology, Theology Proper, Anthropology, Christology, Soteriology, Ecclesiology, and Eschatology (*Systematic Theology,* Wayne Grudem).

[15] Boyd, *Indian Christian Theology*, 258.

[16] These ideas are similar to the Gnosticism refuted in the New Testament epistles, which claimed that knowledge was to be found beyond Scripture in "mysteries" (cf. Col.2:18).

this is compatible with the idea that "Truth shines through all true formulations but can never be exhaustively defined."[17]

2. Integrating Pagan Texts with the Gospel

In a proposed attitude of humility, sacred writings from other religions are used to trace lines of unity between the Christian gospel and other religions. J.N. Farquhar (1861-1929), a Scottish Missionary to India said, "If Christ is able to satisfy all the religious needs of the human heart, then all the elements of pagan religions, since they spring from these needs, will be found reproduced in perfect form, completely fulfilled, consummated in Christ."[18]

Evangelism in the India context began to use the Hindu Scriptures such as the Vedas and the Bhagwad Gita. Sadhu Sundhar Singh developed this trend by saying, "Christianity is the fulfillment of Hinduism. Hinduism has been digging channels. Christ is the water to flow through these channels."[19] With this borrowing of terminology from Hinduism, Christ is seen as the Ganges River purifying our sins.[20] Other terms "baptized" from Sanskrit writings into gospel expressions include *Brahman* for "God," *Karma* for "sin," *Moksha* for "salvation," and *Sabha* for "Church."[21] While this may seem like mere linguistic efforts, these integrationist trends continued to develop an evangelistic methodology that uses the Hindu sacred texts as source material. A present day, popular Indian evangelist, Sadhu Chellapa (1934-present)[22] identifies a Hindu Vedic Deity, *Prajapati* as Jesus, and preaches forgiveness of sin through *Prajapati.*[23]

---

[17] Boyd, *Indian Christian Theology*, 259.

[18] Eric J. Sharpe, *Not to Destroy but to Fulfil, The Contribution of J. N. Farquhar to Protestant Missionary Thought in India before 1914* (Uppsala: Gleerup, 1965), 311.

[19] A. J. Appasamy and Burnett Hillman Streeter, *The Sadhu: A Study in Mysticism and Practical Religion* (London: Macmillan, 1922), 232.

[20] Boyd. *Indian Christian Theology*, 113.

[21] Sunand Sumithra, *Christian Theologies From An Indian Perspective* (Bangalore: Theological Book Trust, 1990), 244-247.

[22] www.agniministries.org.

[23] Roger E Hedlund, ed. *Quest for Identity, India's Churches of Indigenous Origin: The "Little Tradition" in Indian Christianity* (Delhi: ISPCK, 2000), 78.

One of the common defenses of such integration is Paul's use of Epimenides (a poet from Crete) and Aratus (A Macedonian poet) in his evangelistic sermon to the Athenians in Acts 17. The two quotes are: "In Him we live and move and have our being," and "We also are his offspring" (Acts 17:28). As William Hendrickson explains, "By quoting these poets Paul is not intimating that he agrees with the pagan setting in which the citations flourished. Rather, he uses the words to fit his Christian teaching."[24] Paul does not preach Christ from these secular poets, but merely affirms with general revelation that God is our Creator. Christ and Him crucified can only truly be preached from the inspired Word of Christ (1 Cor. 1:23). Contextual integration of biblical truth with pagan ideas inevitably erodes our view of the uniqueness of divine revelation.

The Ecumenical Movement and Reductionism in Doctrinal Essentials

Contextualization began to influence not just the message but also the nature of the church in India. Indian religious philosophy emphasizes ecumenism and unity as a noble goal. This began to become an influence in Indian Christian missionary thought in the early twentieth century.[25] In 1910, under an American missionary John Mott, the National Christian Council formed to build co-operation between different missions groups and denominations in India. This cooperation was unique in that it included Anglicans, Presbyterians and Congregationalists. The influence of Indian thinking on this enterprise (in 1910) is seen in C.B. Firth's statement, "To seek a union of such different traditions was no ordinary enterprise. Perhaps it could not have succeeded anywhere except in India."[26] A four-point term of union was drawn up:

(1) The Holy Scriptures of the Old and New Testaments, as containing all things necessary for salvation
(2) The Apostles' Creed and the Nicene Creed

---

24 William Hendriksen, and Simon J. Kistemaker, *Exposition of the Acts of the Apostles*, vol. 17, New Testament Commentary (Baker Book House, 1953–2001), 637.

25 C.B. Firth, *Indian Church History* (Delhi: ISPCK, 1976), 235

26 Ibid., 240.

(3) The two sacraments ordained by Christ Himself

(4) The Historic Episcopate, locally adopted[27]

Even this simplistic paring down of truth did not make unity an easy task. An example of the discussion and debate can be seen in the formation of the association of the Church of South India, which came about after twenty-eight years of dialogue.[28] A crucial factor seen in the unification process was the use of organized evangelistic programs of co-operation under regional councils.[29] Evangelism became a focal point and catalyst of unity. On September 27, 1947 the Church of South India (CSI) was formed with about 220,000 Methodists, 500,000 Anglicans, and 290,000 Presbyterians and Congregationalists uniting under a common liturgy and central governing body.[30] Churches across the globe hailed the union of such a diverse group of churches and traditions as historic. The essentials of the gospel became central while defining other details of doctrine secondary.

A practical outflow of this was seen in the matter of baptism. Both infant baptism and believer's baptism were practiced based on individual preference.[31] The 1957 edition of Church practice (CSI) had an Appendix B titled, "Guiding Principles in regard to the alternative practices of Infant Baptism and Believer's Baptism'.[32] This was a paradigm shift that demonstrated the Indian philosophical attitude of unity without detailed definition of faith and practice. This challenges the biblical idea that unity is rooted in the "One Faith" (Eph 4:5) that was once for all delivered to the church. This simplification of doctrinal essentials can cause the Church to eventually weaken her voice in the world.[33]

---

[27]   Ibid., 240-41.

[28]   Ibid., 241.

[29]   cf. http://www.nccindia.in/nccinew/index.php/about-us/history (accessed on 11/12/2014).

[30]   R .D. Paul, *The First Decade, an Account of the Church of South India*, (Madras: CLS, 1958), 209.

[31]   Firth. *Indian Church History*, 246.

[32]   Ibid., 256.

[33]   This is sadly evident in the Church of South India, which in a 1998 survey was seen to struggle with nominalism and internal political struggles. Glenn Myers. *Briefings: India*, (Carlisle: Paternoster, 2001), 17.

Accuracy and Relevance in Bible Translation

The translation of Scripture into the native languages of India has been an essential foundation stone of missions since the days of William Carey. His mission at Serampore produced a large body of early Indian Bible translations: Bengali (1801-1809), Urdu (1805-1843), Sanskrit (1805-1819), Oriya (1809-1815), Hindi (1811-1818), Punjabi (1815-1826), Assamese (1810-1833), and the New Testament in Telegu (1818), Konkani (1819), Gujarati (1820), Nepali (1821), Marwari (1821), Kanarese (1822), and Pali (1935).[34] The Bible is now available in fifty Indian languages, with portions available in about fifty more languages and dialects.[35]

While the translation work influenced by Carey became a great catalyst for gospel work in its time, it came under criticism by missionaries of the contextual generation. For instance, William Smalley states:

> Carey believed that 'accuracy' was enhanced by as literal a translation as possible, with the working and the grammatical structure of the translation geared to the wording and grammatical structure of the Greek or Hebrew original. Ironically, as with many other translators his overwhelming drive to make the Scriptures accessible in the languages of India and beyond was thwarted by the distortion he introduced through fear of distorting the Bible by making it truly accessible.[36]

The adaptation of Scripture to the native language and culture was formalized by Eugene Nida, a leader in the Bible Society and the father of the dynamic equivalence method of translating the Bible. He distinguishes dynamic equivalence by saying, "In such a translation one is not so concerned with matching the

---

[34] Leonard Fernando and G. Gispert-Sauch, *Christianity in India: Two Thousand Years of Faith*, (Delhi: Penguin Books, 2004), 17.

[35] Ibid., 17. There are still 150 language groups in India that do not have a Scripture translation.

[36] William Allen Smalley, *Translation as Mission: Bible Translation in the Modern Missionary Movement*, (Georgia: Mercer University Press, 1991) 49-50.

receptor-language message with the source-language message."[37] The principle followed in translation becomes, "What would the author have said if he/she had been using a contemporary language instead of Greek or Hebrew?" The emphasis is on giving the sense of the text for the reader. This type of translation is valuable at times, but it has some serious handicaps. For instance, a translation is likely to be based on the translator's ideas of the text and consequently he will insert his personal interpretation of it.

A comparison between the text of the Marathi translation of Ratnakar Kelkar[38] and the World Bible Translation Center (ERV)[39] shows the following:

John 1:1a

पूरारंभी शब्द होता **(Kelkar)**

Beginning Word was **(literal English Rendering)**

जगाची उत्पत्ता होण्यापूर्वी शब्द अस्तित्वात होता (ERV)

World before came to be Word existence was

As one can see the dynamic text of the Marathi ERV adds to the basic idea in interpretive and explanatory material. In doing so, the emphasis on the idea of the pre-existing Word is minimized while the added nuance of the creation of the world is brought forward. This tendency in dynamic translation can often overshadow the sense of the original words and the syntax of the biblical text. Readability is emphasized over accuracy and the author's original intent.[40]

---

[37] Eugene A Nida, *Toward a Science of Translating: With Special Reference to Principles and Procedures Involved in Bible Translating* (Lieden: Brill, 1964), 159.

[38] Ratnakar Hari Kelkar translated the New Testament into Marathi from Greek (1968).

[39] Produced in 1993, and translated into Marathi from their English Easy to Read Version (ERV).

[40] In personal conversation with an Indian Bible translator, she expressed her struggle with the publisher's overriding concern that the translation was audience friendly rather than accurate to the wording of the original text.

Shifts in Preaching Paradigms

Authoritative preaching has been the hallmark of the minister's work in the gospel. In 2 Timothy 4:2 we have the clear mandate that Christian preaching must herald the objective Scriptures as its basis and source. Texts such as Colossians 1:28 set Christ as the theological constancy of all our preaching. These mindsets were in contradistinction to the Asian patterns of teaching that preferred narrative formats and informal argumentation. In addition, missionaries preaching in the Indian context with orthodox, biblical forms seemingly generated a lack of interest from a Hindu audience and their ministries showed little visible fruit. This led to observations like, "Every preacher should study Hinduism and Mohammadanism, not to attack but to use the fragments of truth in them as helps to preach the gospel with great power and success."[41] Sadhu Sundar Singh developed a model of evangelistic preaching that involved *Anubhava* (personal religious experience) as the hermeneutical principle for Christian preaching in the Indian context.[42] Among the missionaries, James Macnair produced a manual for "village preaching" in the Telugu language and later in English, where he emphasized simplicity and storytelling as an indigenous method of the people.[43] Following Macnair, Henry Marshall wrote *Devadoss and His Preaching Problems*, as a textbook for his students in Burma and India.[44] He stressed the importance of situations of life as the context of preaching, and using that to focus on people's needs and problems.[45]

Indian preaching began to take on a form of its own, with nationals like Narayan Vaman Tilak, N. Goreh, and Brahmabandhab

---

[41] Mathura Nath Bose, Report of the *Second Decennial Missionary Conference Held at Calcutta 1982-83* (Calcutta: Baptist Mission Press, 1983), 27.

[42] Surya P Prakash, *The Preaching of Sadhu Sundhar Singh – A Homiletical Analysis of Independent Preaching and Personal Christianity* (Bangalore: Wordmakers for the Author, 1991), 251.

[43] James I Macnair, *Village Preaching – Being a Simple Course of Homiletical Instruction for Christian Workers Among Illiterate People*, (Madras: Christian Literature Society of India, 1924), 26

[44] Henry I. Marshall, *Devadoss and His Preaching Problems*, (Madras: The Diocesan Press, 1932)

[45] Ibid., p. 93.

Uphadyay, expounding Indian poetry and religious philosophy, and de-emphasizing historic Christian preaching.[46] Criticism of Hindu thought was avoided and the use of Hindu texts in the sermon was encouraged. Sermons became less polemical and more "evangelistic." The result is pointed out by the words of Firth, "There came a great awareness of the Church, and a shift in emphasis from 'Mission' to 'Church,' so that the evangelization to India was no longer seen as primarily the task of the missionary societies, whether foreign or Indian, but as a function of the ordinary church in its various regions and through its various organs."[47]

Contextualization with Indian philosophy made preaching weak in Scripture and overly emphatic on missions and relevance. The pulpit in churches was directed more to the lost than to the saints. The needs of sinners became the goal and cultural philosophy became the source text for preachers. Evangelistic preaching has a vital function in the church (2 Tim.4:5), but never at the expense of sermons that edify the saints (2 Tim.4:2). In this model, preaching as a function of discipleship was eclipsed. This ultimately caused the weakening of Scripture's voice in preaching and eventually led to the doctrinal weakening of the Indian Church. Paul's words in 2 Corinthians 4 are particularly relevant:

> But we have renounced the things hidden because of shame, not walking in craftiness or adulterating the word of God, but by the manifestation of truth commending ourselves to every man's conscience in the sight of God.[48]

Considerations from Contextualization in Missions

Adaptation in missions to the recipient culture has been a part of gospel work since the Apostle Paul, who stated, "I have become all things to all men so that by all possible means I might save

---

[46] Dandapati Samuel Satyaranjan, *The Preaching of Daniel Thambirajah Niles: Homiletical Criticism*, (Delhi: ISPCK, 2009), 15.

[47] Firth, *Indian Church History*, 249.

[48] *New American Standard Bible: 1995 Update* (LaHabra, CA: The Lockman Foundation, 1995), 2 Co 4:2.

some" (1 Cor. 9:22). But when Paul says, "just as we have been approved by God to be entrusted with the gospel, so we speak, not as pleasing men, but God who examines our hearts" (1 Thess.2:4), he demonstrates his unwavering commitment to the purity of the gospel message over the ideas of men.

William Carey showed similar concerns when he wrote in 1817:

> The pecuniary resources and the requisite number of missionaries for the Christian instruction of Hindustan's millions can never be supplied from England, and India will never be turned from her idolatry to serve the true and living God, unless the grace of God rests abundantly on converted Indians to qualify them for mission work, and unless, by those who care for India, these be trained for and sent into the work. In my judgment it is on native evangelists that the weight of the great work must ultimately rest.[49]

Carey's concern for accurate translations led him to only commence a Bible translation when he had a team of native speaking pundits (scholars) working with him.[50] He was convinced that it would be slow and faithful work, without compromising the orthodox truths of the Bible that would win India to Christ.

In this sense, contextualization[51] is helpful to the evangelical mission of the church. Unfortunately, much of the contextualization that took place in India did not seem to have a healthy undergirding respect for scriptural authority and orthodoxy. When an emphasis is placed on integrating Scripture with culture and philosophy, the Scriptures will inevitably be undermined. These trends of contextualization in missions that now dominate contemporary church practice have done more to erode rather than enhance our view of Scripture in the gospel ministry.

---

[49] S. Pearce Carey. *William Carey*, London: Wakeman Trust, 1923, 326.

[50] Ibid., 394

[51] Which could be defined as aiding a new language and people towards understanding the context and meaning of the unchangeable, inerrant Word of God.

Tracing the Path of Roman Catholicism's Abandonment of Inerrancy

By Massimo C. Mollica (Italy)

W hen Protestants consider their major doctrinal differences with Roman Catholicism, they usually don't think of inerrancy. As church historian Greg R. Allison states:

> The early church, the church in the Middle Ages, and the divided church at the time of the Reformation were all united in their belief in the full truthfulness of Scripture. This remarkable consensus, strongly held for over a millennium and a half, began to unravel at the beginning of the seventeenth century.[1]

However, the Roman Catholic view of inerrancy has changed since the Reformation. With the rise of modern science, rationalism, historical-critical approaches to Scripture, and theories of

---

[1] Gregg R Allison. *Historical Theology*, (Grand Rapids: Zondervan, 2011), 109-110. Similarly Robert D. Preus states, "That the Bible is the Word of God, inerrant and of supreme divine authority, was a conviction held by all Christians and Christian teachers through the first 1,700 years of church history ("The View of the Bible Held by the Church: The Early Church Through Luther," In *Inerrancy*, ed. Norman L. Geisler (Grand Rapids: The Zondervan Corporation, 1980), 357.

partial inspiration of the Bible, Rome has gradually changed its view regarding the inerrancy of the Bible.[2]

Rome's Official Teaching on Inerrancy

According to the Second Vatican Council[3], the authoritative statement on inerrancy, the Scriptures must be acknowledged "as teaching solidly, faithfully and without error that truth which God wanted put into sacred writings for the sake of salvation." This statement is presented in essentially the same language in the Roman Catholic Catechism which states that all that the Bible affirms "should be regarded as affirmed by the Holy Spirit, we must acknowledge that the books of Scripture firmly, faithfully, and without error teach that truth which God, for the sake of our salvation, wished to see confined to the Sacred Scriptures."[4] Both express the official, authoritative teaching of the Roman Catholic Church on the Bible's truthfulness.[5]

There has been some debate over the statement "for the sake of our salvation" in the above citations from official Church documents.[6] This phrase seems to introduce ambiguity into the Roman Catholic position. What exactly did Vatican II intend to teach? Does Vatican II affirm the comprehensive inerrancy of the Bible, thus asserting its truthfulness not just in matters of faith and practice, but also in science and history? Or does Rome leave

---

[2] Sinclair Ferguson. "Scripture and Tradition," In *Sola Scriptura! The Protestant Position on the Bible*, ed. Don Kistler (Morgan, PA: Soli Deo Gloria Publications, 1995), 187-192.

[3] Vatican II Council, *Dei Verbum* (Dogmatic Constitution on Divine Revelation), November 18, 1965, in *The Documents of Vatican II*, Vatican Website, sec. 11, http://www.vatican.va/archive/hist_councils/ii_vatican_council/documents/vat-ii_const_19651118_dei-verbum_en.html (accessed November 6, 2014).

[4] *Catechism of the Catholic Church: With Modifications from the Editio Typica* (New York: Doubleday, 1995), sec. 107.

[5] These definitions could be compared to Protestant Paul D. Feinberg's helpful definition of inerrancy, "Inerrancy means that when all facts are known, the Scriptures in their original autographs and properly interpreted will be shown to be wholly true in everything that they affirm, whether that has to do with doctrine or morality or with the social, physical, or life sciences" ("The Meaning of Inerrancy," In *Inerrancy*, ed. Norman L. Geisler (Grand Rapids: The Zondervan Corporation, 1980), 294).

[6] Pontifical Biblical Commission, *The Inspiration and Truth of Sacred Scripture*, trans. Thomas Esposito and Stephen Gregg (Collegeville, MN: Liturgical Press, 2014), sec. 63, iBooks.

the door open to admitting historical inaccuracies and scientific errors by limiting inerrancy to those truths of Scripture essential for salvation?[7]

The Historical Development of Rome's Doctrine on Inerrancy

In order to fully understand Vatican II's statement about the truthfulness of Scripture, it is essential to view the statement in a broader historical context. If one looks at the footnotes of the Vatican II statement, the authors cite sources like St. Augustine, the Council of Trent, Pope Leo XIII, and Pope Pius XII, which seems to imply that Vatican II should be interpreted in the trajectory of the historical position on the comprehensive truthfulness of Scripture.[8] In this section, I survey Roman Catholic statements on inerrancy over the last 120 years. I will show that the Roman Catholic Church has consistently confirmed the inerrancy of the Scriptures. However, there has been a gradual acceptance of modern scholarship, such as historical criticism and rationalism. As these ideologies have increased in their influence, the doctrine of inerrancy has been redefined toward a form of limited inerrancy.

---

[7] For example, Protestant John Warwick Montgomery identifies the use of historical critical ideologies in the works of various post-Vatican II scholars and discusses various drafts of the Vatican II documents that appear to evidence a debate among the council members. From this, he concludes that Vatican II presents a shift in trajectory from the Classic Catholic position of a more comprehensive form of inerrancy, whereas now Roman Catholic scholarship, "displays a very different alignment: with the historical-critical method which won the day among non-evangelical Protestant scholars during the Modernist era. . ." ("The Approach of New Shape Roman Catholicism to Scriptural Inerrancy: A Case Study for Evangelicals," *Bulletin of the Evangelical Theological Society* 10, no. 4 (Fall 1967), 216).

[8] For these reasons, André Marie at Catholicism.org argues that these statements on the truthfulness of the Bible must be interpreted with a hermeneutic of continuity with past statements, per the encouragement of Pope Benedict XVI. Thus, Marie argues for a comprehensive view on Biblical inerrancy, not limited to faith and salvation. ("Biblical Inerrancy," Catholicism.org. http://catholicism.org/biblical-inerrancy.html (accessed November 3, 2014).

Providentissimus Deus (1893)

In 1893 Pope Leo XIII wrote an Encyclical letter entitled *Providentissimus Deus*. In this letter, cited in the footnotes of Vatican II, the pope unequivocally affirms Scripture's comprehensive inerrancy when he states:

> But it is absolutely wrong and forbidden, either to narrow inspiration to certain parts only of Holy Scripture, or to admit that the sacred writer has erred... For all the books which the Church receives as sacred and canonical, are written wholly and entirely, with all their parts, at the dictation of the Holy Ghost; and so far is it from being possible that any error can co-exist with inspiration, that inspiration not only is essentially incompatible with error, but excludes and rejects it as absolutely and necessarily as it is impossible that God Himself, the supreme Truth, can utter that which is not true. This is the ancient and unchanging faith of the Church, solemnly defined in the Councils of Florence and of Trent, and finally confirmed and more expressly formulated by the Council of the Vatican [here a reference to the first Vatican Council (1868-1870)].[9]

In addition to affirming inerrancy, various statements in the Encyclical suggest that Leo XIII is seeking to definitively shut the door to theories of partial inspiration, historical-critical methodologies, and to secular science. For example, he describes those who oppose the Catholic Church as follows:

> ... they set down the Scripture narratives as stupid fables and lying stories: the prophecies and the oracles of God are to them either predictions made up after the event or forecasts formed by the light of nature;

---

[9] Leo XIII, *Providentissimus Deus* (Encyclical Letter on the Study of Holy Scripture), Vatican Website, November 18, 1893, sec. 20, www.vatican.va/holy_father/leo_xiii/ encyclicals/documents/hf_l-xiii_enc_18111893_providentissimus-deus_en.html (accessed November 6, 2014).

the miracles and the wonders of God's power are not
what they are said to be, but the startling effects of
natural law, or else mere tricks and myths; and the
Apostolic Gospels and writings are not the work of
the Apostles at all.[10]

Four key observations can be gleaned about this pope's view
of inerrancy in 1893. First, Leo XIII seems to assume a view of
truth that the factual assertions of Scripture correspond with what
really took place. The above citations explain this to be a natural
consequence of Scripture being inspired. He states that because
God is the author of Scripture, "nothing can be proved either by
physical science or archaeology which can really contradict the
Scriptures. . . truth cannot contradict truth."[11] He is here operating
on the assumption that Scripture, science, and archaeology, when
rightly understood, will correspond to reality.

Second, Leo XIII is concerned to uphold the historical view of
inerrancy passed down through the ages. He states, "The Professor
of Holy Scripture. . . must be well acquainted with the whole circle
of Theology and deeply read in the commentaries of the Holy
Fathers and Doctors, and other interpreters."[12] Leo XIII asserts that
to admit error in the text is not consistent with the Catholic view
of the Bible. He states, "It follows that those who maintain that
an error is possible in any genuine passage of the sacred writings,
either pervert the Catholic notion of inspiration, or make God the
author of such error."[13]

Third, this Encyclical encourages Catholic scholars to learn the
ancient languages, the art of historical criticism, and to be aware of

---

[10]   Ibid., sec. 10. In 1993, Pope John Paul II asserted that *Providentissimus Deus*, was a
response to the attacks of rationalistic science and liberal exegesis which made use of "all
the scientific resources, from textual criticism to geology, including philology, literary
criticism, history of religions, archaeology and other disciplines besides." "Address on
the Interpretation of the Bible in the Church," April 23, 1993, sec. 3, in *The Interpretation
of the Bible in the Church*, Pontifical Biblical Commission, trans. Vatican (Sherbrooke,
Quebec: Editions Pauline, 1994), 9.

[11]   Leo XIII, *Providentissimus Deus*, sec. 23.

[12]   Ibid., sec. 14. In this particular paragraph, Leo XIII cites extensively St. Augustine's
approach to Scripture.

[13]   Ibid., sec. 21.

modern physical science.[14] Regarding the original languages and historical criticism, Leo XIII states:

> The clergy, by making themselves more or less fully acquainted with them as time and place may demand, will the better be able to discharge their office with becoming credit; for they must make themselves "all to all," always "ready to satisfy everyone that asketh them a reason for the hope that is in them."[15]

Leo XIII continues, "Hence to the Professor of Sacred Scripture a knowledge of natural science will be of very great assistance in detecting such attacks on the Sacred Books, and in refuting them."[16] The use of science and historical-critical methods was for apologetic purposes.

Finally, Leo XIII believed that when no mistake was detected in the interpretation of Scripture and history and science still disagreed, then judgment must be suspended for the time.[17] This was because, "there have been objections without number perseveringly directed against the Scripture for many a long year, which have been proved to be futile and are now never heard of."[18]

Pascendi Dominici Gregis (1907)

Following the 1893 Encyclical, Leo XIII established the Pontifical Biblical Commission in 1902 to work on Scriptural problems. His successor, Pius X released an Encyclical, *Pascendi Dominici Gregis* (1907), aimed at addressing the challenges presented by modernism and its atheistic anti-supernatural presuppositions, especially with regards to the life of Christ. This pope, as did his predecessor, seems to also affirm a view of truth that historical

---

[14] Ibid., sec. 17-19.

[15] Ibid., sec. 17.

[16] Ibid., sec. 18. Leo XIII also expressed a concern for the unreliability of science when he states that the Catholic interpreter must "always bear in mind, that much which has been held and proved as certain has afterwards been called into question and rejected."

[17] Ibid., sec. 23.

[18] Ibid., sec. 23.

and scientific factual affirmations of the Bible, rightly understood, correspond with reality.[19] The most significant contribution Pius X makes to the discussion at hand is when he addresses Catholics who, having been influenced by Modernism, have admitted the existence of historical and scientific errors and contradictions in the Bible. These Catholics do so to make their faith more acceptable to those exploring the faith. According to Pius X, they reason as follows:

> In the Sacred Books there are many passages referring to science or history where manifest errors are to be found. But the subject of these books is not science or history but religion and morals. In them history and science serve only as a species of covering to enable the religious and moral experiences wrapped up in them to penetrate more readily among the masses.[20]

Thus, these Catholics would admit errors into the lesser important details of science and history and thereby limit the Bible's inerrancy more to what pertains to religion and morals. Pius X goes on to explicitly condemn such a position when he immediately says, "We, Venerable Brethren, for whom there is but one and only truth, and who hold that the Sacred Books, *written under the inspiration of the Holy Ghost, have God for their author* (Conc. Vat., *De Revel.*, c. 2) declare that this is equivalent to attributing to God Himself the lie of utility or officious lie."[21] Therefore, according to Pius X, limiting inerrancy to spiritual matters and admission of historical and scientific errors is tantamount to calling God a liar. In 1909, Pius X founded the Pontifical Biblical Institute to continue higher levels of study of the Sacred Scriptures.[22]

---

[19] Pius X, *Pascendi Dominici Gregis* (Encyclical Letter on the Doctrines of Modernists), Vatican Website, September 8, 1907, sec. 30-31, http://www.vatican.va/holy_father/pius_x/encyclicals/documents/hf_p-x_enc_19070908_pascendi-dominici-gregis_en.html (accessed December 1, 2014).

[20] Pius X, Pascendi Dominici Gregis, sec. 36.

[21] Ibid., sec. 36.

[22] Pope John Paul II, "Address on the Interpretation of the Bible," sec. 2.

Spiritus Paraclitus (1920)

In 1920 the next pope, Benedict XV, celebrated the 1500th anniversary of St. Jerome's death (to whom we owe the Latin Vulgate) with the Encyclical *Spiritus Paraclitus*. This Encyclical continues in the same trajectory of the previously analyzed encyclicals. Benedict XV celebrates Jerome's devotion to Scripture. He affirms Jerome's view that "the immunity of Scripture from error or deception is necessarily bound up with its Divine inspiration."[23] While Benedict XV commended the use of historical-critical methods to discover new ways to help explain the difficulties of Scripture, he clearly condemned those Catholics that would limit the Bible's inerrancy to primary and religious matters. He says these people affirm that inspiration extends to every word and phrase of the Bible, but "the effect of inspiration – namely, absolute truth and immunity from error – are to be restricted to that primary or religious element."[24] Benedict XV too understood Biblical truth in the same way as his predecessors, saying that the historical affirmations of the Bible must correspond to the facts. He says those "who hold that the historical portions of Scripture do not rest on the absolute truth of the facts but merely upon what they are pleased to term their relative truth, namely, what people then commonly thought, are. . . out of harmony with the Church's teaching."[25] Furthermore, Benedict XV approved of Jerome who, if alive, "would sharpen his keenest controversial weapons against people who set aside what is the mind and judgment of the Church, and take too ready a refuge in such notions as 'implicit quotations' or 'pseudo-historical narratives,' or in 'kinds of literature' such as cannot be reconciled with the entire and perfect truth of God's word."[26]

---

[23] Benedict XV, Spiritus Paraclitus (Encyclical Letter on St. Jerome), Vatican Website, September 15, 1920, sec. 13, http://www.vatican.va/holy_father/benedict_xv/encyclicals/documents/hf_ben-xv_enc_15091920_spiritus-paraclitus_en.html (accessed December 1, 2014).

[24] Benedict XV, Spiritus Paraclitus, sec. 19.

[25] Ibid., sec. 22.

[26] Ibid., sec. 26.

Divino Afflante Spiritu (1943)

In 1943 Pope Pius XII released the Encyclical *Divino Afflante Spiritu*. It reveals a constant affirmation of inerrancy but a growing openness to historical-critical methods of interpretation. The pope once again refuted the idea that inerrancy could be limited. In agreement with his predecessors, Pius XII condemned those who "ventured to restrict the truth of Sacred Scripture solely to matters of faith and morals, and to regard other matters, whether in the domain of physical science or history."[27] However, in this Encyclical, the pope opened the doors for Catholic exegetes to use historical-critical methodologies, while condemning their anti-Christian presuppositions. Speaking of historical-critical methodologies, he states that it "today has rules so firmly established and secure, that it has become a most valuable aid to the purer and more accurate editing of the sacred text and that any abuse can easily be discovered."[28] The letter expresses a greater appreciation for various literary modes and encourages the interpreter to consider the various forms of expression "whether in poetic description or in the formulation of laws and rules of life or in recording the facts and events of history."[29] Literary analysis can help solve problems in Scripture. Pius XII states,

> . . . when some persons reproachfully charge the Sacred Writers with some historical error or inaccuracy in the recording of facts, on closer examination it turns out to be nothing else than those customary modes of expression and narration peculiar to the ancients, which used to be employed in the mutual dealings of social life and which in fact were sanctioned by common usage.[30]

---

[27] Pius XII, *Divino Afflante Spiritu* (Encyclical Letter on Promoting Biblical Studies, Commemorating the Fiftieth Anniversary of Providentissimus Deus), Vatican Website, September 30,1943, sec. 1, www.vatican.va/holy_father/pius_xii/encyclicals/documents/hf_p-xii_enc_30091943_divino-afflante-spiritu_en.html (accessed November 6, 2014).

[28] Pius XII, *Divino Afflante Spiritu*, sec. 18.

[29] Ibid., sec. 36.

[30] Ibid., sec. 38.

By the time Vatican II discussed the issue of inerrancy, *Dei Verbum* (1965) affirmed that the Bible taught truthfully and without error that which was needed "for the sake of salvation." Furthermore, *Dei Verbum* emphasizes literary form as the key to interpretation. It states,

> To search out the intention of the sacred writers, attention should be given, among other things, to "literary forms." For truth is set forth and expressed differently in texts which are variously historical, prophetic, poetic, or of other forms of discourse. The interpreter must investigate what meaning the sacred writer intended to express and actually expressed in particular circumstances by using contemporary literary forms in accordance with the situation of his own time and culture.[31]

The Interpretation of the Bible in the Church (1993)

As stated, Vatican II left the door open to a limited view of inerrancy derived from the results of historical-critical interpretation. In 1993 the Pontifical Biblical Commission (hereafter PBC), released a document entitled *The Interpretation of the Bible in the Church*. This document affirms,

> The historical-critical method is the indispensable method for the scientific study of the meaning of ancient texts. Holy Scripture, inasmuch as it is the "Word of God in human language", has been composed by human authors in all its various parts and in all the sources that lie behind them. Because of this, its proper understanding not only admits the use of this method but actually requires it.[32]

---

[31] *DV*, sec. 12.

[32] Pontifical Biblical Commission, *The Interpretation of the Bible in the Church*, 34.

Not only does the PBC require the use of historical-critical methods, it says that these methods have "made it possible to understand far more accurately the intention of the authors and editors of the Bible, as well as the message which they addressed to their first readers. The achievement of these results has lent the historical-critical method an importance of the highest order."[33] One hundred years after Pope Leo XIII permitted the use of the historical-critical method for apologetic purposes, these methods were now understood to be indispensable and required for determining the author's intention.

The Inspiration and Truth of Sacred Scripture (2014)

In early 2014, fifty years after Vatican II, a document entitled *The Inspiration and Truth of Sacred Scripture* was released by the PBC in order to explain what Vatican II meant. In this document, the PBC attempts to address various historical, social, and ethical dilemmas presented by the Scriptures. This document confirms the intent of Vatican II when it states, "it is undeniable that *Dei Verbum*, with the expression 'the truth...for the sake of our salvation' (n. 11), restricts biblical truth to divine revelation which concerns God himself and the salvation of the human race."[34] Regarding Biblical inerrancy, the PBC states,

> Theologians have had recourse to the concept of "inerrancy," applying it to Sacred Scripture. If it is taken in its absolute sense, this term would suggest that there can be no error of any kind in the Bible. But with the progressive discoveries in the field of history, philology, and the natural sciences, and because of the application to biblical research of the historical-critical method, exegetes have had to recognize that not everything in the Bible is expressed in accordance with the demands of the contemporary sciences, because the biblical writers reflect the limits

---

[33] Ibid., 36-37.

[34] Pontifical Biblical Commission, *The Inspiration and Truth of Sacred Scripture*, sec. 105.

> of their own personal knowledge, in addition to those
> of their time and culture. The Second Vatican Council
> had to confront this problem in the preparation of the
> dogmatic constitution Dei Verbum.[35]

Thus, the writers state, "In the Bible, we encounter contradictions, historical inaccuracies, implausible narratives, and, in the Old Testament, moral precepts and behavior in conflict with the teachings of Jesus. What is the 'truth' of these biblical passages? Without doubt, we are faced with real challenges for the interpretation of the Word of God."[36]

The PBC's most recent study provides analyses of specific passages and how they are to be interpreted. The following summary shows how far the PBC's view of inerrancy has been influenced by modern science and historical-critical methodologies.

Genesis

The PBC states, "The first creation account (Gen 1:1–2:4a), through its well-organized structure, describes not how the world came into being but why and for what purpose it is as it is. In poetic style, using the imagery of his era, the author of Genesis 1:1–2:4a shows that God is the origin of the cosmos and of humankind."[37] The Commission continues, "The distribution of the various works of creation over six days does not intend to affirm as a truth to be believed that the world really took form in six days, while God rested on the seventh; it intends to communicate, rather, that there exists an order and a purpose in creation."[38] The PBC explains the driving force behind their interpretation,

> Much misunderstanding results from reading these
> texts from a modern perspective, seeing them as
> affirmations of "how" the world and humanity were

---

[35] Ibid., sec. 63.

[36] Ibid., sec. 104.

[37] Ibid., sec. 67.

[38] Ibid.

formed. To respond more adequately to the intention of the biblical texts, it is necessary to oppose such a reading, but without putting their assertions in competition with the knowledge that has come from the natural sciences of our time. These do not suppress the Bible's claim to communicate the truth, because the truth of the biblical accounts of creation concerns the meaningful coherence of the world as a work created by God.[39]

Regarding the unfolding of the opening chapters of Genesis, the PBC states,

> The narrative of Genesis 1–11, the traditions dealing with the patriarchs and the conquest of the land of Israel, the stories of the kings down to the Maccabean revolt certainly contain truths, but they do not intend to propose a historical chronicle of the people of Israel. The protagonist in salvation history is neither Israel nor other peoples but God. The biblical accounts are theologized narratives.[40]

Regarding, Genesis 15, the Commission states, "An episode like that of Genesis 15—essential for the thesis of Paul on justification by faith alone independent of works of the Mosaic law (cf. Rom 4)—does not describe the events in the precise way in which they took place, as its redactional history shows."[41] The biblical record is merely the interpretation of the facts that inspired the faith of ancient Israel as they reflected on the original events. The PBC states, "The interpretation of the concrete facts, the sense which emerges from their interpretation in the "today" of the rereading, counts more than the facts themselves."[42]

---

[39] Ibid.

[40] Ibid., sec. 104.

[41] Ibid., sec. 106.

[42] Ibid., sec. 107.

The Exodus

The PBC continues its goal of emphasizing the theological intention of texts by turning next to the Exodus narrative. The biblical account is an "oral tradition, put down in writing" and "was the object of multiple 'rereadings' and, in the end, was inserted into the narrative of the Exodus and into the Torah."[43] As with the previous narratives, factual truth is de-emphasized. "The truth of the account does not reside, therefore, solely in the tradition which it commemorates. . . but also in the theological interpretation which accompanies it."[44] The Exodus account communicates the truth that God is present to save his people, but it "does not intend primarily to transmit a record of ancient events in the manner of an archival document."[45]

Joshua

The Commission also tries to sort out the apparent ethical dilemma created by God's sending Israel to exterminate the inhabitants of the land of Canaan. In the explanation, the book of Joshua is described as having no real historical value. (?)

> From the outset, it is necessary to note that these narratives do not have the characteristics of a historical account: in a real war, in fact, the walls of a city do not come crashing down at the sound of trumpets (Josh 6:20), nor is it evident how a peaceful distribution of lands by lottery could really take place (Josh 14:2). . . One must, therefore, reconsider carefully the literary genre of these narrative traditions. As the best interpreters of the patristic tradition had already suggested, the narration of the conquest epic should be seen as a sort of parable presenting characters of symbolic value. . . The appeal to God's right to distribute the

[handwritten marginal note: and what they do for the cost that the Omnipotence of God]

---

[43] Ibid., sec. 108.

[44] Ibid.

[45] Ibid.

land, thus privileging his own elect (Deut 7:6-11; 32:8-9), is certainly not convincing, because it disavows the legitimate claims of the native populations.[46]

and that was the purpose of it

Jonah

Another Biblical text explained by the Commission is the book of Jonah. While confirming the historicity of the person of Jonah, it states,

> In the account, however, there are not only details but also structural elements which we cannot consider as historical events and which lead us to interpret the text as an imaginary composition with deep theological content.
>
> A few improbable details—as, for example, that Nineveh was an extremely large city, a three-day journey across (Jonah 3:3)—may be considered hyperbole; among the structural elements, however, some are implausible—the fish which swallows Jonah and keeps him alive in its belly for three days and three nights before vomiting him up (2:1, 11) and the supposed conversion of the entire city of Nineveh (3:5-10), of which there is no trace anywhere in Assyrian records.[47]

Why do you think they would like to keep the records?

Christ's Birth Narratives

The document seems to uphold the historical reliability of the NT accounts to a greater degree than it does the OT. Of the four gospels, it states, "they are not to be reduced to the status of symbolic, mythical, poetic creations of anonymous authors, but are a reliable account of events in the life and ministry of Jesus."[48]

---

[46] Ibid., sec. 127.

[47] Ibid., sec. 110. Elsewhere in the document, the Commission states, "In the case of Tobit and Jonah, we noted that texts which do not recount what really happened are nevertheless accounts full of edifying, didactic, and theological significance" (sec. 135).

[48] Ibid., sec. 84.

It nevertheless exhibits a lack of certainty as to the historicity of some of the events. For example, the birth narratives of Christ are said to be irreconcilable,

> According to Matthew, Mary and Joseph live in Bethlehem before the birth of Jesus, and it is only after the flight into Egypt and following a particular warning that they go to Nazareth. According to Luke, Mary and Joseph live in Nazareth, the census brings them to Bethlehem, and they return to Nazareth without a flight into Egypt. It is difficult to find a solution for such differences.[49]

The Earthquake at Christ's Death

The earthquake after Christ's death probably did not occur,

> It is likely, therefore, that Matthew uses this "literary motif." By mentioning the earthquake, he wishes to underline that the death and resurrection of Jesus are not ordinary events but "traumatic" events in which God acts and achieves the salvation of the human race. . . The Evangelist does not speak, then, of an earthquake whose force could be measured according to the grades of a specific scale but seeks to awaken and direct the attention of his readers toward God, highlighting the most important fact about the death and resurrection of Jesus: their relationship with the saving power of God.[50] *J-l will shake again!*

Authorship of New Testament Books

Regarding the authorship of various NT books, the PBC states,

---

[49] Ibid., sec. 111.

[50] Ibid., sec. 120.

This traditional form of reception was followed also for the New Testament writings, which were all seen as coming from the inner circle of the apostles. Today, thanks to the converging results of researchers using literary and historical methodologies, we cannot maintain the same perspective as the ancients; the science of exegesis has actually demonstrated with convincing arguments that the various biblical writings are not the exclusive product of the author indicated in the work's title or recognized as such by the tradition.[51]

Observations about the Development of the Doctrine of Inerrancy

Three observations from this document can be made that will help define Rome's position on the doctrine of biblical inerrancy. First, Rome's definition of truth has undergone a significant shift over the last 120 years since Leo XIII's *Providentissimus Deus* in 1893. As was observed various times in the Papal Encyclicals in the first half of the twentieth century, the underlying assumption of the popes seemed to be that historical or factual affirmations of the biblical texts must correspond with what happened in reality. The popes used words like "absolute truth," "immunity from error," and "entire and perfect truth" in an effort to safeguard the historical and scientific integrity of the Bible. It is clear that the RCC has moved away from this correspondence view of truth to emphasize the theological or salvific truth.

Multiple times in the above excerpts, there is either a de-emphasis or clear denial of the factual truth of the text. At times, the PBC is clear the text does not correspond to what really happened. At other times, facts are relegated to a position of secondary importance relative to the intended theological truth. Thus, the PBC explains its understanding of truth, "Among these is the fundamental one of attesting the truth, understood, however, not as an aggregate of exact information on the various aspects of human knowledge but as a revelation of God himself and his

---

[51] Ibid., sec. 140.

salvific plan."[52] The document admits that certainty is difficult regarding the Bible's factuality,

> At first glance, many narrative texts of the Bible appear to have the character of a precise record of what actually happened. Corresponding to this impression is a way of reading the Bible which sees in all the events recounted things that really occurred. . .
> On the contrary, the reading of Scripture which takes account of the modern sciences (historiography, philology, archeology, cultural anthropology, etc.) complicates the understanding of the biblical texts and appears to propose less certain results. We cannot, however, ignore demands of our time and interpret the texts of the Bible outside their historical context; we must read them in our time, with and for our contemporaries.[53] *in different to reach the truth of God.*

Therefore, in the mind of the PBC, by restricting truth to the Bible's theological or salvific intent, it can be both truthful and factually erroneous at the same time. For example, notwithstanding the historical inadequacies, the Exodus story still teaches that God is present to save his people. It teaches that theological truth without error. Therefore, inaccurate facts do not prevent the saving intent from being true. This, I suggest, displays a gradual redefinition of truth over the last 120 years.

Second, while the PBC affirms the full inspiration of the Bible, it seems at times to arrive at the same negative consequences that partial inspiration theories bring, the very consequences that previous popes warned of.[54] Partial inspiration means that the religious and moral aspects of the Bible are inspired, but the historical and scientific parts are not necessarily inspired, thus leading to the apparent discrepancies in these portions. By appealing to partial

---

[52] Ibid., sec. 144.

[53] Ibid., sec. 136.

[54] I am not saying here that the PBC has embraced a theory of partial inspiration, only that partial inspiration and their view of truth have the same consequence. The RCC affirms the full inspiration of Scripture.

inspiration, a Catholic could avoid impugning God's integrity because God did not inspire the errant parts.

However, Pius X and Benedict XV were concerned because they knew that God inspired the entire Bible, not just parts. The admission of errors would still call into question God's integrity and limit the Bible's truthfulness. In 1907, Pius X was not simply condemning partial inspiration, but also a restricted view of the Bible's truthfulness when he said "this is equivalent to attributing to God Himself the lie of utility or officious lie."[55] In 1920, Benedict XV actually condemned those who affirm the full inspiration of the Bible, but limit the Bible's absolute truthfulness. These people say "the effect of inspiration—namely, absolute truth and immunity from error—are to be restricted to that primary or religious element."[56]

By affirming full inspiration, by admitting the presence of factual inaccuracies, by de-emphasizing the factuality of secondary elements, and by restricting truth to its primary saving purpose, the PBC has fallen into the exact consequence of partial inspiration condemned by Benedict XV. According to Benedict XV, immunity from error must extend even to those elements that are not primary, that is, those elements that have a subordinate function. Regarding the gospels, the PBC states, ". . . the theological affirmations about Jesus have a direct and normative import, the purely historical elements have a subordinate function."[57]

Interestingly, Benedict XV also warned about justifying errors in the text by appealing to literary features. He, along with Jerome centuries earlier, condemned those who "take too ready a refuge in such notions as 'implicit quotations,' 'pseudo-historical narratives,' or 'kinds of literature' such as cannot be reconciled with the entire and perfect truth of God's word."[58] However, by frequent appeals to literary genre to justify its conclusions, the PBC appears to have done just this. There are multiple ways to arrive at a restricted view of the Bible's truthfulness. One way is through a theory of partial

---

[55] Pius X, *Pascendi Dominici Gregis*, sec. 36.

[56] Benedict XV, *Spiritus Paraclitus*, sec. 19.

[57] Pontifical Biblical Commission, *The Inspiration and Truth of Sacred Scripture*, sec. 123.

[58] Benedict XV, *Spiritus Paraclitus*, sec. 26.

inspiration, another way is how the PBC has done it. No matter how you justify it, this kind of restricting of the Bible's truthfulness was what the early 20th century popes warned against.

Third, the PBC reveals that the Roman Catholic Church has steadily adopted more and more of the presuppositions of historical-criticism and naturalistic science. It is always doubtful how much one can apply a method without being influenced by its presuppositions. While the PBC often appeals to literary genre to support its interpretation, at times its skepticism over the Biblical text comes out. This is nowhere more clearly seen than with Joshua when it says, "in a real war, in fact, the walls of a city do not come crashing down at the sound of trumpets (Josh 6:20), nor is it evident how a peaceful distribution of lands by lottery could really take place (Josh 14:2)." It is their skepticism over the supernatural in this case that leads to their decision on literary genre, "One must, therefore, reconsider carefully the literary genre of these narrative traditions."

Additionally, in the excerpt on the Genesis 1 creation narrative, the document does not hide how much it has been influenced by modern science. The foreword to the document states, "To respond to the questions that arise in the interpretation of these difficult texts, it is necessary to study them carefully, taking into account the findings of the modern sciences and, simultaneously, the main theme of the texts, namely, God and his plan of salvation."[59] However, modern science, through its naturalistic assumptions, rules out *a-priori* conclusions that would invoke the supernatural. Thus, to allow your interpretation to be driven by modern science's conclusions is to be influenced by anti-supernatural assumptions.

In making these three observations, Rome is no longer on the trajectory that has been set throughout church history by St. Augustine, St. Jerome, the various Catholic Church Councils, or the popes of the late nineteenth and early twentieth centuries. After being infected by biblical criticism for so many decades and with the release of *The Inspiration and Truth of Sacred Scripture* in 2014, it is difficult to imagine Rome turning back to its stronger

---

[59] Pontifical Biblical Commission, *The Inspiration and Truth of Sacred Scripture*, 24.

affirmations of biblical inerrancy from the early 20th century.[60] If the historical view of truth entails both factuality and theological or saving truth, then the RCC restricts or reduces truth to the latter, a position known as Limited Inerrancy in evangelical circles.[61] Rome's position is outside of the trajectory set by the Bible,[62] the early church's understanding of the Bible,[63] and the trajectory of the Roman Catholic Church's own tradition, as this paper has demonstrated.

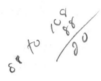

---

[60] The document *The Inspiration and Truth of Sacred Scripture* should not be seen as an authoritative pronouncement by the church. The foreword to the document states, "The present document of the Biblical Commission does not constitute an official declaration of the Church's Magisterium on this topic, nor does it intend to set forth a complete doctrine regarding inspiration and the truth of Sacred Scripture. It only wishes to report the results of an attentive exegetical study of the biblical texts regarding their origin in God and their truth." (24-25).

[61] American theologian John M. Frame says that Limited Inerrancy "claims that Scripture is inerrant only in matters of salvation" in John Frame, *The Doctrine of the Word of God* (Phillipsburg, NJ: P&R Publishing, 2010), 167. Another American Evangelical theologian John D. Woodbridge, describes the position as follows, "The central purpose of God's written communication is to reveal salvation truth about Christ. God did not intend that the Scriptures should be read for technically correct information about the world" in John D. Woodbridge, *Biblical Authority: A Critique of the Rogers/McKim Proposal*. (Grand Rapids: Zondervan, 1982), 21.

[62] For a more detailed discussion of Scripture and truth, see Roger Nicole, "The Biblical Concept of Truth," in *Scripture and Truth*, ed. D.A. Carson and John D. Woodbridge (Grand Rapids, MI: Zondervan Publishing House, 1983), 287-298.

[63] See Woodbridge's *Biblical Authority* for a detailed analysis of church history with respect to the Limited Inerrancy position.

THE COMING WAR IN MALAWI AGAINST BIBLICAL AUTHORITY

By Brian Biedebach and Gideon Manda (Malawi)

A frica is becoming more like the West. In Malawi, this is noticeable in every sector of society. For better or for worse, the younger generation of Malawians is less traditional. Malawian politics, social trends, and religious views are highly influenced by the United States, England, and other Western countries. In some instances, this change can be viewed as positive. For example, economically, Malawi seems to be moving its way out of the list of "top ten poorest countries in the world." When it comes to Christianity, however, Malawians should be careful not to accept all that Western churches offer but should rather attempt to avoid various pitfalls that have plagued the West. The authors of this article are both pastors in Malawi[1] who are familiar with how biblical authority has been attacked in the West. We are calling out to fellow pastors to protect the church in Malawi from similar attacks.

Today, the vast majority of pastors in Malawi believe that the Bible is the authoritative, inerrant, infallible Word of God. It is common for a pastor to quote Isaiah 40:8, "The grass withers, the flower fades, but the Word of our God stands forever." Many quote

---

[1] Brian Biedebach first came to Malawi for a year in 1997. After pastoring in Johannesburg, South Africa for eight years, he returned in 2007 to pastor a church in Lilongwe, where he currently serves. Gideon Manda is a Malawian who was trained in South Africa and has been pastoring in Blantyre for more than ten years.

that text immediately after they read any Old Testament or New Testament passage in public. In contrast to what we see around us, they maintain that God's Word will endure forever, just as His Word states. This unwavering belief in God's Word used to be universal among pastors in Western churches as it is in Malawi today. However, that belief began to change in the West in the 1800's and early 1900s.

Key Definitions and Terms

The foundation for all evangelical Christian doctrine and belief is the Word of God. The mere fact that someone would refer to the Bible as the *Word of God* implies that in his or her view, the Bible is inerrant. As one writer puts it, the Bible's original autographs "cannot contain error for the simple reason that God cannot lie."[2] Or, as another said, "The Bible, as a whole and in its parts, contains nothing but God-breathed truth; evangelicals have simply affirmed what the church universal had affirmed for well over a millennium – *when the Bible speaks, God speaks.*"[3] Inerrancy is the historical view of the Christian church which recognizes the Bible to be without error in its original manuscripts. It is important to note that although we do not have the original manuscripts today (but only copies and translations), we do have a:

> wealth of biblical manuscripts in the original languages and with the disciplined activity of textual critics to establish with almost perfect accuracy the content of the autographs, any errors which have been introduced and/or perpetuated by the thousands of translations over the centuries can be identified and corrected by comparing the translation or copy with the reassembled original. By this providential means, God has made good His promise to preserve the Scriptures. We can

---

[2]   Gordon H. Clark, *Journal of the Evangelical Theological Society*, 09:1 (Winter 1966), 2.

[3]   R. Albert Mohler in *Five Views on Biblical Inerrancy*, J. Merrick and Stephen M. Garret, eds. (Grand Rapids: Zondervan, 2013), 29.

rest assured that there are translations available today which indeed are worthy of the title, The Word of God.[4]

The key issue surrounding inerrancy relates to authority: Can the Bible be trusted as the ultimate authority for Christian belief and practice? Closely related to biblical authority is the issue of inspiration. If the Bible is the inspired Word of God, then it must be inerrant, and we are obligated to submit to its authority.

Biblical Authority's Erosion in the West

More than a hundred years ago, one of the most significant threats to inerrancy (and biblical authority) in the Western world was Darwinism.[5] Many Protestants during that time found it difficult to reconcile supposedly scientific theories, like evolution, with Scripture. Liberal theology provided an outlet that would allow the acceptance of Darwinism and the Bible, because the Bible could be interpreted in light of modern science. Many pastors began to accept the teaching of evolution as something compatible with Christianity because they viewed the biblical accounts of creation merely as stories, the details of which were not necessarily true.

Throughout the 1900s, more and more pastors were influenced by liberal theology, and eventually the majority of them in many Christian denominations questioned whether the Bible was really reliable. In 1979, James Montgomery Boice published an important booklet entitled, "Does Inerrancy Matter?" In that booklet he published some shocking statistics from a questionnaire sent out to 10,000 U.S. clergymen from Western Reserve University. One of the questions was, "Do you believe the Bible to be the inspired Word of God?" Out of 7,442 responses:

82% of the Methodists

---

[4] John MacArthur, ed. *The MacArthur Study Bible* (Nashville, TN: Word Pub., 1997), xvi, electronic ed.

[5] As Justo L. Gonzalez has noted, "Protestant Liberalism was an attempt to couch Christianity in the mold of those [evolutionistic] ideas. . . most liberals were committed Christians whose very commitment drove them to respond to the intellectual challenges of their time, in the hope of making the faith credible for modern people." Justo Gonzalez, *The Story of Christianity*, vol. 2 (San Francisco: Harper & Row, 1985), 256.

89% of the Episcopalians
81% of the United Presbyterians
57% of the Baptists
57% of the Lutherans

Answered, "NO!"[6]

Boice went on in his booklet to remind his readers that the Bible teaches inerrancy, Jesus affirmed inerrancy, historically the church has believed inerrancy, and God's character demands inerrancy.[7]

Warning Signs that Should Alarm Malawian Pastors

Currently, in Malawi, in spite of the widespread verbal acknowledgement that the Bible is the authoritative Word of God, there are already a number of issues that undermine this belief. Like termites gnawing away at a wooden pulpit, from the outside the Malawian church appears to be united in a high view of biblical authority. But current issues are actually eating away at this belief from within.

One such issue is the "health, wealth, and prosperity gospel." This false teaching that has ravished so many churches in Malawi is a serious concern. It appears that the proponents of this movement put too much trust in their so-called "prophet" and, consequently, abandon the Bible as their authority. Granted, there are those with different views on prophecy. The authors of this article believe that God's Word is complete and that there is no further revelation being given today. But even our colleagues who believe differently can give numerous examples of Malawian pastors who have clearly made false prophecies. What is concerning to us is not only that false prophecies are common in Malawi, but that very few speak out against it. This should alarm all of us.

Another issue that is causing Protestant pastors to question the authority of Scripture is the ecumenical movement. There is

---

6 James Montgomery Boice, *Does Inerrancy Matter?* (Carol Stream, IL: Tyndale House, 1980), 9

7 Ibid., 14-20.

great pressure for many Malawian pastors to partner with Roman Catholics, Muslims, and leaders of other faiths. This is especially true when it comes to social causes like AIDS education.

A third issue that is a hot topic in Malawi is the ordination of women. Politically, in Sub-Saharan Africa, most countries have set a goal that at least 30% of their parliament members should be female. That cultural mandate has encouraged many churches to strive for a similar goal in the church. Many churches have already appointed female pastors. Other churches are wrestling with the issue. One of the synods for the largest denomination in Malawi, the Central African Presbyterian Church (CCAP), recently approved the decision that women could serve as elders. Later they reversed that decision, allowing for current female elders to complete their term but not allowing any more female elders to be nominated into the position of elder. Perhaps the most concerning part of the debate in Malawi over women in ministry is that society, rather than the Bible, seems to be determining what people should believe about women in ministry.

Observations that Hinder Malawian Pastors from Seeing the Coming Attacks on Biblical Authority

Whether the issue is the "health and wealth gospel," ecumenism, women in ministry, or any other issue that questions the authority of God's Word, one question that should be asked is, "Why is it that very few have connected these issues with inerrancy (biblical authority)?" Concerning discernment in relation to inerrancy, John MacArthur warns:

> The inability to discern is the final problem. It is like having spiritual AIDS. You can die of a thousand diseases because your immune system does not function. The church can perish at the hands of a thousand heresies because it can't discern, and the only way you can discern is to have the truth by which everything is measured, and that is Scripture. If you equivocate on whether Scripture is true or not, then you are

⎧ hopelessly removed from discernment because you ⎫
⎩ are hopelessly removed from the truth.[8] ⎭

The issues that attack biblical authority in Malawi will change from year to year. A high view of inerrancy does not usually die with one big blow from a *panga* ("machete"), rather it is a thousand issues that act like paper cuts, slowly draining the blood out of one's biblical view. In order for pastors to protect themselves from "slowly bleeding to death," two observations should be kept in mind.

Observation 1: Pastors in Malawi are often dependent on the West.

Colonialism is sometimes blamed for all the current problems in Africa. While that would be an unfair overstatement, background does matter when it comes to understanding how pastors are influenced in Malawi. Malawians are generally grateful for missionaries like Livingstone and others who helped preserve them from Portuguese slave traders and brought them the message of salvation through faith in Christ alone. However, because those early missionaries were so closely associated with colonialism, when African countries like Malawi were gaining their independence, there was great pressure for the "colonial missionaries" to leave.[9] Many missionaries were pressured to hand over their churches and ministries to national men, and they had not adequately prepared the congregations nor the men for this transition.

Many Malawians relied on missionaries to assist them with physical needs during famines and other difficult times. Unfortunately, when the missionaries left, the people then looked to the newly appointed pastors for these same needs. Today in Malawi, it is almost a foreign concept that a congregation should take care of their pastor's physical needs so that he could devote

---

[8]   John MacArthur, "Biblical Inerrancy and the Pulpit," *Expositor Magazine*, October 1914, 41.

[9]   Several missiologists suggest that the term missionary was so despised by many Africans because of colonial associations in the 1960s and 1970s that many missionaries began to use other terms to identify themselves. Willem Saayman references books such as *Missionary Go Home! and The Ugly Missionary* in his 2010 article "Missionary or Missional? A Study In Terminology." http://hdl.handle.net/10500/7094

himself to their spiritual needs. Most Malawian church members look to their pastors to help them with both spiritual and physical needs. Most Malawian pastors are not fully supported by their local congregation.

It is common to find Malawian pastors looking for financial provision from some other means than their own congregation. Some of them rely on their denomination to help support them financially. Therefore, many denominations do not have enough ministers to shepherd their congregations, forcing them to put one pastor over many congregations. It is not uncommon for a denominational pastor to shepherd a dozen or more churches, each congregation consisting of hundreds of people. Other pastors, not associated with a particular denomination become circuit riders. They plant numerous churches, expecting lay leaders to do the bulk of the teaching while they visit each "branch" once every two or three months to preach and collect an offering. Other pastors are forced to be bi-vocational, many of them managing a farm by hand while pastoring a congregation. Some privileged pastors receive individual support from Christians outside of Malawi. Unfortunately, this has encouraged other pastors to spend a lot of time each week in internet cafés scouring the web for potential benefactors from the West.

Though almost all pastors in Malawi say that ideally they would like to preach each week to the same congregation and be completely supported financially by that one body, in reality a small minority of pastors in Malawi are in that position. Thus, the financial circumstances facing pastors in Malawi put them in a difficult spot when faced with a decision that may involve compromising their beliefs, including their view of biblical authority, in order to gain financial support for their families.

Whether an individual pastor or an entire denomination requires financial support from the West, the sponsors from the West have a tremendous influence on the church in Malawi. Recently, some American missionaries in Malawi helped the General Secretary of a certain Presbyterian synod in Malawi to make contact with pastors in the United States who are more conservative Presbyterians. Their fear was that if they did not intervene and help the Malawian General Secretary find financial support from conservative churches, the liberal Presbyterian churches in the United States would be the only option for the Malawian General Secretary to partner with. Of course, the liberal side would be gently pressuring the General Secretary in Malawi to consider a myriad of issues that attack biblical authority. This leads us to a second observation.

Observation #2: Church councils and associations often have agendas of which most Malawian pastors are not aware.

Independent churches are not common in Malawi. Association with a certain denomination or a group of churches is almost universal. In addition to this, many Malawian churches and denominations value association with organizations such as the Evangelical Association of Malawi (EAM) and the Malawi Council of Churches (MCC). Since EAM is the more conservative of the two, one would hope that inerrancy would be an issue that they would champion in Malawi. Unfortunately, it is unlikely that inerrancy would be a topic of discussion in either EAM or MCC. These organizations tend to stay away from issues that could be seen as divisive by some.

The MCC is associated with the World Council of Churches and has a much more liberal agenda, including issues of social action, environmental issues, and human rights. The members of MCC and the Roman Catholic Church have formed a relief and development organization called Christian Service Committee.[10] Ironically, some churches in Malawi are members of both EAM and MCC, and they are unaware that the two organizations might have separate agendas. They would be surprised, for example, to learn that key members of the World Council of Churches are denominations that see homosexual marriage as a human right.

Nevertheless, as councils, associations, or other para-church organizations determine to mobilize pastors in Malawi to assist them in a social project (for example, AIDS education), pastors are often lured in to participate when finances are provided. Instead of the Bible guiding pastors on how they might best minister to the needs of the communities, organizations tend to set the course for pastoral ministry. Pastors are under enormous pressure to find money for

---

[10]   J. Tengatenga, *The UMCA in Malawi*, (Zomba, Malawi: Kachere Books, 2010)

ministry and their personal needs. So if an organization decides to roll out a social program in a community, they often involve the established churches. Such organizations offer funds to pastors for the administration of the project. They can buy computers, provide office supplies, and sometimes even purchase vehicles. This can be a great temptation for many church leaders. And of course, the organization will call the shots. If they decide that Muslim leaders and Christian leaders should work together for a project, that is what will happen. If they decide that condoms should be distributed by church leaders, the condoms will arrive at the pastor's home and he will be involved in the distribution of condoms.

Why Inerrancy is not Easy to Recognize as an Important Issue

Social agendas of organizations and Western benefactors often become the smoke and mirrors that divert Malawian pastors away from the real issue – the attack on the inerrant, authoritative Word of God. Historically, when church councils have met, it has been to discuss issues like inerrancy, doctrine, and truth. Even a hundred years ago, it used to be that only liberals integrated human philosophy with the rules of hermeneutics while conservatives generally agreed that there could only be one correct interpretation for a particular Scripture passage.[11] Though conservatives might have disagreed on the correct meaning of a particular text, the rules of interpretation would help them to dialogue with one another. But in Malawi, rules of interpretation are rarely discussed at meetings where the authority of Scripture is questioned. Because of this, no meaningful discussion can take place.

There is one main example of this rule: Not long ago, a group of conservative pastors in Malawi were invited to meet with a group of various leaders. Attending the meeting were conservative Protestants, liberal Protestants, and Roman Catholics. The issue happened to be the distribution of condoms to prevent the spread of HIV/AIDS, but it could have been any social issue. In the meeting,

---

[11] For a detailed discussion on the changes in evangelical hermeneutics during the 20th century, see Robert L. Thomas, *Evangelical Hermeneutics: The New Versus the Old* (Grand Rapids: Kregel, 2002), beginning on p 17.

various leaders were given the opportunity to speak. Some spoke about abstinence as God's plan for those who are not married. Some were more pragmatic and spoke about the fact that if people use condoms, even if they are involved in immorality, they will be saved from HIV/AIDS and therefore live longer and have more time to be converted to Christianity. Others spoke about their church's view that birth control is wrong. After a lengthy meeting, all the leaders returned home.

Later, some of the church leaders wondered why they were unable to come to any agreement at the meeting as to what the Bible says about this issue. The answer is because the meeting was never intended to consider what the Bible says. The meeting was only about letting people voice their opinions in order to demonstrate that different people had different opinions on this issue. Once that was established, the organization had the green light to move ahead with their program because at least some people were of the opinion that it was a good idea for churches to distribute condoms.

If the intention of that meeting had been to determine what the Bible teaches about the distribution of condoms, the leaders should have first been required to agree on the rules of biblical interpretation and authority of Scripture. If two groups meet that have two different systems of interpretation, there is no way that they will be able to have any meaningful dialogue. It would be as if the Malawi Flames soccer team was invited to a sporting competition with the ABC Lions basketball team and no rules were discussed prior to the competition. You can imagine the two teams showing up, some with football boots, others with high-top tennis shoes. Some of the athletes will be kicking the ball in one direction while others are picking up the ball and looking for a hoop in which to shoot. While some could say that an athletic event took place that day, others would rightly say that no meaningful competition occurred. That is what it is like at an ecumenical meeting of pastors in Malawi because "the two systems are incapable of meaningful dialogue with each other, because they use different rule books."[12]

---

[12] In Robert L. Thomas' book, *Evangelical Hermeneutics: The New Versus the Old,* he uses a similar illustration involving a baseball team and a basketball team (p. 19). Thomas was referring to the modern day evangelicals who have a new hermeneutic meeting with other evangelicals who maintain a traditional hermeneutic, but the situation is even worse

What are Malawian Pastors to Do?

In Lilongwe, Malawi's capital city, there is a large open market right in the center of town. The Lilongwe River happens to run right through the market, dividing the market so that half of the market is in Area 2 and the other half is in "Old Town." Some years ago, some entrepreneurial Malawians took wooden "gum poles" and timber "off-cuts" and constructed a rickety bridge to enable shoppers to pass from one side of the market to the other without having to leave the market. They, of course, charged a small fee for shoppers to use their bridge. Others thought this was a grand idea and they also built their own bridges. The only problem was that during the rainy season, as the Lilongwe River surged, one or two storms a year would completely wash away the bridges.

After seeing their bridges washed away and having to rebuild them several years in a row, the bridge owners learned two key realities. One was obvious: storms will come. The other lesson learned required some cooperation. The bridge builders learned that if they built their bridges right next to each other and tied them together, the bridges were strong enough to endure the annual storms. We hope that this article will help pastors in Malawi to realize two similar realities. One, attacks on our view of biblical authority are bound to come. Two, if we plan for them together, we will be better prepared for them.

There are no easy solutions to this problem. Malawi is one of the poorest countries in the world and it is easy for pastors to be diverted from ministering to spiritual needs and getting caught up in the social agendas even of some very good works. Obviously, pastors cannot ignore physical needs of those who are suffering around them, but the key is to make sure that the Bible sets the agenda for the priorities of ministry. Malawian pastors, like any pastor, can usually tell when someone is only coming to his church in search of financial gain. In a similar way, he should try to recognize when organizations are trying to use him for their purposes. He must not get involved in social projects to the extent that they

in Malawi. The rules of biblical interpretation are never discussed. The organizers of the meeting have set the agenda, and it doesn't really include a meaningful discussion about biblical authority.

in any way divert him from the priority of the proclamation of the authoritative Word of God.

A Similar Situation in 2 Timothy 3

In Paul's second letter to Timothy, he begins chapter three with a warning that in the last days, difficult times will come as "imposters" infiltrate the church and divert it from its focus. These difficult times will be characterized by selfish men who have ungodly characteristics. Paul's instruction to young Timothy is three fold. First, he is to avoid such men (v. 5). Second, he is to carry on with what he learned from Paul, even in the midst of persecution as things go from bad to worse (vv. 10-14). This includes both godly behavior and biblical teaching. Third, while avoiding evil men and carrying on with righteous behavior, Timothy was to esteem the Word of God – the "sacred writings" (v. 15). Why should Scripture have such a high place in this pastor's life? Because "All Scripture is inspired by God and profitable for teaching, for reproof, for correction, for training in righteousness; so that the man of God may be adequate, equipped for every good work" (2 Tim. 3:16-17).

Paul's warnings to Timothy were against apostasy within the church. The selfish and ungodly men that Paul warns about are men *within* the church. They "have a form of godliness although they have denied its power" (v. 5). This passage should be a startling reminder that pastors need to be cautious regarding partners in ministry. For starters, when Malawian pastors are invited to a meeting to discuss a theological or social issue, the first question should revolve around the authority of Scripture. Does Scripture speak towards the issue and are all the leaders present willing to submit to the authority of the inerrant word of God? Or is this merely a meeting where "personal opinions" might be voiced. Secondly, what rules of interpretation should be applied if there is disagreement as to what the Scripture teaches on an issue? Furthermore, pastors need to be bold enough to recognize that even if something is permitted by Scripture, it may not be a priority for pastors. As the early church leaders devoted themselves to "prayer and ministry of the word," not allowing themselves to be deterred by the noble and important work of looking after certain widows (Acts 6), so pastors need to keep their priorities in Malawi today. In John MacArthur's commentary on 2 Timothy, he notes:

> Paul had three overriding priorities in his life: to know Christ, to defend Christ's truth (Scripture), and to minister in Christ's name. A major part of both of his letters to Timothy focuses on the second priority, defending God's revealed truth. There is much relational preaching today that attempts to make people feel better about themselves and about how God might feel about them, but there is little forceful defense of full truth. As in most periods of church history, strong and effective defenders of the truth are at a premium. Not many pastors and teachers cry out for doctrinal and moral purity, for right belief and right living.[13]

Today, Malawi needs these defenders of truth more than ever, men who devote themselves to faithfully preaching the Word of God in one pulpit. The way to bring about spiritual growth among a certain congregation is through the proclamation of God's Word in that church. Immediately following Paul's hallmark statement about the inspiration and authority of the Word of God (2 Tim. 3:16-17), Paul commands Timothy, "Preach the word; be ready in season and out of season; reprove, rebuke, exhort, with great patience and instruction" (2 Tim. 4:2). This is a reminder to us that the faithful exposition of God's Word is the proper response from someone who recognizes its inspiration, inerrancy, and authority.

As it is, in Malawi today, the godliest men with the most theological training typically do the least amount of preaching in an individual church. They are too busy running around trying to cover a dozen or more pulpits. The end result is that all twelve congregations are missing out on the faithful, consistent preaching of the Word.

Malawi needs men who know God's Word and are willing to plant themselves before a single congregation. They must

---

[13] John MacArthur, "2 Timothy", *The MacArthur New Testament Commentary* (Chicago: Moody, 1995), 125.

tenaciously hold to the promise to care for the spiritual needs of their congregation as their congregation commits to provide for their pastor's physical needs. These men need to be willing to suffer. A missionary from another country once told a story about a pastor he trained and then offered financial support as the pastor was determined to plant a church in his home village. The pastor turned down the offer for financial support saying, "I want the people in my village to know that I am there for them, and if they value the Word preached to them, they will make sure I don't starve." Though it would not necessarily be wrong for a pastor to receive outside financial assistance (at least for a time), the focus on the proclamation of God's Word should never be hindered. Malawian pastors who are devoted to proclaiming the truth may suffer persecution from "impostors" (2 Tim 3:13) who are in the church but not concerned about the truth going forth. Persecution in Malawi may very well manifest itself in the withholding of money and resources from those who would stand firm on biblical inerrancy. Nevertheless, the truth must be proclaimed. Pray earnestly for Malawi.

Renewalism

"hermeneutic of the Spirit"

Affirming Inerrancy but Undermining Authority: Dangerous "Renewalist" Theology in Latin America

By Jim Dowdy (Mexico)

It is commonly accepted that Charismatic and Pentecostal movements represent the fastest-growing segments of global Christianity.[1] According to the _World Christian Database,_ over five hundred million people throughout the world are thought to be members of the Charismatic Movement. In Latin America, there are approximately one hundred and forty million charismatics.

In Latin America, charismatics represent a diverse branch of Christianity that is difficult for even religious scholars to describe. Most agree, however, that it includes two major groups: Pentecostals and charismatics. Taken together they are sometimes referred to as "renewalists" because of their common belief in the renewing gifts of the Holy Spirit. This term will be used to refer to

---

[1] Most also agree that they have their roots in the American Pentecostal religious revivals of the early 20th century through people such as Charles Fox Parham, William Joseph Seymour, W.H. Durham, Agnes Ozman and Aimee McPherson.

both movements. Three out of every four Evangelical Christians in Latin America are renewalists.[2]

The argument could be made that renewalist movements, despite their affirmation of biblical inerrancy, actually undermine the authority and sufficiency of Scripture by their acceptance of certain aberrant practices within their churches. First, we will present an overview of the doctrinal distinctions of these movements, and then discuss the hermeneutics of Bernardo Campos, a leading figure in the movement. We will conclude with a discussion of various leaders and practices in the Latin American renewalist movements and show how they undermine the authority and sufficiency of Scripture.

Charismatic Doctrinal Distinctives

We should note that while there are some doctrinal and practical differences between the various groups of renewalists throughout Latin America, they are generally characterized by their belief in, and practice of, the spiritual gifts that were operational during the first-century apostolic church. While some evangelical Protestant Christians believe that spiritual gifts such as apostles, prophets, miracles, healings and tongues were unique to the foundational period of the church in the first century (2 Cor. 12:12; Eph. 2:19-20; Heb. 2:3-4) and thereafter ceased (1 Cor. 13:8-11; Heb. 2:3-4),[3] modern day renewalists believe such spiritual gifts are still operational today among Christians.

Guillermo Maldonado—a well-known and respected Pentecostal-charismatic leader who appears frequently on *Enlace*, Trinity Broadcasting Network's Latin America media division— recently authored a book entitled "*El Reino de Poder: Cómo Demostrarlo Aquí y Ahora*" (The Kingdom of Power: How to

---

[2]   Pew Forum on Religion and Public Life, "Spirit and Power: A 10-Country Survey of Pentecostals" (October 2006) accessed October 13, 2014 http://www.pewforum.org/uploadedfiles/Orphan_Migrated_Content/pentecostals-08.pdf

[3]   This is known as cessationism. The author of this paper holds to a Classical Cessationist position. Classic Cessationism teaches that the sign gifts have ceased since the apostolic age and the completion of the biblical canon (Heb. 1:1-2; 2:3-4; Jude 3; Rev. 22:18-19). While God still can and does do miracles in a general sense, the *miraculous gifts* are no longer in operation today.

Demonstrate it Here and Now). The book is based on the thesis that given that "the Kingdom of God is His will and dominion carried out on earth as it is in heaven . . . wherever the kingdom of God governs, it is *visibly* demonstrated." This visible demonstration is in the form of miracles, signs, healings and liberations *exactly the way Jesus did it*.[4] Maldonado argues that each time Jesus announced the gospel of the Kingdom, sin, sickness, poverty, demons and even death were defeated. Therefore, he believes that Christians today should do the same.

Latin American renewalists are generally distinguished by their claims to speak in tongues, prophesy new revelation from God, heal, exorcise demon spirits, and more. While not every renewalist claims to be the recipient of such miraculous spiritual gifts, there would be near unanimous agreement regarding their modern-day continuation. At a minimum, most renewalists profess to have witnessed the practice of such miraculous gifts in their churches and other Pentecostal-Charismatic religious events.

To support their actions, all renewalists trace their beliefs to the Bible. While the most common proof text is Acts 2, which involves the events of Pentecost, another reference is the New Testament gospels on the supernatural acts of Jesus and the apostles. While Classic Pentecostalism tends to see the modern-day ministry of apostles and prophets in a secondary way,[5] many renewalists throughout Latin America, such as Cash Luna and Guillermo Maldonado believe there is a direct correspondence between their practice of the miraculous signs and wonders and that of Jesus and the apostles in the first century.

---

[4] Guillermo Maldonado, *El Reino de Poder: Cómo Demostrarlo Aquí y Ahora* (The Kingdom of Power: How to Demonstrate it Here and Now), (New Kensington, PA: Whitaker House, 2013), Kindle e-book. All translations from Spanish to English are my own.

[5] Pedro Olvera, *Credo: Perfil Doctrinal* (Creed: Doctrinal Profile), Iglesia Cristiana Independiente Pentecostés A.R. (Independent Christian Pentecostal Church: Apizaco, Tlaxcala, Mexico), icipar.net/web/ (accessed November 22, 2014). Classic Pentecostalism throughout Latin America believes in the uniqueness and unrepeatability of the original twelve apostles, yet sees apostolic power in a secondary sense in certain church leaders. Nevertheless, they do not see a one-to-one direct correspondence between Jesus' apostles and current day renewalists.

Post-Pentecostal "Hermeneutic of the Spirit"

In the past twenty-five years Latin American renewalist theologians have developed a post-Pentecostal "hermeneutic of the Spirit." Distinguished Peruvian Pentecostal theologian and professor, Bernardo Campos, has written extensively regarding this new interpretive model.[6] He comments, "The hallmark of Pentecostal theology lies in its creative capacity of a body of doctrine that is pragmatic, malleable, functional, perfectible and even changeable, without regard to its source, depending more on the considerations of the social context in which it is developed."[7] In other words, according to Campos, the interpretive rules (hermeneutics) that we should apply to the biblical text to determine meaning are flexible and changeable. All of this depends on local social context and the practical, cultural and philosophical issues on the ground at any given moment.

As Campos launches his argument for a "hermeneutic of the Spirit," he first states it is important to differentiate between an *a priori* epistemological point of departure and an *a posteriori* experiential point of departure. While he acknowledges that an *a priori* epistemology is the basis for our theological reflection, and that all Christians affirm that the Holy Scriptures "are and contain the Word of God revealed to men throughout history," he states that the Scripture only constitutes a "referential point of departure and horizon from where we construct our theory of religious knowledge."[8] In other words, while the Scripture is sufficient to help launch our understanding of God, salvation and sanctification, we must go *beyond* the Scripture to complete our understanding of what God is doing *today*.

Campos states that to have a correct and complete understanding of what God is doing in the world *today* it is necessary to add an *a posteriori* "existential point of departure" to our interpretive

---

6 Bernardo Campos, *El Post Pentecostalismo: Renovación de Liderazgo y Hermenéutica del Espíritu* (Post Pentecostalism: Leadership Renewal and Hermeneutic of the Spirit), CyberJournal for Pentecostal-Charismatic Research, 2003, http://www.pctii.org/cyberj/cyberj13/bernado.html (accessed November 20, 2014).

7 Ibid.

8 *Campos, El Post Pentecostalismo, 20.*

model. That is, we must include both individual as well as collective religious *experiences* to the interpretative process. Campos notes, "Different from the epistemological point of departure, the existential point of departure comes historically *before* [Divine] Revelation."[9] In other words, God does something supernatural and mysterious in the world today and then we are left to figure out what and why He is doing it by employing a "hermeneutic of the Spirit." *But d hus to be in harmony with the Scripture not depending from them*

After noting that our daily lives pose a series of existential questions and demand answers "that fill or satisfy the thirst of feeling that we have as created beings," Campos says therefore that *There is point of departure backwards* "it is natural that in the exegetical process, *the point of departure is, our life situation and not the author of the [biblical] text*."[10] After referring to Elisha receiving a double portion of Elijah's spirit (2 Kings 2:9, 14) and to the events of Pentecost (Acts 2), Campos continues to make astounding hermeneutical claims:

> The criteria of [interpretive] judgment *changes* in the wake of new experiences in the religious life, producing a kind of . . . new rationale to explain the new experience of the supernatural. . . .The explanation of the new logic is not now possible with traditional standards of interpretation [historical-grammatical], for which there is made necessary a distinct instrument [hermeneutic of the Spirit]. *If the hermeneutic of the Spirit was similar to the one of the Scripture we have then is find the problem many.*

Not only does he propose a new hermeneutical model ("of the Spirit"), but these mystical rules are not even being employed to interpret the Scripture, but rather the new contemporary mystical charismatic *experiences*. In other words, in light of the more unusual charismatic manifestations occurring among renewalists today (i.e. miraculous healings, exorcisms, prophetic declarations, etc.), they have been given a new "hermeneutic of the Spirit" that explains what God is doing through such unusual manifestations.

---

9 Ibid.

10 Ibid.

Specifically, Campos identifies this new distinct instrument of interpretation as modern-day prophecy. By prophecy Campos means "that mystical religious experience through which God communicates his will [today] through direct revelation to his spokesmen called 'prophets' or 'seers.'"[11] According to Campos, the discovery of this "hermeneutic of the Spirit" has brought about substantive changes in the organic leadership of the church. Campos claims that there has been what he calls "a novel, provocative and fascinating reaffirmation of the five ministries of Ephesians 4:11", including apostles and prophets. Campos notes that as a result of the restoration of this five-fold ministry, Latin American Christians have begun to experience more unusual charismatic manifestations. These include spontaneous falling to the floor, laughing, shouting, whistling, vomiting, dancing, prophetic declarations, liberation from demon possession and sorceries, and the miraculous inlay of gold or marble dentures in faithful Christians. One charismatic pastor even reports that he physically levitates to the ceiling when he prays.[12]

Campos claims that these charismatic manifestations:

> Are easily confused with the apparent practices of the New Age such as precognition, regressionism, magic, esoterism, mind control, theories of positive thinking, and others. Although on occasion, the difference can be very fine and can appear to coincide with the world of magic . . . nevertheless, according to Campos, true believers can perceive a substantive difference. Theologically speaking, the difference is qualitative, due not only to the nature of the experience, but above everything, due to the motives and intentions that accompany such practices.[13]

This is an astounding assertion! Campos tells us that the unusual charismatic manifestations occurring among renewalists

---

[11] Ibid., 1.

[12] Marco Antonio Peralta-Correa, e-mail message to author, December 3, 2014. Used by permission of author.

[13] Campos, *El Post Pentecostalissmo*, 20.

today can be so similar to unbiblical New Age and magical practices, that they can be easily mistaken for them. Campos assures us there is no need to worry, however, because the Spirit mystically helps true believers perceive a "substantive" and "qualitative" difference between the two apparently similar manifestations. This supposed spiritual discernment, however, does not come via a careful examination of the Scriptures. Rather, as long as the true renewalist's motives and intentions are pure, these contemporary charismatic experiences are "of the Spirit" and not the devil. Contrary to Campos, however, a comparison of these contemporary charismatic manifestations with the Scriptures indicates they are either of the flesh, or even Satanic (Matt. 7:15, 21-23; 2 Pet. 2:1-3).

In responding to Campos' "hermeneutic of the Spirit," a number of things should be noted. Firstly, God's Word is not situational or culturally determined. Societies cannot relativize the message of the Bible by accommodating it to changing cultural situations. The Chicago Statement on Biblical Hermeneutics states:

> We *affirm* that the Bible contains teachings and mandates which apply to all cultural and situational contexts and other mandates which the Bible itself shows apply only to particular situations. We *deny* that the distinctions between the universal and particular mandates of Scripture can be determined by cultural and situational factors. We further *deny* that universal mandates may ever be treated as culturally or situational relative.[14]

The Holy Scriptures transcend all cultural barriers and, correctly interpreted, are binding on all men everywhere.

Secondly, Campos' hermeneutical model "of the Spirit" produces doctrinal confusion and error since it denies a closed and completed biblical canon (Heb. 1:1-2; Jude 3; Rev. 22:18-19). It rejects the *a priori* epistemology of the objective, propositional, and historical truth of Scripture through the faithful and meticulous

---

14 Chicago Statement on Biblical Hermeneutics, November 1982, http://www.bible-researcher.com/chicago2.html (accessed November 29, 2014).

application of the historical, grammatical and contextual rules that have governed the church for the past 2,000 years. It replaces the authoritative and sufficient Word of God (2 Tim. 3:16-17; 2 Pet. 1:3-5, 16-21) with subjective and mystical experiences and new "revelations" from God.

Thirdly, several biblical passages that Campos points to as indicating the need for the implementation of this "hermeneutic of the Spirit," actually point to something quite different. Ironically, citing Paul's statement that there will come a time when people will not put up with sound doctrine (2 Tim. 4:3-5), Campos says we will therefore be required to implement this new "hermeneutic of the Spirit." Contrary to Campos, however, apostle Paul says that when the religious culture of the day is characterized by intolerance for sound doctrine along with tolerance for unsound doctrine, what the church must do is "preach the Word" (v. 2).[15] Earlier, Paul referred to the "Word" as "the pattern of sound words that you have heard from me" (1:13), and as "the good deposit entrusted to you" (v. 14). In 2:9, he specifically refers to it as "the word of God" which the faithful Bible interpreter must give his maximum effort to interpret so that he can impart God's word accurately and clearly to his hearers (2:15). In chapter 3 Paul refers to the Word of God as "the sacred writings, which are able to make you wise for salvation through faith in Christ Jesus" (3:15). Then, to leave no doubt, apostle Paul says that "All Scripture is breathed out by God and profitable for teaching, for reproof, for correction, and for training in righteousness, that the man of God may be competent, equipped for every good work" (3:16-17). Therefore, when Paul comes to 4:2 and writes, "preach the word," there is no doubt that he is referring to the scriptural Word of God contained in the Old and New Testaments of the Bible. This is the true "hermeneutic of the Spirit." The Holy Spirit is the giver of Scripture. Men spoke from God "as they were carried along by the Holy Spirit" (2 Pet. 1:19-21). He is the one who divinely inspired its giving to man (2 Tim. 3:16). He is the one who illuminates the Holy Scriptures to our hearts and minds (1 Cor. 2:6-16).

---

[15] All quotes from the Bible are from the English Standard Version.

Moreover, Campos points to the apostle Peter's warning regarding the rise and appearance of false prophets and teachers (2 Peter 2:1), and then says that in order "to be able to detect these false teachers implies we must employ this new 'hermeneutic of the Spirit.'" Further, pointing to 1 John 2:18-29, he states that only a "hermeneutic of the Spirit" can free us from the seductive error of the antichrist. The biblical reality is, however, that it is the self-pronounced renewalist "apostles," "prophets," and "evangelists" whose false teachings seduce, mislead and trouble so many Christian congregations throughout Latin America.

Is the Gospel Really Complete Without Miracles

Perhaps the most serious attack on the authority of Scripture by well-known renewalist leaders throughout Latin America is their corruption of the gospel of Jesus Christ. This has the most serious consequence of any of their hermeneutical errors. It is the difference between eternal damnation and eternal life.

In Latin America, renewalists are often defined by their belief in the "prosperity" or "health-and-wealth" gospel. A majority of renewalists believe that God grants good health and relief from sickness along with material prosperity to those who have strong enough faith.[16] While most charismatics sense a divine duty to evangelize (and there remains among them a widespread belief that faith in Jesus Christ represents the exclusive path to eternal salvation), the "gospel" that predominates much of their evangelism has little to do with the forgiveness of sin through the redemptive work of Jesus Christ at Calvary and more to do with receiving the (temporal) blessings of good health and material prosperity. "The message of health-and-wealth is now the message multitudes think of when they hear the word *gospel*."[17]

Many have accurately observed that the rapid growth of the Renewalist Movement in Latin America has more to do with the

---

[16] Pew Forum. "Spirit and Power", 10. This Pew Forum data suggests that the prosperity gospel is actually a defining feature of all Pentecostalism, with majorities of Pentecostals exceeding 90 percent in most countries holding to these beliefs.

[17] John MacArthur, *Strange Fire: The Danger of Offending the Holy Spirit with Counterfeit Worship* (Nashville: Thomas Nelson, 2013), 157.

popularity of the prosperity gospel than the true convicting work of the Holy Spirit. Allan Anderson wrote:

> To what extent have contemporary forms of Pentecostalism become 'popular religion', in that they present only that which the masses want to hear and omit important fundamentals of the gospel of Christ? The reasons for crowds of people flocking to the new [renewalist] churches have to do with more than the power of the Spirit. . . .The offer of a better and more prosperous life often gives hope to people struggling in poverty and despair.[18]

Harvey Cox, speaking of the global growth of Pentecostalism, notes that the single practice that initially draws most people to these renewalist groups, and the one that characterizes them more than any other, is that they offer healing of mind, body and spirit.[19]

Charismatic-Pentecostal pastor, Guillermo Maldonado, teaches that accompanying miracles are a *requirement* to preach the complete and powerful gospel. He asks, "What should happen when we preach the 'gospel of the kingdom'?" He answers, "The same good thing that happened when Jesus preached. He demonstrated the power of the kingdom with miracles, signs, healings and the casting out of demons." Maldonado later adds, "The gospel of the kingdom can never be separated from salvation, healing, and the exorcism of demons."[20] Then Maldonado adds, "If you do not see the power of God doing what He did through Jesus, then you are preaching an *incomplete and substitute gospel*."[21] Maldonado conditions the power and integrity of the gospel on its being accompanied by healings, exorcisms, signs, and wonders. He places an unbiblical burden on all Christians, causing them to believe that if their

---

[18] Allan Anderson, *Introduction to Pentecostalism: Global Charismatic Christianity* (Cambridge: Cambridge University Press, 2013), 280.

[19] Harvey Cox, *Global Pentecostal and Charismatic Healing* (Oxford: Oxford University Press, 2011), xviii).

[20] Guillermo Maldonado, *El Reino de Poder: Cómo Demostrarlo Aquí y Ahora (The Kingdom of Power: How to Demonstrate it Here and Now)*, (New Kensington, PA: Whitaker House, 2013) Kindle.

[21] Ibid.

proclamation of the gospel is not accompanied by the same signs and wonders that Jesus did, they are not preaching a true gospel.

The discerning Christian (Acts 17:11), however, needs to ask, "Is the preaching of the biblical gospel incomplete unless it is accompanied by the exorcism of demonic spirits? Does the Bible require these miraculous manifestations today in order for our gospel proclamation to be 'powerful'"? The biblical answer is clearly "no." *Right answer*

First, the miracles of Jesus and his apostles did not "complete" the message of the gospel. The gospel is a historical reality that is complete in itself (1 Cor. 15:3-4). At its very core, the gospel sets forth the substitutionary and redemptive work of Christ on the cross for sinners (Rom. 3:21-26; 2 Cor. 5:21; 1 Pet. 3:18). Paul said the focus of his preaching to unbelievers was "Jesus Christ and him crucified" (1 Cor. 2:2). The purpose of Jesus' miraculous signs was not to complete the gospel, but rather to *testify that he came from God*: "Jesus of Nazareth, *a man attested to you by God* with mighty works and wonders and signs that God did through him in your midst" (Acts 2:22). Likewise, the apostles healed people to confirm to Israel that Jesus was the Messiah: "Let it be known to all of you . . . that by the name of Jesus Christ of Nazareth . . . by him this man is standing before you well" (Acts 4:10). The signs, wonders, and miracles done by Jesus and his apostles divinely authenticated Jesus, his message, and his apostles: "The signs of a true apostle were performed among you with utmost patience, with signs and wonders and mighty works" (2 Cor. 12:12: Rom. 15:18-19; Heb. 2:3-4). Patricio Ledesma accurately says, "Today the *Bible* testifies to Christ and there are no longer [living] apostles to endorse him. Therefore, if we do not see the supernatural power in us doing the same that he did through Jesus . . . the gospel that we proclaim is still complete. Whoever adds requirements to this gospel is the one who really brings additional [extra-biblical] elements."[22]

---

[22] Patricio Ledesma, *Reseña del libro "El Reino de Poder"—Explorando las enseñanzas de Guillermo Maldonado* (Review of the book "The Kingdom of Power"—Exploring the teachings of Guillermo Maldonado), November 16, 2014, es.9marks.org/resena/resena-del-libro-el-reino-de-poder-explorando-las-ensenanzas-de-guillermo-maldonado/ (accessed November 28, 2014).

Secondly, the Bible does not link the power of the gospel with miraculous signs and wonders such as exorcisms and healings, but rather with the salvation of rebellious sinners and their sanctification. "For I am not ashamed of the gospel, for it is the power of God for salvation to everyone who believes, to the Jew first and also to the Greek. For in it, the righteousness of God is revealed" (Rom. 1:16-17). Only God's power through the gospel of Jesus Christ is able to overcome man's sin and give him new life (Rom. 5:6; 8:3; 1 Pet. 1:23). Although Maldonado cites 1 Cor. 4:20 ("For the kingdom of God does not consist in talk but in power") and then 1 Thess. 1:5 (". . .our gospel came to you not only in word, but also in power") to defend his position that the gospel of the Kingdom is power and not just words,[23] these verses do *not* talk about healings and exorcisms at all. Rather, the context of both of these passages refers to the reality that the power of the gospel results in a sanctified life (see context of 1 Cor. 4:18-21; 1 Thess. 1:5-10).

While the health-and-wealth prosperity gospel is definitely popular in Latin America, we must recognize that it is *not* the true biblical gospel. David Jones and Russell Woodbridge clarify the stark contrasts between the true and false gospels:

> The message preached in some of the largest churches in the world has changed. A new gospel is being taught today. This new gospel is perplexing—it omits Jesus and neglects the cross. Instead of promising Christ, this gospel promises health and wealth, and offers advice such as: declare to yourself that everything that you touch will prosper, for, in the words of a leading prosperity gospel preacher, "There is a miracle in your mouth." According to this new gospel, if believers repeat positive confessions, focus their thoughts, and generate enough faith, God will release blessing upon their lives.[24]

---

[23] Guillermo Maldonado, *El Reino de Poder.*

[24] David Jones and Russell Woodbridge, *Health, Wealth, and Happiness* (Grand Rapids: Kregel, 2011), 14.

This false prosperity message empties the cross of Christ of its power (1 Cor. 1:17), rendering it impotent to save. What happened to the apostolic message of Jesus Christ and him crucified for sinners? It has been co-opted by the false message that sounds like wisdom to the world, but can't deliver forgiveness of sins and eternal life.

Clarifying a Contradiction in Terms

Latin American renewalists claim to have a high view of Scripture. They profess belief that the Bible is the Word of God and should be read in a literal way.[25] The doctrinal statement of Guillermo Maldonado states: "We believe that the Bible is the inspired, infallible and unchangeable Word of God from Genesis to Revelation (2 Tim. 3:16)."[26] Cash Luna also affirms: "We believe that the Bible was inspired by the Holy Spirit and is the living Word of salvation."[27] They are unlike the liberal children of the Enlightenment who outright deny that the Holy Scriptures are the inerrant and inspired Word of God. However, as we have already seen—and shall yet see—their professed belief in the inerrancy and inspiration of the Bible is for the most part a contradiction in terms. While they affirm inerrancy, they undermine both the Scripture's authority and sufficiency by their actual practice. They subordinate sound doctrine to their unbiblical spiritual experiences and drive a wedge between the Bible and their extra-biblical revelations.

Even though the renewalist movements affirm the importance of the Word of God, in the day-to-day preaching and teaching within the movement, too much attention is given to extravagant claims about what God is doing through supposed miraculous charismatic manifestations instead of giving careful attention to the Bible. Let us consider the case of Cash Luna, perhaps the most influential leader in Latin America's Renewalist Movement. He explains the genesis of his own ministry:

---

[25] Pew Forum. *"Spirit and Power"*, 25.

[26] Guillermo Maldonado, http://www.elreyjesus.org/acerca-de-nosotros/nuestro/credo/ (accessed November 22, 2014).

[27] Cash Luna, http://cashluna.org/index.cfm/page/conocenos/show/202/Declaracion-de-Fe/ (accessed November 22, 2014).

> We were born as a congregation on September 11, 1994, after the Lord called Pastors Cash and (wife) Sonia Luna to undertake a ministry to which He had called them. . . .the Lord *spoke* saying that this church had not been born in the heart of man, but in the heart of God, and that it would be known, in the same way as the Ark of the Covenant, for manifestations of His presence.[28]

It is common to hear Luna and his renewalist counterparts claim to receive new revelation from God. In his book, *En honor al Espiritu Santo: ¡No es un algo, es un alguien!* (In Honor of the Holy Spirit: He is not something, He is someone!), Luna tells us that it contains "unique lessons of life that you will not find anywhere else about the theme [of the Holy Spirit]."[29] Among these "unique lessons" that we are to learn are Luna's fantastical claims that he made a leg grow on a man, that people fell down before his presence while he was walking in the airport, and even one episode where he was in a large stadium and when he looked toward the balcony, all of the people fainted.[30] This is blasphemous.

Luna writes of over a dozen "conversations" that he has had with God; conversations in which God purportedly spoke to him in an audible way. For example, the Spirit told him that "wherever you go, tell my people that I love them just as they are, with their virtues, strengths, defects and weaknesses." On another occasion the Spirit asks Luna if he believes that he will lose his divine unction "because you play with your children and fulfill your role as a father." During a dream in which the guru of prosperity and positive thinking, Kathryn Kuhlman, appeared to Luna, he claims to have received his greatest unction from the Holy Spirit. Following this transformative unction, the Spirit promised him on

---

[28] Ministerios Cash Luna (Cash Luna Ministries), 2014, *Casa de Dios, tu casa* (House of God, your house),http://www.cashluna.org/index.cfm/page/conocenos/view/Ministerios Cash Luna (accessed November 22, 2014).

[29] Cash Luna, *En honor al Espiritu Santo: ¡No es un algo, es un alguien!* (Miami, FL: Editorial Vida, 2010), Kindle edition.

[30] Ibid.

three consecutive nights a pair of shoes, a house, and a new temple for the growing church, all of which he later received.[31]

The Renewalist Movement, through its belief in modern-day apostles, prophets and their claims to receive extra biblical revelations from God, encourages people to look for divine revelation outside of the Bible. MacArthur speaks to the danger of such "revelation" saying, "The ramifications of that faulty premise are disastrous—destroying the doctrine of Scripture's sufficiency and effectively ignoring the close of the canon."[32] The Holy Spirit who conceived and inspired the Scriptures "acts through *it* today to work faith in *its message*."[33] The Holy Spirit is not only the source of Scripture, but works to produce faith in the Scripture, not in alleged "revelations" which are both contrary to and outside of Scripture. The Chicago Statement on Biblical Hermeneutics correctly states, "No matter how sincere or genuinely felt, no dream, vision, or supposed revelation which contradicts Scripture ever comes from the Holy Spirit."[34]

As a result of renewalists' focus on prophecies and miracles, the Bible does not receive the proper place it should have in the life of the church. The most compelling proof of the low position of the Bible among them is the fact that so few charismatics and Pentecostals actually read and study the Word of God. One report reveals that as low as 10% of renewalists in Latin America say they read their Bible on a regular basis.[35] Further, few if any of their leaders actually apply a sound grammatical-historical hermeneutic to the biblical text. Dr. Marco Peralta spent 18 years in the Renewalist Movement in Mexico City and notes:

> I never heard expository preaching while I was in the Charismatic Movement. They only used isolated verses as a trampoline to accommodate what they wanted to say. Otherwise, they used psychological and

[31] Ibid.

[32] MacArthur, *Strange Fire*, 68.

[33] Chicago Statement on Biblical Hermeneutics, www.bible-researcher.com/chicago2.html, November 1982 (accessed November 29, 2014).

[34] Ibid.

[35] Pew Forum. *"Spirit and Power, 15.*

humanistic arguments, shared personal testimonies, commented on political issues, told jokes and only referred to isolated parts of the Bible to accommodate their themes. . . .They try to study the Bible but do not actually do it in an exegetically appropriate manner because they don't know how . . . because of this they make many [interpretational and applicational] mistakes.[36] (Of course!)

While the "Ten-Country Survey of Pentecostals" indicates that few charismatics read their Bibles and even fewer study them carefully, high majorities profess to have received a direct *extra-biblical* revelation from God and overwhelming majorities report receiving direct prophecies from God.[37] Adding to this doctrinal confusion is the reality that most Latin American charismatics get most of their information about what they believe from charismatic religious media such as television, radio or internet. An example of this is the popularity of Trinity Broadcasting Network's Latin America affiliate, *Enlace*.[38]

Latin American renewalists' practice of "revelation" and "prophecy" has led them even further away from one of the key Reformation features: *Sola Scriptura*. The canon of Scripture was closed with the death of John (*c.* 100 AD) and, with it, the sole authority of apostolic-inspired testimony, the New Testament Scriptures. MacArthur comments, "The writings of the New Testament constitute *the only true apostolic authority in the church today*. (emphasis in original)"[39] This is primarily why the renewalists' purported extra-biblical revelation is a dangerous threat to the church. It is an attack on the historic Protestant Reformation conviction that the canon of Scripture is closed and no new revelation is needed. The sixty-six inspired and inerrant books of the Old (Matt. 5:17-18; Luke 24:44; John 10:34-35) and New (John 14:16;

---

[36] Marco Peralta, e-mail message to author, October 16, 2014. Used by permission of author.

[37] Pew Forum. *"Spirit and Power"*, 15.

[38] TBN Enlace USA. *Wikipedia*. http://en.wikipedia.org/wiki/TBN_Enlace_USA (accessed October 18, 2014).

[39] MacArthur, *Strange Fire, 96*.

16:13) Testaments of the Bible are complete, divinely authoritative and totally sufficient both for our salvation and sanctification (2 Tim. 3:15-17; 2 Pet. 1:3). The Bible is "the faith that was once for all delivered to the saints" and therefore needs to be faithfully defended and publicly proclaimed (Jude 3; 2 Tim. 4:1-5; see also Rev. 22:18-19).

MacArthur writes, "I believe the charismatics attack the Bible when they add all their visions and revelations to it. It is a subtle and often unintentional attack, but it is an attack just the same. They say that Jesus told them this, and that God told them that. In the meantime, they are undermining the Bible because they no longer see it as the single authority."[40] Divine authority is the central issue. The logical corollary of belief in the inerrancy of Scripture is belief in both its authority and sufficiency. Charismatics repeatedly undermine their professed belief in inerrancy by failing to carefully interpret and faithfully proclaim the Holy Scriptures. They live on a steady diet of supposed extra-biblical revelations and "fresh" prophesies that are fallible and errant, and therefore false. This approach to "prophecy" and "new revelations" from supposed contemporary apostles and prophets is blasphemous "because it ascribes to God that which did not come from Him."[41]

Apostle Paul says clearly that the church is "built on the foundation of the apostles and prophets, Christ Jesus himself being the cornerstone" (Eph. 2:20); that is, the *New Testament* apostles and prophets, not supposed modern-day ones. Further, the writer of Hebrews states, "How shall we escape if we neglect such a great salvation? It was declared at first by the Lord, and it was attested to us by those who heard, while God also bore witness by signs and wonders and various miracles and by gifts of the Holy Spirit distributed according to his will" (Heb. 2:3-4). The supernatural signs, wonders and various miracles were God's authentication and confirmation of the gospel of Jesus Christ (see also John 10:38; Acts 2:22; Rom. 15:19; 2 Cor. 12:12). The past-tense forms of the verbs "was declared" and "was attested," indicate these confirmatory

---

40 John MacArthur, *The Master's Plan for the Church* (Chicago: Moody Publishers, 2008), 24.

41 MacArthur, *Strange Fire*, 128.

signs and wonders occurred in the past and are not occurring in the present.

Jesus appointed his apostles to be his spokesmen, and after his ascension back to heaven, they presented their preaching and teaching as the very word of God, given by Christ through the Spirit, not by any human source (John 14:26; 15:26; 16:13). This is why Paul reminded the Thessalonian church that when they heard him preach they accepted it "not as the word of men but as what it really is, the word of God" (1 Thess. 2:13). It is also why obedience to his letter is a matter of church discipline (2 Thess. 3:14-15), and why he commanded his letters be read to all the Christians (Col. 4:16; 1 Thess. 5:27). It is for these reasons that John Frame writes, "There can be no doubt, then, that the apostles functioned as prophets, not only in their oral preaching and teaching, but in their written ministry as well. As there is an authoritative written account of the old covenant, there is also an authoritative written account of the new. These are both God's personal words to us."[42]

Yet another incongruity among renewalists is that their leaders claim authority based on the Bible, but don't allow the Bible to limit their authority or even sanction them when they are outside the bounds of Scripture. A common and glaring example of this is their repeated refusal to step down when they are no longer qualified for ministry according to scriptural qualifications, such as being above reproach (1 Tim. 3:1-7; Titus 1:6-9). A recent example of this in Mexico is that of "Apostle" Roger Wolcott, founder of the mega church, *Castillo del Rey* (Castle of the King). After he was widowed, Wolcott remarried, but within a few short months divorced. Meanwhile, he continued serving as an "apostle" in the church.[43] Unfortunately, renewalist leaders are well known for their moral failures and financial excesses (Titus 1:6-7; 1 Tim. 3:2-3). Practically speaking, then, while they claim personal and spiritual authority based on the Bible, they reject the authority of Scripture to govern their own lives and ministries.

---

[42] John Frame, *Systematic Theology: An Introduction to Christian Belief* (Phillipsburg: P & R Publishing, 2013), 585.

[43] E-mail to author from Dr. Marco Antonio Peralta-Correa, December 3, 2014. Used by permission of author.

Inerrancy Linked to Authority and Sufficiency

Scripture teaches that God's words are truth (John 17:17), that God cannot lie or speak falsely (Num. 28:19: Heb. 4:12-13), and that the Old and New Testaments of the Bible are God's written words (2 Tim. 3:15-17; 2 Pet. 1:19-21; Heb. 1:1-3). Moreover, the New Testament teaches that redemptive history has reached a pinnacle with the incarnation, death, burial and resurrection of Jesus Christ. John Frame writes, "The work of Christ is final, in a way that the work of Abraham and Moses are not. In Christ, God has spoken, (past tense, Heb. 1:2) a final word to us and this was attested to (also past tense, Heb. 2:2) by Jesus' original hearers. As the redemptive work of Christ is once for all, so the word of Christ and the apostles is once for all."[44]

[handwritten margin note: Very important]

The link between inerrancy and authority is so strong that historically most writers of systematic theologies have included the subject of inerrancy under the title of authority. Wayne Grudem, defending his inclusion of a separate chapter on inerrancy in his *Systematic Theology* writes, "Most books on systematic theology have not included a separate chapter on the inerrancy of the Bible. The subject has usually been dealt with under the heading of the authority of Scripture, and no further treatment has been considered necessary."[45] Nor should it be. If, in fact, all of the words in Scripture are God's words, and if God cannot lie or speak falsely, then all the words in Scripture are completely true and contain no error (Ps. 12:6; Prov. 30:5; Ps. 119:89; Matt. 24:35: Num. 23:19). The undeniable corollary between *inerrancy* and *authority*, therefore, is that the written Word of God in the 66 books of the Old and New Testaments of the Bible cannot be improved upon or added to, but rather trusted, obeyed and faithfully proclaimed in the power of the Holy Spirit (1 Cor. 2:4-5; 1 Thess. 1:5).

The Old Testament prophets repeatedly warned of false prophets (Deut. 13:1-5; 18:20-22; Jer. 23:16-32), as did New Testament writers (Matt. 24:11, 24; Acts 20:28-30; 2 Peter, Jude). On the other hand, when God speaks, it is always true (without error

---

[44] Frame, *Systematic Theology, 590.*

[45] Wayne Grudem, *Systematic Theology* (Grand Rapids: Zondervan, 1994), 90.

in part or in whole) (John 10:35; Titus 1:2). Consequently, when renewalists claim "new revelations" and "prophecies" from God when, in fact, He has not really spoken to or through them, they mislead many and dishonor both God and His Word. MacArthur makes this point well:

> Truth is the lifeblood of Christianity. Thus, false prophecy (and the false doctrine that accompanies it) represents the single greatest threat to the purity of the church. The Charismatic Movement provides false prophets and false teachers an unguarded entry point into the church. More than that, the movement puts out a welcome mat for those who proliferate the error of their own imaginations, inviting them inside the camp with open arms and affirming their sin with a hearty amen. But the prophets of the Charismatic Movement are not true prophets. So what does that make them? . . .According to 2 Peter and Jude, they are dry wells, fruitless trees, raging waves, wandering stars, brute beasts, hideous stains, vomit-eating dogs, mud-loving pigs, and ravenous wolves.[46] *(wow!)Very strong word*

Conclusion: A Diminished View of God and His Word

The Bible reveals that the one true and triune God is a divine being, self-exists, is majestic, good, eternal, righteous, holy, everywhere present, all-knowing and all-powerful. The apostle Paul said to the Athenians, "The God who made the world and everything in it, being Lord of heaven and earth, does not live in temples made by man, nor is he served by human hands, as though he needed anything, since he himself gives to all mankind life and breath and everything" (Acts 17:24-25). The God of the Bible is the blessed and only Sovereign, King of kings, and Lord of lords, who alone has immortality (1 Tim. 6:15-16). *(from past to future)*

Sadly, this one and only true God who graciously and mercifully reveals himself in the pages of Scripture, is not the "god" of many

---

46 MacArthur, *Strange Fire, 130.*

in the Renewalist Movement. The true Word of God contained in the sixty-six books of the Old and New Testaments of the Bible, is not the "word" that many renewalists proclaim and follow. While some renewalist leaders speak of the gospel in orthodox terms, they undermine both the Scripture's authority and sufficiency by actually preaching "another gospel" (Gal. 1:6-9). They subordinate sound doctrine to their unbiblical spiritual experiences and drive a wedge between the Bible and their extra-biblical revelations. They affirm biblical inerrancy on the one hand, but deny it on the other by undermining its unique divine authority through their erroneous teachings and practices.

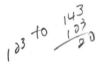

AN APPEAL TO AVERT THE DECLINE OF THE DOCTRINE AND APPLICATION OF INERRANCY IN NEW ZEALAND

By Various Faculty of The Shepherd's Bible College (New Zealand)

The recent New Zealand (NZ) census indicates that approximately 30% of New Zealanders are affiliated with at least a broad form of Protestant Christianity.[1] This is a 15% decline since the 1996 census.[2] It has been our experience[3] that matters appear grimmer on the ground, yet not without hope. On one hand, we are grateful that the voice of the inerrant, authoritative, sufficient Scriptures may still be heard in public forums. Our concern, however, is how the doctrine and application of the unlimited inerrancy of Scripture appears to be undergoing erosion among evangelicals

---

[1] 32%, to be exact (1,345,749 of the 4,242,051 of NZ). Based on the 2013 NZ Census (2013 Census Regional Summary Tables Part Two:http://www.stats.govt.nz/Census/2013-census/data-tables/regional-summary-tables-part-1.aspx), including Anglican, Baptist, Methodist, Pentecostal, Presbyterian, Christian (not further defined), and other Christian religions, but omitting Catholic and Latter-day Saints.

[2] Wikipedia. "Christianity in New Zealand." http://en.wikipedia.org/wiki/Christianity_in_New_Zealand

[3] Through the consistent reports we hear from throughout NZ through The Impact Bible Conference and The Shepherd's Bible College (TSBC); and through the combined pastoral experience of the Riverbend Bible Church and TSBC staff in various parts of NZ.

in New Zealand. This is our appeal, as fellow reflections in the mirror of the word (cf. Jas. 1:23-25) let us consider our ways (cf. Hag. 1:7).

"Unlimited inerrancy" refers to how the Scriptures, in their original autographs, tell the truth *equally in every part* (2 Tim. 3:16; Ps. 119:160) and with *every word* (1 Cor. 2:13) in *all* that it teaches *explicitly and implicitly* (Mt. 5:18; Lk. 24:25), because they are the words of God (Matt. 4:4; Rom. 3:2) who cannot err (Dan. 4:37; Titus 1:2; Heb. 6:18). This truth is foundational and essential to that formal principle of the Protestant Reformation, summed up in the Latin phrase *Sola Scriptura* ('Scripture alone'), meaning that the Old and New Testament Scriptures are the *sole* and *sufficient authority* for our faith and practice. What's vital for us Kiwi Bible-believing Evangelicals to appreciate is how inerrancy and *Sola Scriptura* are inextricably tied. Without inerrancy, we cannot have *Sola Scriptura*. If inerrancy falls, so do the interrelated doctrines and practices with it. While, thankfully, evangelicals in NZ still seem to confess the inspiration and authority of Scripture, inerrancy is commonly unmentioned or, if mentioned, is done so inexplicitly.[4] The contention of this article is, "Our brothers, this ought not to be so."

Much like some classical stone pillars consisted of a capital and base with multiple sections of stone mortared or dry-fit together in between, so the capital of the doctrine of *Sola Scriptura* is intimately tied together with several underlying supporting doctrines. Each section-stone doctrine rests on top of the other and depends on each other for its overall stability. If any of these segments are weakened so will the sole authority and sufficiency of Scripture be weakened. Accordingly, the purity of *Sola Scriptura* rests on the biblical fidelity of the undergirding doctrines including: special revelation,

---

[4] One telling testimony to this is the Statements of Faith of the significant Christian training institutes of NZ. See: Laidlaw College (http://www.laidlaw.ac.nz/en/college-informa-tion/our-statement-of-faith); Elim Ministry Training College (http://www.mtcnz.org.nz/about_us/statement_of_faith); Vision College (http://www.visioncollege.ac.nz/schools/leadership/church-connections); Carey Baptist College's statement of faith is nowhere posted on their website, but through personal inquiry, they said they affirm that of the Baptist Union (http://www.baptist.org.nz/general/Being-a-Baptist/); Pathways College affirms the Scriptures as "true and fully reliable" which may or may not be affirming unlimited inerrancy (http://www.pathways.ac.nz/site_files/1747/upload_files/2014Aca-demicProspectusV3.pdf?dl=1).

inspiration, canonicity, preservation, perspicuity, hermeneutics, and, of course, *inerrancy*. Thus, to the degree that one's view is less than the biblical view of these doctrines, similarly the authority and sufficiency of Scripture will be less than what it ought to be. If one's view, for instance, allows for man's involvement to *taint or introduce error* into God's revelation whether in the receiving of it (special revelation), writing it (inspiration), gaining unlimited truthfulness (inerrancy) and clarity (perspicuity) resulting from that process, recognizing and collecting of it (canonicity), or preserving (preservation) or interpreting it (hermeneutics), to that same degree the authority of Scripture would be inescapably impaired and limited, unable to speak adequately or authoritatively to all aspects of our faith and practice. In fact, according to Titus 1:1-3, the very hope of the gospel ("the hope of eternal life") is inseparably grounded in the inerrancy of Scripture ("the God who cannot lie. . . who has disclosed His message at the proper time"). Beliefs have consequences.

How consistent or prudent is it then, for example, if leading Christian training institutes of NZ on the one hand affirm the authority and inspiration of Scripture, but on the other, glaringly omit any clear affirmation of the doctrine of inerrancy or even relegate it to a level commensurate with the mode of baptism?[5] What good does it do to say Scripture is inspired and authoritative if a foundation of that confession is left open to attack or to slow decay through neglect? As NZ becomes increasingly post-Christian, it is not the time to be silent or leave the foundations of the authority of our faith open to attack or erosion. Rather, it is imperative to act and speak up about inerrancy! How else will the church of the living God in our day fulfil its calling to be "the pillar and mainstay of the truth" (1 Tim. 3:15)? Let us consider our ways and see to our foundations.

However, a mere addendum to our confessions of faith would hardly be a sufficient response. The cardinal truth of inerrancy must also be consistently applied in our practice. To the degree that the Scriptures breathed out by God are inerrant, they will be

---

5   Mark Keown, (New Testament lecturer at Laidlaw College), 2013. "Is Laidlaw College 'Liberal'?" Posted July 15, 2013. http://drmarkk.blogspot.co.nz/2013/07/is-laidlaw-college-liberal.html.

"profitable for teaching, for reproof, for correction, for training in righteousness" and able to make the man of God "*sufficiently [artios] and completely equipped [exartizō]* for _every_ [emphatic in the Greek] good work" (2 Tim. 3:16-17). Since the Scriptures are completely and fully inerrant, the sufficiency of their equipping for every good work is complete and full. Therefore, no other source is necessary. Accordingly, the fully inerrant Scriptures ought to be the *sole* voice in driving and determining our approach to ministry (i.e. "every good work"). They alone should determine *what* we do, *why* we do it, and *how* we do ministry from pulpit to programs. They *alone* are to be the church's compass, road map, filter, plumb line, and measuring tape. They alone ought to dictate our "philosophy of ministry." When the Scriptures, as the word of the One who is the Truth (Jn. 14:6), don't sit *alone* on the throne over our ministries, it creates a vacuum to be filled by all manner of competing *errant* authorities. Could this be why pragmatism, humanistic psychology, feminism, and other forms of culturalization have been integrated into evangelicalism in NZ? Let us then consider our philosophy of ministry as well, particularly in four areas: evangelism, counselling, the role of women, and pulpit ministries in the church.

The year 2014 marked the two hundredth anniversary of the gospel having been proclaimed in New Zealand. In that bicentennial year, a multi-church effort was made to proclaim the gospel to every household through literature, the Internet and television. The effort was off to a rousing start, as many churches contributed to and supported the work. A piece of literature was produced which would be delivered to every mail box. This booklet entitled "The Invitation: Hope for All"[6] contained stories of Christian people past and present, scientific evidence for Intelligent Design, and a presentation of "the Christian message of hope." However, there was one rather conspicuous thing missing—the Bible! Not a single Bible verse was cited or explained. Yet Scripture makes it clear that saving faith comes by the Word of God: "Faith comes by hearing and hearing through the word of Christ" (Rom. 10:17); "You have been born again. . .through the living and enduring word of God" (1 Pet. 1:23); "He gave birth to us by means of the word of

---

6   "The Invitation: Hope for All", 2014. http://hopeproject.co.nz/e-book/

truth" (Jam. 1:18). If this is so, and the Scripture is without error, then shouldn't a significant portion of our bicentennial "gospel" proclamation include the unfolding of that gospel as revealed in the actual word of God? Or do we think it cannot do what it says it can? Does our approach to evangelism demonstrate a genuine, consistent belief that "the holy writings. . .are able to make you wise for salvation" (2 Tim. 3:15)? Or does it err on this point? If it doesn't and *is* fully inerrant, then let us proclaim the gospel as revealed in Scripture in accordance with the exhortations and examples of the sufficient Scriptures.

Now it also follows that if the Bible is *not* fully inerrant, then it is impossible for it to be the sufficient source and means of counsel for "all things necessary for life and godliness" (2 Pet. 1:3) and for "every good work" (2 Tim. 3:17). The "all things" and "every" would be diminished to whatever degree the Bible was not fully inerrant. Therefore, it would be unable to address people's deepest emotional and spiritual problems and would open the door for other "authorities" to supplement the Scriptures. This is fundamentally what has happened in Christian counselling in NZ. The more inerrancy has been let go of or not understood, the more errant humanistic psychology has entered to erode and destroy biblical truth. New Zealand has followed the path of the world by integrating secular psychology with biblical truth in regard to Christian counselling, which is being replaced with "Christian psychology." There are very few trained *biblical* counsellors but many trained Christian *psychologists.* The trend continues to gain credibility with the Christian populace because of the subtle blend of biblical-sounding and appealing theological ideas. Although Christian psychologists claim to offer biblical counsel, they often offer secular-based psychology disguised behind proof-texted Bible verses. Psychology has the effect of destroying the church's confidence in the inerrancy, authority, and sufficiency of Scripture. The Bible becomes viewed as the Home Guard during wartime – nice, but not really effective or sufficient when facing a battle. Scripture is relegated to a mere book of good ideas or a place to get some general direction, but when serious mental or emotional trouble occurs, it simply doesn't provide adequate answers. Those who integrate humanistic psychology with the Bible fail to appreciate that it strikes at the very heart of biblical inerrancy.

The erosion of inerrancy in NZ is occurring in more subtle, fundamental ways as well. As indicated in the opening paragraphs, just as inerrancy is intricately connected with *Sola Scriptura*, so is inerrancy linked with all the other underlying interrelated doctrines, including hermeneutics. Perhaps the three most prevalent foreign authorities that seem to have made inroads into Kiwi evangelical hermeneutics include naturalism[7], subjectivism[8], and feminism. This last one is as telling as it has been controversial. The rise of feminism in NZ over the last several decades has placed tremendous social-cultural pressure and influence on the churches in NZ. An example of how this pressure has influenced the church in NZ may be seen in a report published in the *Christian Reality Magazine*[9], in which those interviewed attribute opposition to women leading pastors in the church in terms of "gender discrimination" and "gender prejudice." A part of the problem indicated is that "leadership has been redefined in masculine terms and the Church is no longer able to see beyond its own narrow interpretation." But nowhere are any relevant biblical texts discussed as to what God has to say about the matter and His definition of leadership in His church. A shift has occurred from what the Lord says to what the culture states.

This is perhaps no more clearly seen than in how churches handle 1 Timothy 2:11-15. What wasn't difficult to interpret and apply in 1 Timothy 2:11-15 several decades ago has in recent years been subject to a number of creative and subtle methods of dismissing its clear divine trans-cultural mandate for the church-age. Paul the Apostle, in addressing proper conduct when

---

[7] The explaining away of the supernatural in favor of a more natural reinterpretation results in such things as the denial of a supernatural literal six-day creation.

[8] The shift from discerning the original authorial meaning of the text to what the interpreter "feels" it means, results in such things as eisegesis (reading a meaning into the text), proof texting (removing a text out of its context to prove a point foreign to its original meaning), allegorizing (reading symbols into the text where none were originally intended), and spiritualizing (plucking out phrases or concepts from their context and reading spiritual principles into them).

[9] Sally Wise, "New Zealand Women and Church Leadership" *Reality Magazine* (Issue 66, 2004. http://www.reality.org.nz/article.php?ID=407.

the mixed-gender church is gathered, (1 Tim. 3:15) grounds the divine prohibition of female leadership and teaching (1 Tim 2:11-12) in the trans-cultural grounds of the created order (1 Tim. 2:13). Nevertheless, some insist that Paul was addressing a specific cultural issue of his day in Ephesus (which no longer is applicable today) even though nothing in the text even intimates that. Others muster cross-references about the genders from different contexts, addressing things such as spiritual equality (Gal. 3:28) or spiritual gifting (1 Cor. 12:4-31; 1 Pet. 4:10-11) and not gender-roles, and then allow them to override the plain sense of 1 Timothy 2:11-15. More subtly, some confuse the trans-cultural principle of verse twelve ("I do not permit a woman to teach or to exercise authority over a man") with a culture-specific application of a principle (like "braided hair" is to the principle of "modesty and self-control" in v. 9) and by so doing make the application of the principle of verse twelve a matter that is *culturally,* rather than biblically, defined.[10] In each case, what drives the interpreter away from the plain authorial meaning of the text is not the text itself, but an extraneous influence of culture determining the meaning and application of Scripture. This culturalization of Kiwi hermeneutics will continue and multiply unless we return to a sound biblical grammatical-historical hermeneutic that is consistent with a clear and accurate understanding of the doctrine and application of full inerrancy.

Perhaps the erosion of inerrancy in NZ is no more publicly demonstrated than from pulpits. Yet few voices rise above the silent approval to decry the general sad state of preaching in NZ. The Scriptures are increasingly being set aside in sermon addresses. Preaching that seeks to proclaim, explain, and reprove and exhort from the intended meaning of the text of Scripture (2 Tim. 4:2) is a rarity in NZ, as are those who can discern the difference. Instead the authority base of the content of sermons has shifted to more effective ways to motivate people, such as stories, testimonies,

---

[10] The result of such an approach includes the notion that since in NZ today women teaching men does not necessarily symbolize taking authority over them, a woman may teach when the church is gathered and men are present as long as she does so in a submissive manner "under the Elders" and isn't an "Elder" or a "Senior Pastor" herself (however, she may be a "pastor" since the term in NZ culture doesn't necessarily mean "Elder").

psychological concepts, quotes from secular or pagan sources, and dramatic monologues. Sermons are turning away from sound teaching and inerrancy of the Bible and turning to myths (cf. 2 Tim. 4:3-4; Jer. 5:31). But let us consider this. If every word of the original inspired words of God in Scripture are fully inerrant and infallible, should they not hold precedence over the fallible stories and philosophies of men? Shouldn't the inerrant points of the passage be the determiner of the points of the sermon, rather than errant speech? We are not more effective than He is, are we?

What we have seen are just some of the symptoms of the decline of the conviction of and fidelity to the inerrancy of Scripture in NZ. The link between inerrancy and *Sola Scriptura* and our practice is a chain of immeasurable importance. It is a chain which when held, holds orthopraxy within orthodoxy and assures the flock they are feeding on good pasture. Biblical inerrancy is a foundation stone that needs to be returned and reinforced in the foundation of our church doctrine and practice. When such a foundational stone is dislodged then that particular building is surely set to fall. Let those that are in accord with the "once for all delivered to the saints' faith" (Jude 3) continue, flourish, and spread. Let the gaps between inerrancy (and consequently *Sola Scriptura*) and our practice become smaller and fewer. Let us not grow weary or weak in doing good. We should not sit idly as rust and decay corrode the foundations. Christ's house will still stand (Matt. 16:18), not necessarily those in which we minister (Rev. 2:5, 16, 22-23; 3:3).

BUILDING ON THE INERRANT WORD: THE SOLUTION FOR SYNCRETISM

By Allan Luciano (The Philippines)

I n John 18:38, Pilate asked the perennial question, "What is truth?" He was not the first to make such an inquiry, nor was he the last. From the dawn of human civilization to the present day, mankind has endeavored to distinguish truth from falsehood. In a moment of tragic irony, Pilate uttered this now-famous question to Jesus of Nazareth, who claimed to be the very truth that Pilate dismissed as unknowable. He stood in the presence of truth incarnate but did not see. We now have the truth of Jesus recorded in Holy Scripture; but like Pilate, there are those today who stand in the presence of the truth and still do not see.

In the Philippines one of the greatest obstacles to seeing the exclusive and objective truth of Jesus as recorded in the Bible is the seductive spirit of syncretism. Syncretism is the blending of Christian beliefs and practices with those of the dominant culture resulting in Christianity losing its distinctiveness and speaking with a voice reflective of its culture.[1] Alternatively, syncretism combines elements of Christianity with folk beliefs and practices in such a

---

[1]   Gailyn Van Rheenen, "Syncretism and Contextualization: The Church on a Journey Defining Itself" in *Contextualization and Syncretism: Navigating Cultural Currents* (Pasadena: William Carey Library, 2006), 7-8.

way that the gospel loses its integrity and message.[2] The truth of Jesus is obscured when His message is tainted by the association of falsehood. This is typically exposed when supposed Christian converts continue to practice elements of local religions.

The Philippines, with its history of colonization by Spain and the United States, provides abundant examples of syncretism both among Catholics[3] and Protestants. Old animist beliefs that pre-date Spanish colonization in the sixteenth century continue to influence Filipino Catholics and Protestants. For a country that is predominantly Catholic, it is surprising that only an estimated ten to fifteen percent of baptized Catholics practice their religion in officially sanctioned ways.[4] This led one author to conclude, "Apparently the Filipino is still an animist at heart, in spite of four centuries of Roman Catholicism."[5] Protestant churches have not been exempt from the influence of indigenous beliefs. Research found elders of a Protestant church consulting the *baylan* or medium for their sickness in spite of repeated instruction from their pastor that they go to the doctor.[6] A recent conversation with a local pastor just outside of Manila confirmed that such behavior is not uncommon among church members today.

At its core, syncretism is the deceptive attempt to combine truth with error. Truth from the Word of God is merged with beliefs and practices from false religion, inventing a Christ that is more palatable to pagans, while resulting in what one author calls "Christopaganism."[7] The danger here is that people may be deceived into thinking that they have embraced Christianity when in reality they have merely added elements of Christian philosophy or morality to their lives but remain unaffected by radical,

[2]   David Hasselgrave, "Syncretism: Mission and Missionary Induced?" in *Contextualization and Syncretism*, (Pasadena: William Carey Library, 2006), 71.

[3]   John Schumacher, "Syncretism in Philippine Catholicism," *Philippine Studies* 32, 1984: 251.

[4]   Melba Maggay, *A Clash of Cultures: Early American Protestant Missions and Filipino Religious Consciousness* (Manila: Anvil, 2011), 166.

[5]   Rodney Henry, *Filipino Spirit World: A Challenge to the Church* (Mandaluyong: OMF Literature, 1986), 12.

[6]   Ibid., 167.

[7]   Paul Hiebert, *Anthropological Insights for Missionaries* (Grand Rapids: Baker Book House, 1985), 184.

paradigm-shifting, world view-shattering gospel truths. Syncretism deceives people into believing that they are on their way to heaven, when in reality it is the broad road of destruction that they walk. The eternal destiny of souls is at stake.

Also at stake is the holiness of God. Holiness is a fundamental attribute of God; it is basic to everything about Him.[8] To say that God is holy is to recognize that He exists entirely apart from all that is creaturely, earthly, or human.[9] God demands that His holiness be recognized by His people. After killing Nadab and Abihu with fire for offering Him "strange fire," God said, "Among those who are near me I will be sanctified, and before all the people I will be glorified" (Leviticus 10:2). New Testament believers are called to the same standard as Old Testament saints: "but as He who called you is holy, you also be holy in all your conduct, since it is written, 'You shall be holy, for I am holy'" (1 Peter 1:15-16). To worship God in ways derived from pagan worship is to deny the truth of His holiness. It is to say that He is no different from the pantheon of false gods around the world. It is to proclaim and practice the opposite of what God has said in Isaiah 42:8, "I am the Lord; that is my name; my glory I give to no other, nor my praise to carved idols." Syncretism is idolatry done in the name of the Lord. It is inherently blasphemous and threatens both the holy name of God and the eternal destiny of man.

Error, lies, and deceit are at the heart of syncretism. The only arsenal against these is the truth of Jesus Christ proclaimed exclusively and boldly. Truth repels error in the same way that light dispels darkness. The only antidote to the poison of relativistic syncretism in the Philippines is an unwavering commitment to the truth of God as revealed in Holy Scripture.

Truth is at the heart of the doctrine of the inerrancy of Scripture. To say that the Bible is inerrant is to affirm that it is truthful and reliable.[10] Inerrancy simply means that the Bible always tells the truth concerning everything it discusses.[11] A commitment to

---

[8] Robert Culver, *Systematic Theology* (Roth-shire: Mentor Imprint, 2005), 95.

[9] Ibid., 96.

[10] Wayne Grudem, *Systematic Theology* (Grand Rapids: Zondervan Publishing House, 1994), 90.

[11] Ibid., 91.

inerrancy is a commitment to truth. To fight against the error of syncretism, it is absolutely crucial to have a strong commitment to the truthfulness of the Bible. Heeding the objective, authoritative truth of the Word of God will protect the Filipino church from syncretistic influences.

What the Inerrant Word Says About Syncretism

The dangerous concept of religious syncretism is addressed throughout the Bible. Exodus 32 records one such example, along with God's harsh response.[12] After Moses had been away receiving instruction from God on Mount Sinai for forty days and forty nights (Exodus 24:18; 32:1), the Israelites demanded that Aaron make them a god (32:1). Aaron complied and fashioned a molten calf from the gold of the earrings of the people (32:2-3). The choice to create an image of a calf was likely an influence of Egyptian religion, particularly the Egyptian god Apis.[13] But when he introduced his creation to the Israelites, Aaron made it clear that this idol was not a depiction of any of the Egyptian gods. This was an image of Yahweh Himself: "This is your god, O Israel, who brought you up from the land of Egypt" (32:4). Here is where idolatrous practices are appropriated by God's people and incorporated into Yahweh worship—the essence of syncretism. In doing this, they had corrupted themselves (Exodus 32:7); they clearly disobeyed His commands (32:8); and they successfully provoked His wrath (Exodus 32:10). Because of their defiled syncretistic worship, 3,000 Israelites died (Exodus 32:28) and God sent a plague to the people as judgment (Exodus 32:33).

In another example found in John 4:1-26, Jesus converses extensively with a woman from a religiously syncretistic background.[14] She was a Samaritan woman whose ancestors adopted Israel's religion and combined it with their own polytheism (2

---

[12] John J. Davis, *Moses and the Gods of Egypt*, Old Testament Studies (Grand Rapids: Baker Book House, 1983), 285.

[13] C.F. Keil and Franz Delitzsch, *Commentary on the Old Testament*, vol. 1, *The Second Book of Moses* in *The Pentateuch* (Peabody: Hendrickson Publishers, 1996), 466.

[14] Merrill C. Tenney, "John" in *The Expositor's Bible Commentary*, ed. Frank E. Gaebelein et al., vol. 9 (Grand Rapids: Zondervan Publishing House, 1981), 56.

Kings 17:24-41).[15] In the course of their conversation, Jesus graciously and carefully reveals to her that He is the Messiah. He also shows her the character of true worship.[16] Jesus' assessment of the Samaritan's religious syncretism is that they worship out of ignorance (4:22). In contrast to this, Jesus explains what is absolutely essential in worshipping God—it must be done in both spirit and truth (4:24). To worship in spirit means rendering such homage to God that the entire heart enters into the act. Worshipping in truth means doing so in full harmony with the truth of God as revealed in His Word.[17] God has clearly laid out the standard for worship that He desires, and He will not compromise His perfect standard. God desires worshippers who are genuine in their devotion to Him, and who worship Him in accordance to His revealed Word. Offering syncretistic worship to God, like the Samaritans who mixed biblical ideas with pagan idolatry, is futile and ultimately rejected by God.

Additionally, in 2 Corinthians 6:14-7:1, Paul tells Christians to avoid relationships that foster syncretism.[18] He opens this section with a clear command in verse 14: "Do not be unequally yoked with unbelievers." While this verse is frequently used to teach against believers marrying or going into business with unbelievers, the primary thrust of this command, given its context, is to teach about the separation of the Christian religion from pagan religion.[19] After giving the command, Paul asks five rhetorical questions that contrast Christianity with false religion. Christianity is as incompatible with pagan religion as righteousness is with lawlessness, as light is with darkness, as Christ is with Belial, as a believer is with an unbeliever, and as the temple of God is with idols (vv. 14-16). It is irrational and devastating to the soul to seek to combine the worship of God with false religion. Aside from the inherent incompatibility of Christianity with pagan religion, God

---

[15]   Allen Myers, ed., The Eerdmans Bible Dictionary (Grand Rapids: William B. Eerdmans Publishing Company, 1987), s.v. "Samaritans."

[16]   William Hendriksen, "John", *New Testament Commentary* (Grand Rapids: Baker Academic, 2007), 169.

[17]   Ibid., 167.

[18]   Murray J. Harris, "2 Corinthians" in *The Expositor's Bible Commentary*, ed. Frank E. Gaebelein et al., vol. 10 (Grand Rapids: Zondervan Publishing House, 1976), 360.

[19]   Simon J. Kistemaker, "2 Corinthians", *New Testament Commentary* (Grand Rapids: Baker Academic, 1997), 228.

has specifically commanded His people to separate themselves from false religion (vv. 16-18). The reason for this separation is the special relationship that exists between God and His people: He dwells and walks among His people, He is their God, and they are His people (v. 16). He is a father to His people and His people are sons and daughters to Him (v.18). Integrating pagan beliefs and practices in the lives of believers undermines the special and unique relationship God has graciously extended to His redeemed people. On the basis of God's great promises, Paul commands all Christians to purify themselves from all defilement, which refers to religious defilement, or unholy alliances with idols, idol feasts, temple prostitutes, sacrifices, and festivals of worship[20] that pollute the entire person (body and spirit). In other words, succumbing to syncretism is irrational (vv. 14-16), irreverent (16-18), and disobedient (7:1). It is completely inconsistent with biblical Christianity to seek to incorporate pagan idolatry in the lives of believers.

Stemming the Tide of Religious Syncretism

From the Old Testament to the New, the Bible expressly condemns syncretism of any kind. Syncretistic worship is not worship at all, but is actually a bold act of disobedience and irreverence against God. Falsehood is incompatible with truth. To mix the truth of God's Word with lies from false religion is a compromise of the Christian faith. The result of such a union is a false religion that is not Christian. A firm conviction about the truthfulness and trustworthiness of Scripture will protect the church, and missions, from the dangers of syncretism.

Eventually, incompatible beliefs and practices conflict. A person cannot consistently hold to the exclusive truth of Christ while simultaneously affirming a plurality of religious expression. It is essential that the Filipino converts are taught the inerrancy of the Word of God, for whenever their former beliefs and practices come into conflict with what Scripture claims, they will know that the objective source of all unerring truth is Holy Writ alone.

---

[20] MacArthur, *The MacArthur Bible Commentary*, 1634.

In this way, the inerrancy of Scripture is inextricably linked to the authority of Scripture. As is stated in the preamble of the Chicago Statement on Biblical Inerrancy, "recognition of the total truth and trustworthiness of Holy Scripture is essential to a full grasp and adequate confession of its authority."[21] In other words, a commitment to the inerrancy of Scripture paves the way for submission to its authority. Only when the Filipino understands that Scripture alone is without error, and that all other truth claims must be subjected to the Bible will he be able to yield himself to its authority in sanctification. Because Scripture has a divine source (2 Timothy 3:16) and because God cannot lie (Hebrews 6:18), the Bible is completely truthful and reliable. Because of its veracity and divine origin, the Bible has authority. "When the Bible speaks, God speaks."[22] When ministry is done under submission to the authority of Scripture, the work of the ministry as well as the ideas that influence ministry are evaluated under the lens of the Word of God. This gives the church discernment to protect itself against syncretistic influences that come in the form of man-made philosophies, tradition, and religion.

To counter the influence of syncretism, discernment must be cultivated. The conviction of the Bible's inerrancy combined with a commitment to both the responsible interpretation of Scripture and the development of a mature biblical theology are the necessary prerequisites for gaining discernment.[23] In other words, a robust ministry that is resistant to syncretism will be built upon sound doctrine and faithful exposition and application of the Word of God. All of this is built upon the conviction that the Bible is true. Inerrancy is the foundation upon which a biblically faithful ministry is built. This means that everything about that ministry—its goals, criteria for success, reason for existence, and methodologies—are all derived from and evaluated through Scripture. Various cultural traditions as well as new ideas and trends that come up in the

---

[21] Norman L. Geisler, ed. *Inerrancy* (Grand Rapids: Zondervan Publishing House, 1980), 493.

[22] Albert Mohler, "When the Bible Speaks, God Speaks: the Classic Doctrine of Biblical Inerrancy" in *Five Views on Biblical Inerrancy*, J. Merrick, et al. eds. (Grand Rapids: Zondervan Publishing House, 2013), Kindle Electronic Edition: Chapter 1, Location 882.

[23] Ibid., Chapter 1, Location 878.

field of ministry (whether local or overseas) must pass through the scrutiny of Scripture to determine its usefulness or its danger.

In the context of missions, it is crucial to equip national church leaders to have this level of discernment. This means that they need to take hold of the underlying convictions that yield discernment— the commitment to faithful and accurate Bible interpretation, the development of biblically faithful theology, and the absolute truthfulness and reliability of Scripture. In order for national church leaders to gain these convictions, the training of faithful men must take priority in missions. This model of ministry was practiced and taught by Paul. He appointed elders to lead the churches he planted (Acts 14:23). He entrusted both Titus and Timothy with the task of equipping and appointing qualified elders to lead local churches (1 Timothy 3; 2 Timothy 2:2; Titus 1:5).

National leaders, by the fact that they are native to the culture and society, will have an insider's perspective in evaluating culture and tradition. Couple that native-level understanding of culture with biblical discernment and godly character befitting elders (1 Timothy 3; Titus 1:6-9) and the result is a national leadership that is equipped to protect local churches from syncretism. They will be shepherds who are equipped to adequately feed and protect God's sheep. Such men will be in position to carry out Paul's model of multi-generational duplication of leadership mentioned in 2 Timothy 2:2, "and what you have heard from me in the presence of many witnesses entrust to faithful men who will be able to teach others also." With leaders such as these, churches will have ample protection against syncretistic influences.

Conclusion

Syncretism is a serious problem with grave consequences. Syncretism dilutes truth with subtle lies from false religion. This can deceive people into falsely thinking that they are Christian. However, the infinitely greater danger in religious syncretism is the blasphemy done to God's holy name. Syncretism rejects this most basic attribute of God, bringing Him down to the level of false idols. With such great consequences at stake, this problem must be addressed. The only proper response is to combat relativistic falsehood with the exclusive and objective truth of Jesus Christ in Holy Scripture. A commitment to the inerrant Word of God is the foundation upon which the solution to syncretism must be built.

This is consistent with our Lord's teaching. When Jesus preached the Sermon on the Mount, He closed with the illustration of the two builders. The wise builder was the one who built his house upon the rock. The foolish builder was the one who built upon sand. The storm revealed the true quality of their construction. Jesus used this illustration to call His audience to build their lives upon His words, to be "doers" of His word and not just hearers.

In "building" missions, what could be a better foundation than the inerrant Word of God? To build on anything else (various traditions and philosophies of man) is to be the foolish builder who built on sand. It will not last. Ministry built upon God's inerrant Word, however, will be able to withstand anything—even the storms of syncretism.

Russian Evangelical Tradition: A Case Study in Non-Western Adherence to Inerrancy

By Alexander Gurtaev (Russia)

For many centuries the church was united in its affirmation of the complete veracity of Scripture. Inasmuch as this conviction had not been challenged from within, the church treated it largely as an assumption. Consequently, in the early church confessions one does not find the direct references to "inerrancy" — much less the detailed argumentation to support it — as we find in theological discussions today.[1] Nevertheless, we can confidently assert that the *concept* of what is today called "biblical inerrancy" has existed through the ages.[2] An illustration of this historicity can be seen in

---

[1]   Norman L. Geisler and William C. Roach, *Defending Inerrancy: Affirming the Accuracy of Scripture for a New Generation* (Grand Rapids: Baker Books, 2011), 324.

[2]   Jason S. Sexton J., "How Far Beyond Chicago? Assessing Recent Attempts to Reframe the Inerrancy Debate," *Themelios* 34 no. 1 (2009), 46; Norman Geisler, *Systematic Theology*, vol. 1, *Introduction, Bible* (Minneapolis, MN: Bethany House, 2002), 500–502. For detailed arguments see John D. Woodbridge, *Biblical Authority: A Critique of the Rogers/McKim Proposal* (Grand Rapids: Zondervan, 1982); Robert D. Preus, "The View of the Bible Held by the Church: The Early Church Throughout Luther," in *Inerrancy*, ed. Norman L. Geisler (Grand Rapids: Zondervan Publishing, 1980): 357–382; John D. Woodbridge, "Some Misconceptions of the Impact of the 'Enlightenment' on the Doctrine of Scripture," in *Hermeneutics, Authority and Canon*, eds. D. A. Carson and John D. Woodbridge (Eugene, OR: Wipf & Stock Publishers, 1986): 237–270.

the response of Augustine of Hippo (354–430 AD) to possible allegations in his own time that there were errors in sacred Scripture. In a letter to Jerome, he writes:

> I have learned to yield this respect and honour only to the canonical books of Scripture: of these alone do I most firmly believe that the authors were completely free from error. And if in these writings I am perplexed by anything which appears to me opposed to truth, I do not hesitate to suppose that either the manuscript is faulty, or the translator has not caught the meaning of what was said, or I myself have failed to understand it.[3]

However, humanistic influences of the Enlightenment, the expansion of philosophical currents into biblical studies, and the increasing popularity of higher critical approaches slowly eroded the church's long-held view of Scripture in the modern era. Spreading first among liberal Protestants, attacks on biblical inerrancy soon caught up with evangelical world as well, becoming a matter of debate among evangelicals even as early as the start of the twentieth century.[4]

Is Inerrancy Characteristic only of the American Context?

The recent Zondervan Counterpoint publication, *Five Views on Biblical Inerrancy*,[5] illustrates the significant disagreement existing today among confessing evangelical scholars regarding the nature and extent of Scripture's veracity. Presenting his position as an alternative to the traditional evangelical view of total inerrancy, Australian theologian Michael Bird raises challenging questions

---

[3] Millard Erickson, *Christian Theology* (Grand Rapids: Baker Books, 1986), 226.

[4] D. A. Carson, "Recent Developments in the Doctrine of Scripture" in *Hermeneutics, Authority, and Canon*, 6. See also a brief overview of several waves of attacks on inerrancy in Sexton, "How Far Beyond Chicago?" 26–30; S. Andrew, "Biblical Inerrancy," *Chafer Theological Seminary Journal* 8 no. 1 (January 2002), 5–7.

[5] J. Merrick and Stephen M Garrett, eds., *Five View on Biblical Inerrancy*, (Grand Rapids: Zondervan Publishing, 2013).

about the relevance of the "American inerrancy tradition"[6] for the global evangelical community. He attributes this "tradition" to the American tendency to globalize its achievements, as is seen illustrated in American titles like "world champions" for winners of purely *national* contests, or when it claims "international" status to councils or documents which are held or crafted only in the United States. The *Chicago Statement on Biblical Inerrancy*, drawn up by the *International Council on Biblical Inerrancy* in 1978, is thus for Bird an essentially *American* theological statement, expressing only a limited, narrow American view on the nature of Scripture, one which fails to express the convictions of evangelicals in the rest of the world.[7]

According to Bird, many evangelical Christians in other contexts outside of the United States never use the word "inerrancy," and the discussions associated with it are simply not found in their formal teachings and doctrinal statements.[8] He thus focuses his argument on the *terminology* of inerrancy rather than its *concept*. By focusing on the specific absence of the term, or on the absence of the same form of the discussion as observed in American evangelicalism, he concludes that evangelicals from outside North America do not even share the idea of complete inerrancy, nor do they care about the intense discussion surrounding it. For global evangelicals, Bird asserts, inerrancy is simply not an important issue.

In response, Bird offers a revisionist approach to the question of Scripture's nature of truthfulness, free from what he calls "American theological colonialism." He is more satisfied by general descriptions for Scripture such as "truthful," "veracious," or "authoritative." He espouses an understanding of Scripture which justifies his rejection of the plain, literal sense of the text and allows him to minimize or even ignore questions about the veracity of its specific, historical details.[9]

Moreover, Bird laments the absence of international voices in the discussion which could modify or balance the American

---

[6] Michael F. Bird, "Inerrancy Is Not Necessary for Evangelicalism Outside the USA," in *Five Views on Biblical Inerrancy*, 145.

[7] Ibid., 155.

[8] Ibid., 155, 161.

[9] Ibid., 146, 158.

inerrancy tradition.[10] While he has legitimate concerns about this particular deficiency and offers some positive suggestions for overcoming it, his fundamental argument from *terminology* is still problematic. Does the absence of inerrancy terminology in other evangelical traditions around the world imply a lack of understanding or concern for the doctrine it represents? A survey of the Russian evangelical tradition provides a refutation of Bird's premise.

Russian Evangelical History as a Case Study

The Russian evangelical tradition[11] does not boast the same kind of long history which marks evangelical movements in many European countries. The sixteenth century Protestant Reformation never impacted Russia to any notable extent. However, shortly after the middle of the nineteenth century, in three different parts of the Russian Empire, an evangelical awakening began, which later gave rise to multiple associations of evangelical churches which then later merged into a single movement.[12]

By traditional understanding, Russian evangelical believers are a people who recognize the central role of the gospel to save sinners and who confess a clear commitment to the supreme authority of Scripture.[13] They are convinced that their beliefs, religious practices, and behavior for daily life must be based upon the teachings of God's Word. Although it is recognized that the specific terminology related to inerrancy is lacking in the development of this evangelical movement, complete respect for God's written revelation—its nature, qualities, and authority—is in no way difficult to trace.

---

[10] Ibid., 145, 155.

[11] While differences on theological issues existed between the branches of Evangelical Christians, Baptists, and other evangelical groups in Russia in their early development, these differences cannot be discussed here, nor do they affect the central arguments of this essay.

[12] See *История евангельских христиан-баптистов в СССР* (Москва: ВСЕХБ, 1989), 13; and *Евангельские христиане баптисты. Сохранившие верность Евангелию* (Москва: Протестант, 1992), 6.

[13] For example, see Я. Винс, *Наши баптистские принципы* (Харбин: Типо-Литография и Цинкография Л. М. Абрамовича, 1924), 5–9.

Before analyzing its view of Scripture, it is important to note that historians disagree over the precise influences which led to the birth of the evangelical church in Russia. For example, according to the formal position of the Russian Union of Evangelical Christians-Baptists (one of the largest evangelical denominations in Russia today), the evangelical church came into existence on Russian soil primarily due to the workings of the Holy Spirit within Russian Orthodoxy. One official source states:

> The emergence of the first communities of Christian-Baptists in Russia was not the result of foreign missions, meaning, it is not a random phenomenon "brought to people from the outside" as it was believed to be in the past by Orthodox historians. The current understanding of the appearance of the first communities of Christian-Baptists in Russia sees it as a distinct process, originating from deep within the national spirit. Spiritual awakening occurred under the influence of the gospel.[14]

On the other hand, other historians have argued that the evangelical movement in Russia was formed under the direct influence of the fundamentalist wing of American evangelical Christianity. For example, in his influential analysis of the identity and theology of evangelicals in Russia, Andrei Puzynin refers to the influence of western Protestantism which contributed to the beginning of the awakening in different parts of the Russian Empire. He points to personal contacts between early prominent Russian evangelical leaders and Reuben A. Torrey and other representatives of American fundamentalism in the middle of the 1920s. He then concludes that, "The theological trajectory of the tradition of evangelical Christians throughout its history was under the guiding influence of the fundamentalist wing of Anglo-American

---

[14] *История евангельских христиан-баптистов в СССР*, 13; see also С. Савинский, *История евангельских христиан-баптистов Украины, России, Белоруссии* (СПб.: Библия для всех, 1999), 1.11; М. Каретникова, *400 лет баптизма: История в картинках* (СПб.: Библия для всех, 2010), 75.

evangelical theology."[15] Puzynin continues to see the influence of American fundamentalism on Russian evangelicalism continuing in the present day, an observation which in no way encourages him considering his anti-fundamentalist, postmodern convictions.[16]

Ultimately, the origin of Russian evangelicalism is most likely to be found somewhere in the middle. While the evangelical awakening occurred from within the Russian Orthodox Church, it was subsequently influenced by western Protestantism. And while it is not the purpose of this essay to analyze carefully these origins and influences, it is important to note that the Russian evangelical church's view of Scripture developed along these same lines. Certainly, Western influences did affect the Russian evangelical church's view of Scripture, but only in that they strengthened and affirmed that which already existed in the hearts and minds of its first adherents.

Included below are excerpts from several influential statements of faith composed by Russian evangelicals throughout the history of the movement. The portions selected express their attitude towards the Bible. Brief observations will be made concerning the terminology they used and the nature of their convictions regarding Holy Scripture.

Did American Evangelicalism Impose Its View of Inerrancy on the Russian Church?

Before surveying these statements, it is important to make several general observations on the terminology in the larger discussion. This is important since those who take the revisionist approach to inerrancy often exaggerate the issues surrounding strict terminology, attempting to repudiate the concept of inerrancy by claiming that the term "inerrancy" itself is so awkward and unclear that it requires countless qualifications.[17]

---

[15] А. Пузынин, *Традиция евангельских христиан: Изучение самоидентификации и богословия от момента ее зарождения до наших дней* (Москва: ББИ, 2010), 412; see also 302–303, 420.

[16] Пузынин, *Традиция*, 419–24.

[17] For example, see Bird, "Inerrancy Is Not Necessary for Evangelicalism Outside the USA," 162–63.

First, it is regularly stated that the term "inerrancy" is not a biblical term and is not found anywhere in Scripture itself. Opponents to strict inerrancy also contend that the term is inadequate since it is only a *negation*—a statement of what something is *not*, i.e., not errant—rather than a positive expression of truth. Some also contend that "inerrancy" is a modern, scientific term, or that it is too artificial to represent the spiritual nature of the Bible, etc.[18] Yet once all of the emotional responses and theological prejudices are put to the side, the term functions well in what it is intended to express, and should continue to be used especially in theological contexts where assertions are regularly being made that Scripture is precisely the opposite—i.e., that it contains errors.[19]

Consequently, it should again be emphasized that the essence of the debate is really not a dispute about the term "inerrancy" or other terms used in the discussion, but about the teaching these terms represent. If the Bible really contains a considerable number of claims about the quality of the written revelation it provides, then to find a term—even one not found in Scripture itself—to summarize this testimony is perfectly warranted. We need only to look to such fundamental terms as "trinity," "incarnation," and "substitutionary atonement" to confirm the validity of such a practice from the earliest centuries of the church. What matters is that the *concept* it represents *is* clearly taught on Scripture's pages.[20] It is not a sign of weakness when a term requires qualification and explanation. *To express it more clearly!*

The same principles apply to the theological terminology used in any given tradition. The attack on the term "inerrancy"—whether because of how it is used in the West, or because of its strict absence in non-Western, non-English evangelical traditions—cannot be allowed to dismiss the validity of the concept itself, or to conclude that the ideas it represents are foreign to those contexts. *It is implied in Scripture as being part of the fundamentals of the faith?* [marginal note: *2 Tim 3:16–17*]

---

[18] These and other arguments are noted by Erickson, *Christian Theology*, 224; Carson, "Recent Developments in the Doctrine of Scripture," 30; Geisler, *Systematic Theology*, 1:506–507; etc.

[19] Wayne Grudem, *Systematic Theology: An Introduction to Biblical Doctrine* (Grand Rapids: Zondervan Publishing, 1994), 95; Paul Feinberg, "The Meaning of Inerrancy," in *Inerrancy*, 289; Geisler and Roach, *Defending Inerrancy*, 319.

[20] Grudem, *Systematic Theology*, 95; Geisler, *Systematic Theology*, 1:499; Geisler and Roach, *Defending Inerrancy*, 319.

Excerpts from Russian Evangelical Statements

While the specific origins of and influences upon the Russian evangelical movement may be debated, the view of Scripture held by its founders and their followers is not difficult to discern from their early theological confessions. Although in these early statements the term "inerrancy" is not encountered, their description of the qualities of written revelation and their highly reverential attitude towards it leaves no doubt that they affirmed Scripture's absolute purity. Establishing this fact, on the one hand, answers the challenge posed by Michael Bird. On the other hand, it encourages and strengthens the foundations of faith for Russian evangelical Christians, since "out of all the doctrines on the theological spectrum—and at the moment one of the most discussed among evangelical believers in Russia today—the doctrine of the infallibility of the Scripture is perhaps most important."[21]

Historians have identified more than a dozen different Russian evangelical confessions of faith that can be classified according to their date and their intended general or private usage.[22] The excerpts listed below contain the most relevant statements concerning the nature of Scripture.[23]

"The Symbol of Faith of St. Petersburg Believers" (1897)[24]

The author of this statement, which was drawn up between 1895 and 1897, is not known. The statement came to be used among evangelicals in the Russian city of St. Petersburg.[25] Its statement on

---

[21] Е. Егоров и А. Прокопенко, "О безошибочности Писания: российский контекст," Альманах «Кафедра» 7 (Май 2014), 7.

[22] Savinskiy explains that "general" confessions were those "which were accepted by the whole brotherhood [of evangelical Christians] or by a majority of its constituents (Baptists, Evangelical Christians, Mennonite Brethren, and Christians of the Evangelical Faith)," while "private" or "local" confessions were those "accepted by independent fellowships or groups" (cf. Савинский, *История*, 1:315).

[23] The specific terms which express the high view of Scripture held by the fathers of the evangelical movement in Russia will be noted below in bold and italics.

[24] *Символ евангельской веры петербургских верующих (1897 г.).*

[25] Савинский, *История*, 1:314.

the nature of Scripture is formulated very succinctly: "I believe that the Sacred Scripture of the Old and New Testament is the divinely inspired revelation of the will of God to people and is the *perfect and the only rule of faith and the God-pleasing life.*"[26] (2 Timothy 3.16)

"A Short Statement of Faith of Christians of the Evangelical Confession" (1903)[27]

This statement was written in 1903 by a Mennonite, Peter Friesen, and was used in several congresses of the denomination of Evangelical Christians in later years.[28] Regarding the Scriptures this statement asserts the following:

> The divinely inspired, canonical books of the Old and New Testament taken together comprise the Sacred Scripture or Word of God, the only *infallible* rule of doctrine, faith and life. All other teachings and writings are to be tested according to the standard of Holy Scripture under the guidance of the Holy Spirit (Acts 15).[29]

"The Confession of Faith of Christians-Baptists" (1906)[30]

This confession was composed in Russian in 1906 on the basis of the "Hamburg Confession of Faith"—a confession written in the middle of the nineteenth century by the German father of the continental Baptist movement, Johann Oncken. The

---

[26] "Верую, что священное писание Ветхого и Нового Завета есть Боговдохновенное откровение воли Божией людям и есть *совершенное* и единственное правило веры и Богоусердной жизни" (http://slavicbaptists.com/2012/02/10/symbolegveng/; accessed November 1, 2014).

[27] *Краткое вероучение христиан евангельского исповедания (1903 г.).*

[28] См. Савинский. *История.* 1:314.

[29] "Богодухновенные, канонические книги Ветхого и Нового Завета в совокупности своей составляют Св. Писание или Слово Божие, единственное *непогрешимое* правило учения, веры и жизни. Всякое другое учение и писание подлежит испытанию на основании Св. Писания под руководством Духа Св. (Деян. 15)" (http://slavicbaptists.com/2012/07/31/1903shortconfession/; accessed November 2, 2014).

[30] *Исповедание веры христиан-баптистов (1906 г.).*

Hamburg confession was first translated into Russian by Vasiliy Pavlov in 1876 for Baptist fellowships in Russia, then published formally by Pavlov in 1906, and then republished again in 1928 by Nicholai Odintsov.[31] The confession's statement on Scripture reads as follows:

> We believe that the Sacred Scripture of the Old Testament... and also the books of the New Testament... are truly inspired by the Holy Spirit (2 Tim 3:16; Exod 19:9; 2 Sam 23:2; Isa 1:2; Jer 1:9; John 10:35; 2 Pet 1:20–21; Heb 1:1–2; Luke 10:16; Matt 10:20; 1 Thess 2:13; Gal 1:11–12; 1 Cor 2:13); so that all these books taken together constitute the only *true* revelation to the human race and must be the only source of the knowledge of God, and also the only rule and measure of our faith and conduct (2 Pet 1:19; Ps 119:105; Luke 16:29–31; 2 Tim 3:15–16; John 9:39; Acts 17:11; Rom 1:16; 1 Cor 14:37; Gal 1:8; Rom 16:25–26; 3:21; Rev 22:18).[32]

"A Statement of Evangelical Faith, or Confession of Evangelical Christians" (1910)[33]

This statement was written by Ivan Prokhanov in 1910 and republished by him again in 1924 for the churches of the Evangelical Christians denomination in Russia.[34] Regarding the Scriptures he writes the following:

---

[31] Савинский, *История*, 1:315; see also Каретникова, *400 лет баптизма*, 67–68.

[32] "Мы веруем, что Священное Писание Ветхого Завета. . . также и книги Нового Завета. . . истинно вдохновенно Святым Духом (2 Тим. 3:16; Исх. 19:9; 2 Цар. 23:2; Ис. 1:2; Иер. 1:9; Иоан. 10:35; 2 Пет. 1:20–21; Евр. 1:1–2; Лук. 10:16; Матф. 10:20; 1 Фес. 2:13; Гал. 1:11–12; 1 Кор. 2:13); так что все эти книги в совокупности составляют единственно *истинное* откровение роду человеческому и должны быть единственным источником богопознания, а также единственным правилом и мерилом веры и поведения нашего (2 Пет. 1:19; Пс. 118:105; Лук. 16:29–31; 2 Тим. 3:15–16; Иоан. 9:39; Деян. 17:11; Рим. 1:16; 1 Кор. 14:37; Гал. 1:8; Рим. 16:25–26; 3:21; Откр. 22:18)" (http://slavicbaptists.com/2012/02/10/pavlovconfession/; accessed November 2, 2014).

[33] *Изложение евангельской веры, или вероучение евангельских христиан (1910 г.)*.

[34] Савинский, *История*, 1:315.

The external (written) revelation of God is the Sacred
Scripture of the Old and New Testament, which
contains in itself words chosen by men—patriarchs,
prophets, through whom God spoke "at many times
and in many ways,"[35] but in these last days—in His
Son (Heb 1:1–2). "All Scripture is breathed out by God
and profitable for teaching, for reproof for correction,
and for training in righteousness, that the man of God
may be competent, equipped for every good work" (2
Tim 3:16–17), "living and active" (Heb 4:12), contains
in itself the ***truth, and only the truth*** (Matt 24:35), and
is completely sufficient for us to be saved and have
eternal life (John 5:39; 17:17; 20:31; Pss 119:138,
142); it has eternality and imperishable meaning, for
it is more likely that heaven and earth will pass away,
but the words of God will not.[36]

"A Short Summary of the Faith of Evangelical Christians" (1913)[37]

Ivan Kargel compiled this document in 1913 for the second
fellowship of Evangelical Christians in St. Petersburg.[38] It included
the following statement:

---

[35] Unless otherwise indicated, all Scripture quotations used in the English translation of
this essay are taken from The Holy Bible, English Standard Version (ESV), copyright
© 2001 by Crossway Books.

[36] "Откровение Божие внешнее (писанное) есть Священное Писание Ветхого и Нового
Завета, которое содержит в себе слова избранных мужей, – патриархов, пророков,
чрез которых Бог говорил «многократно и многообразно», а впоследствии – в Сыне
Своем (Евр. 1:1–2). «Все Писание богодухновенно и полезно для научения, для
обличения, для исправления, для наставления в праведности, да будет совершен
Божий человек, ко всякому доброму делу приготовлен» (2 Тим. 3:16–17); «живо и
действенно» (Евр. 4:12); содержит в себе *истину, и только истину* (Матф. 24:35)
и совершенно достаточно для того, чтобы мы спаслись и имели жизнь вечную
(Иоан. 5:39; 17:17; 20:31; Пс. 118:138, 142); имеет вечное, непреходящее значение,
ибо скорее небо и земля прейдут, а слова Божии не прейдут" (http://slavicbaptists.
com/2012/02/10/prohanovconfession/; accessed November 1, 2014).

[37] *Краткое изложение вероучения евангельских христиан (1913 г.).*

[38] Савинский, *История*, 1:315.

We believe that all the canonical books of the Old and New Testament, comprising together the Bible or Sacred Scripture (excluding the Apocrypha) are inspired by the Spirit of God (2 Pet 1:21) and given by the Lord (Ps 148:8–9) as the necessary, singular (Prov 30:6; Mark 7:13) and perfectly adequate source for the knowledge of God, of our salvation (Heb 1:1–2; John 5:39; 20:31), and of His will with respect to our faith (Phil 1:27) and life (Acts 20:32; 2 Tim 3:15–17).[39]

"Our Baptist Principles" (1924)[40]

"Our Baptist Principles" was a brochure compiled by the Baptist pastor and missionary Yakov Vince in 1924 to acquaint evangelical young people living in the Far East with the seven foundational principles of the Baptist movement. The author adds brief commentary to each of these principles. For example, regarding the first principle—"The Sacred Scripture is our only rule and guide in all matters and questions of faith and life"—he writes:

> Our first principle speaks about our attitude towards the word of God, which must take the form of *an unconditional and absolute* recognition of the divine inspiration of Sacred Scripture. . . . We strongly believe that there is not another book, which by the worthiness of its content and meaning could stand above or beside Sacred Scripture; for the only book which gives us *absolutely faithful information* concerning the will of God, the salvation of sinners, and of responsibilities, benefits, and expectations of all the children of God, and concerning life after the grave, is the book of

---

[39] "Мы веруем, что все канонические книги Ветхого и Нового Завета, составляя в совокупности Библию или Священное Писание (исключая апокрифические) вдохновенны Духом Божиим (2 Пет. 1:21) и даны Господом (Пс. 147:8–9), как необходимый, единственный (Прит. 30:6; Марк. 7:13) и совершенно достаточный источник для познания Бога, нашего спасения (Евр. 1:1–2; Иоан. 5:39; 20:31) и Его воли относительно нашей веры (Флп. 1:27) и жизни (Деян. 20:32; 2 Тим. 3:15–17)" (http://slavicbaptists.com/2012/02/09/kargelconfession/; accessed November 1, 2014).

[40] *Наши баптистские принципы (1924 г.).*

the Bible. . . . [W]e see *the undeniable perfection* of the word of God. . . . We Baptists, remaining faithful to our first principle, place as the foundation of all questions of faith and life *the authoritative* Word of God. . . . Thus, since the Word of God *is holy, perfect and faithful*, we Baptists certainly acknowledge it as such.[41]

"The 1985 Statement of Faith of Evangelical Christians-Baptists"[42]

This statement was adopted in 1985 and remains a key theological document in the Union of Evangelical Christians-Baptists in the present day.[43]

We believe that the Bible, the canonical books of Sacred Scripture of the Old and New Testaments, is the Word of God, written by the inspiration of the Holy Spirit, and consisting of 39 books of the Old Testament and 27 books of the New Testament (John 17:17; Rom 3:22). The Bible—*the perfect* revelation of God to the human race—is *the true* source of the knowledge of God. It opens the will of God, contains the commandments, laws, and prophecies of God and points the path to salvation (2 Tim 3:16; 2 Pet 1:21; Jer 1:9; 27:18; 36:1–4; 2 Pet 1:15–20; Eph 3:3; 1 Thess 2:13; 1 Cor 2:13; John 20:31; Rev 22:18–19). The Bible

---

[41] "Первый наш принцип говорит о нашем отношении к слову Божию, которое должно выразиться в *безусловном и абсолютном* признании боговдохновенности Св. Писания. <. . .> Мы глубоко верим, что нет другой книги, которая по достоинству своего содержания и значения могла бы стать над или рядом с Св. Писанием; ибо единственная книга, которая дает нам *абсолютно верные сведения* относительно воли Божией, спасения грешников и обязанностей, преимуществ и чаяний всех детей Божиих и загробной жизни, – это книга Библия. <. . .> . . .мы усматриваем *неоспоримое совершенство* слова Божия. <. . .> Мы баптисты, оставаясь верными нашему первому принципу, кладем в основание всех вопросов веры и жизни, *исключительно авторитетное* Слово Божие. . . <. . .> Итак, как Слово Божие *свято, совершенно и вечно*, то мы баптисты безусловно признаем" (Винс, *Наши баптистские принципы*, 5–7).

[42] *Вероучение евангельских христиан-баптистов 1985 года.*

[43] *Евангельские христиане баптисты*, 12.

reveals the truth, proclaims God's love and eternal life in Christ Jesus (John 14:6; 1 John 4:10; 5:11; John 20:31). The Sacred Scripture is the source of Christian faith and spiritual guidance to the believers (Rom 10:17; 2 Pet 1:19; Josh 1:7–8; Matt 22:29; Rom 15:4; 2 Tim 3:14–16; Heb 4:12).[44]

A Brief Analysis of the Relationship to Scripture in the Framework of the Russian Evangelical Tradition

Analyzing the excerpts given above, it is important to note several clear facts concerning their relationship to the Holy Scripture.

Brief Statements About Scripture

First of all, it is immediately apparent that these statements do not provide detailed or carefully defined teaching about Scripture in general or about its inerrancy in particular. Russian evangelicals simply did not create anything similar to the *Chicago Statement on Biblical Inerrancy*. In fact, even when compared to the earlier *1689 Baptist Confession of Faith*, it cannot be denied that the above excerpts from Russian evangelical statements reveal a lack of detailed articulation. We see, for example, that for early evangelical leader Ivan Prokhanov it was enough simply to say that Scripture "contains in itself the truth, and only the truth"[45] in order to express his conviction about the absolute truthfulness of the Word of God.

---

[44] "Мы веруем, что Библия, книги Священного Писания Ветхого и Нового Заветов канонические, — является Словом Божиим, написанным по вдохновению Духа Святого, и состоит из 39 книг Ветхого Завета и 27 книг Нового Завета (Иоан. 17:17; Рим. 3:22). Библия — *совершенное* откровение Бога роду человеческому — является **истинным** источником богопознания. Она открывает волю Божию, содержит заповеди Божии, законы и пророчества и указывает путь к спасению (2 Тим. 3:16; 2 Пет. 1:21; Иер. 1:9; 27:18; 36:1–4; 2 Пет. 1:15–20; Еф. 3:3; 1 Фес. 2:13; 1 Кор. 2:13; Иоан. 20:31; Откр. 22:18–19). Библия открывает истину, возвещает о Божьей любви и вечной жизни во Христе Иисусе (Иоан. 14:6; 1 Иоан. 4:10; 5:11; Иоан. 20:31). Священное Писание является источником христианской веры и духовным руководством для верующих (Рим. 10:17; 2 Пет. 1:19; И. Нав. 1:7–8; Матф. 22:29; Рим. 15:4; 2 Тим. 3:14–16; Евр. 4:12)" (*Евангельские христиане баптисты*, 12–13).

[45] "Содержит в себе *истину, и только истину*" (http://slavicbaptists.com/2012/02/10/prohanovconfession/; accessed November 1, 2014).

The reason for such brevity in doctrinal expression was due to the fact that such expressions were not points of contention among evangelicals at the time. Various evangelical groups were united in their convictions regarding the nature, characteristics, and authority of the Bible. Moreover, at the time there were no serious controversies with theologians from the Orthodox Church regarding the issue of the Bible's veracity either. The lack of a polemical context over this issue meant that there was no need to develop complex statements with affirmations, qualifications, and denials.

Agreement With Russian Orthodoxy

At the same time, it is not difficult to notice that practically all of the above-mentioned confessions did clearly indicate the areas in bibliology where there was disagreement with Russian Orthodox views. In particular, this difference lies in Russian evangelicalism's insistence on the authority of the canonical Scriptures *alone*, excluding from this category the contents of the Apocrypha. As for the reliable, perfect, and absolutely truthful nature of the Bible, Russian evangelicals found full agreement with the typical understanding of the common laity and even of the hierarchy of Russian Orthodoxy at that time,[46] with the possible exception being the Orthodox academics.[47] We can see this agreement, for example, in one of the most popular Orthodox catechisms, *The Law of God*, which states:

> Therefore, we—Christians—believe and know that "all Scripture is breathed out by God" and is ***indisputable truth***. . . . God the Holy Spirit Himself invisibly helped them [holy men] so that all that which was written in these books was ***right and true***. . . . All the

---

[46] For example, see Bradley Nassif, "Are Eastern Orthodoxy and Evangelicalism Compatible? Yes," in *Three Views on Eastern Orthodoxy and Evangelicalism*, ed. James Stamoolis (Grand Rapids: Zondervan Publishing, 2004), 61–65.

[47] It is not a secret that "a great gap exists between the mature and popular expressions of [Russian] Orthodoxy" This gap extends also to the attitude towards Scripture. Donald Fairbairn, *Eastern Orthodoxy Through Western Eyes* (Louisville, KY: Westminster/John Knox Press, 2002), 132.

> listed sacred books of the Old Testament are called canonical, that is, **absolutely true** in origin just as in **content**.[48]

The vast majority of evangelical believers came out of the Orthodox environment, bringing with them many of its features—including views about Scripture.[49] Some groups even resisted leaving the fold of the Orthodox Church for a long time, thus combining traditional religious affiliation with evangelical beliefs and practices.[50]

Conservative Influence

Although Russian evangelicals for the most part have Orthodox roots, it cannot be denied that the evangelical awakening in Russia occurred not in isolation from the Protestant West. Historians investigating the origin of the Russian Baptist movement unanimously point to three sources of influence, each characterized by a conservative view of Scripture.[51]

First, in southern Ukraine, German colonists—Mennonite by confession, who first experienced revival in their own communities—gave impulse to the gospel movement when they began to preach to the indigenous people. Second, in the Caucasus region of southern Russia, German Baptists influenced the development and spread of the evangelical faith in areas where the Molocan

---

[48] "Итак, мы – христиане – верим и знаем, что «все Писание богодухновенно» и есть **непреложная истина**. <. . .> Сам Бог Дух Святой невидимо помогал им [святым людям], чтобы все, что в этих книгах написано, было **правильно и истинно**. <. . .> Все перечисленные священные книги Ветхого Завета называются каноническими, то есть, **несомненно истинными** как по происхождению, *так и по содержанию*" (Серафим Слободской, *Закон Божий: руководство для семьи и школы*, 4-е изд. [Репр.; М.: Молодая гвардия, 1990], 9, 490–91; emphasis added).

[49] А. Коломийцев, *Библейская принципиальность в служении* (Ванкувер: Церковь «Слово Благодати», 2012), 12.

[50] See Пузынин, *Традиция*, 202.

[51] See *История*, 13; Савинский, *История*, 1:18–19; Р. Крыжановский, *Кто такие баптисты?* (Ирпень: Духовное возрождение, 2012), 41–46; Пузынин, *Традиция*, 73–78. For example, M. Karetnikova writes the following about German Baptist Johann Oncken: "The theological views of Oncken were conservative. . . and this was evident in the first Baptist confessions in Europe" (Каретникова, *400 лет баптизма*, 71).

movement had been active.[52] This influence is evidenced by the subsequent connections between the Russian Baptist churches that formed in that region and Baptist Johann Oncken from Hamburg. Third, in St. Petersburg, the gospel began to make an impact among the Russian aristocracy due in large part to the ministry of Lord Radstock, a representative of the evangelical wing of the Church of England who also had connections with the conservative Plymouth Brethren.[53]

The distinctive feature of all of these groups was a high view of the Bible, the spirit of pietism, and even some influence from the holiness movement. For example, in analyzing the ministry and preaching of Radstock, it cannot be denied that he "believed in the literal inspiration of Scripture, like all evangelical believers of that time."[54] The same applies to Radstock's successor in the evangelistic effort in St. Petersburg, retired colonel Vasiliy Pashkov, of whom it is said, "In the letters of Pashkov faith in the authority and inspiration of Scripture is clearly expressed. Pashkov believed that the Word of God had no flaw."[55]

Therefore, if indeed there was an influence of American fundamentalism on the Russian evangelical movement and on its view of the nature of written revelation, it had a later character and can be identified because it coincided with the view of Scripture already established among early Russian evangelical believers.[56] The most significant influence came instead from conservative European sources. *It is absolute necessary for the faith to find the image response in authority concept outside of this American so called influence.*

Developing Terminology

Although a lack of necessity meant that a fully articulated doctrine of biblical inerrancy was not developed in the Russian

---

[52] The Molocans were members of a movement within the Russian Orthodox Church which arose in the 1800s and was characterized by an emphasis on the authority of Scripture and the rejection of religious rituals. Although this sect did not avoid many mistakes in their use of the Bible, it nonetheless prepared the soil for the evangelical awakening in the places where it spread. (cf. Савинский, *История*, 48–51).

[53] Пузынин, *Традиция*, 80, 84, 134.

[54] Пузынин, *Традиция*, 97.

[55] See the evidences for this conclusion in Пузынин, *Традиция*, 199, 302–304.

[56] Пузынин, *Традиция*, 261–62.

evangelical context, the terminology chosen by its founders none-theless indicate the existence of this *concept* in their convictions in general. Speaking of Scripture they do not resist emphasizing its exclusiveness, sacredness, absolute perfection, and incontestable faithfulness.[57]

This early attitude towards the Bible formed the basis for the later formulations and expressions in which we do see the terminology of "infallibility" or "inerrancy" begin to appear.[58] For example, the authors of the booklet *Evangelical Christians-Baptists: Retained Faithfulness to the Gospel*[59] in 1992 formulated the first principle of the Baptist movement as follows: "the Bible is the only *infallible* authority in matters of faith and practical life."[60] In 2000, Russian evangelical theologians and historians Reshetnikov and Sannikov approvingly quoted the words of a contemporary confession of faith which stated that "being completely and literally inspired in the original text, the Bible is *absolutely infallible and inerrant* in the meaningful expression of all issues which it touches."[61]

A High View of the Sacred Scriptures

Even the absence of specific terminology in the earlier confessions of faith cannot conceal the general position of the leaders of the Russian evangelical movement with regard to biblical revelation. They boldly declare that the highest authority belongs to the Scriptures alone, they highly honor its character, and repeatedly

---

57 See *История*, 440; Савинский, *История*, 1:317.

58 It should be noted that to this day in Russian theological literature a strict distinction is not maintained between the definition of "infallibility" and that of "inerrancy."

59 *Евангельские христиане баптисты. Сохранившие верность Евангелию.*

60 *Евангельские христиане баптисты,* 4.

61 "Будучи полностью и дословно богодухновенной в оригинальном тексте, Библия является *абсолютно непогрешимой и безошибочной* в содержательном изложении всех тем, которых она касается" (Ю. Решетников и С. Санников, *Обзор истории евангельско-баптистского братства на Украине* [Одесса: Богомыслие, 2000], 22); see also Пузынин, *Традиция,* 381.

emphasize its worth. The same exact attitude is seen in other literature produced by early Russian evangelical leaders.[62]

Thus, the above observations confirm the idea that the lack of specific inerrancy terminology in early Russian confessions of faith does not exclude the presence of conviction in this concept nonetheless. The Russian Baptist movement continually resisted liberal theological tendencies, both at the stage of its origin and formation as well as in subsequent periods. For example, even in the 1920s Russian evangelist Wilhelm Fetler, looking upon Western Christians and, leaning on the experience of the Russian Baptist movement, said he "in his own naiveté assumed that every Baptist believed in the Bible as the Word of God."[63] He boldly offered this call to Baptists from other countries who had already consented to theological compromise:

> When it comes to a confession of faith and the missionary work, which must be connected to the New Testament Church, then I politely say: "Please, hands off. This far and no further." If it is your opinions, alright, you can have these views. But it is not the views of the Baptists. . . . You do not have the right to raise the age-old Baptist banner when you mean something different. You cannot and you must not act under false pretenses. You do not have the right to sell the righteous efforts of the Baptist Church, Baptist seminaries, Baptist Missionary Societies, ordaining and sending such men, filling the pulpits of Baptist churches with "Baptist preachers" who are not Baptists. All we ask is that you be honest. Tell me

---

[62] For example, one cannot fail to mention the high view of Scripture evidenced in the writings of Ivan Kargel (cf. *Собрание сочинений* [Репр; СПб.: Библия для всех, 1997]). From later works it is appropriate to mention those of Yuri Grachov, who not only was a leading Russian evangelist and preacher, but a historian who gathered significant materials on the history of the Baptist movement in Russia (cf. Каретникова, *400 лет баптизму*, 76). See especially Grachov's book about the Christian's relationship to the Bible: *Как ты относишься к Библии?* (Репр.; СПб.: Библия для всех, 2007).

[63] В. Фетлер, "Как я открыл ересь: модернизм среди американских баптистов и почему я основал русское миссионерское общество," Журнал «Друг России» (август – ноябрь 1924); available at http://rus-baptist.narod.ru/dop/fetler.htm (accessed February 5, 2014).

where you stand and in what you believe. Do not use our theological terms for expressions of something entirely different than what they stand for. And do not blame us for being narrow and critical. I believe we are not such. I believe that we are as broad as the Gospel is broad, as sensible as the Apostle Paul, and as friendly as the Good Samaritan. We are ready to do everything we can to save those who have fallen in the hands of the "robber-critics" on the way from the old religious Jerusalem to the Jericho of the modernists. But in our spiritual attitude towards you, do not wait for us to be wider than the word of God.[64] *Amen*

For the same reason, any elderly Christian brought up in the evangelical tradition by default accepts the Bible to be completely free from error. The leadership of the Baptist Union in Russia in 1979 could therefore assert, "The theology of Evangelical Christians-Baptists rests on a fundamental recognition of the divine authority of the Sacred Scriptures—the Bible. . . . Modernist and liberal dogmatic views do not have any circulation among us."[65]

Today, the situation has changed and evangelical believers are being challenged to strengthen their foundations. The time has come in Russia when the doctrine of inspiration is being subject to revision, and the concept of inerrancy is not always considered important nor necessary. If a person today declares his conviction in the full verbal inspiration of Scripture, in total infallibility, in the indisputable authority of Scripture, in the legitimacy of gospel harmonization, it is not unusual to hear accusations of narrow-mindedness, divisiveness, pride, and fundamentalism—even from Russian scholars who consider themselves evangelical. If one critiques the presuppositions of higher criticism and rejects its approaches, it is sadly not surprising to be dismissed as "uneducated" and "prehistoric." Nevertheless, the confession of a high view of Holy Scripture—and the concept of inerrancy—has not

---

[64] Фетлер, "Как я открыл ересь."

[65] *Евангельские христиане-баптисты в СССР* (М.: Изд. ВСЕХБ, 1979), 14.

died out from within the boundaries of the Russian evangelical tradition.[66] [handwritten: Amen]

The Biblical Witness Concerning the Truthfulness of Scripture

A high view of Scripture with a recognition of its absolute perfection and of the absence of any errors was not imposed on the Russian evangelical movement. But neither is it an invention of the Russian church either. Such a view originates in the Bible's own testimony concerning itself. [handwritten: Absolutely true]

As already noted above, "inerrancy" expresses an important biblical concept even though the term itself is not found in the biblical text. Even those who hold to the position of full inerrancy recognize that there is not a precise statement in negative terms that emphasizes the absence of all errors in written revelation. It is openly acknowledged that readers of Scripture cannot expect to appeal to just one or even a couple of key texts which contain particular words or statements which give them quick and effort-less answers. Instead, in answering the question of Scripture's quality seriously, readers must be ready to analyze many texts throughout the scope of written revelation and consider the direct implications of other doctrines intertwined with the doctrine of revelation in order to arrive at an accurate understanding of the nature of God's Word.[67]

It is important to note that in reality, inerrancy — as a negation (i.e., the *denial* of error) — is really the opposite side of the same truth stated in positive terms — that divine revelation is *absolutely true*.[68] This is easily seen in the standard definitions provided for the

---

[66] A testimony to this enduring legacy can be seen in recent publications by Transfiguration Church of the Russian Union of Evangelical Christians-Baptists of Samara, Russia. For example, the May 2014 edition of its journal «Кафедра» (*Pulpit*) is entirely devoted to the doctrine of biblical inerrancy and its history and relevance in the Russian context. See also a recently published book by this author, *Укрепление фундамента: Библейское основание учения о непогрешимости Писания* (СПб.: Библия для всех, 2014), which is devoted to this same theme.

[67] Erickson, *Christian Theology*, 229.

[68] See Ronald McCune, *A Systematic Theology of Biblical Christianity*, 3 vols. (Detroit, MI: Detroit Baptist Theological Seminary, 2008), 1:91. J. I. Packer, "Infallible Scripture

term. For example, Feinberg writes, "Inerrancy means that when all facts are known, the Scriptures in their original autographs and properly interpreted will be shown to be ***wholly true*** in everything that they affirm whether that has to do with doctrine or morality of with the social, physical, or life sciences."[69] Erickson defines inerrancy as asserting that "The Bible, when correctly interpreted in light of the level to which culture and the means of communication had developed at the time it was written, and in view of the purposes for which it was given, is ***fully truthful*** in all that it affirms."[70] Similarly, Wayne Grudem asserts that "The inerrancy of Scripture means that Scripture in the original manuscripts does not affirm anything that is contrary to fact. . . . [T]he Bible ***always tells the truth***, and that it always tells the truth concerning ***everything*** it talks about."[71]

Despite the contentions of some, there is nothing reprehensible in explaining concepts through negation (denials). The biblical authors themselves often employed antithetical parallelism. For example, the apostle John writes, "God is light, and in him there is no darkness at all" (1 John 1:5). Furthermore, there is no shortage of biblical texts which clearly and in positive terms affirm the absolute truthfulness of God's Word. Consequently, in establishing the doctrine of the inerrancy in response to the critics who assert the presence of errors in Scripture, it is not only possible, but necessary, to refer to this positive biblical witness concerning its quality, and then also state this witness in terms of what it excludes.

Therefore, according to definition, inerrancy is the opposite side of the absolute truthfulness of Scripture. Grudem states, "To say that Scripture is truthful in everything it says is to say that it is 'inerrant.'"[72] This absolute truthfulness is emphasized in the

---

and the Role of Hermeneutics," in *Scripture and Truth*, eds. D. A. Carson and John D. Woodbridge (Grand Rapids: Baker Books, 1992), 351.

[69] Feinberg, "The Meaning of Inerrancy," 294; emphasis added.

[70] Erickson, *Christian Theology*, 233–34; emphasis added.

[71] Grudem, *Systematic Theology*, 90–91; emphasis added. See also the helpful formulation in Geisler, *Systematic Theology*, 1:498.

[72] Wayne A. Grudem, "Scripture's Self-Attestation and the Problem of Formulating a Doctrine of Scripture," in *Scripture and Truth*, 58; cf. John M. Frame, *The Doctrine of the Word of God* (Phillipsburg, NJ: Presbyterian & Reformed, 2010), 170.

testimony of the Old Testament prophets, in the testimony of our Lord Jesus Christ, and in the testimony of the New Testament authors.[73]

The Witness of the Old Testament Prophets

The Old Testament prophets highly valued both the oral and written revelation of God. They repeatedly emphasized its *truth-fulness*—no matter what the form.[74] Using different descriptions to refer to the revelation of God, the psalmist David asserted that "the testimony of the LORD is sure, making wise the simple; . . . the rules of the LORD are true, and righteous altogether" (Ps 19:7b, 9b). Describing the splendor of written revelation, the author of Psalm 119 also exclaimed, "Your righteousness is righteous forever, and your law is true" (119:142; cf. also vv. 151, 160, etc.). Similarly, Agur warned, "Every word of God proves true; he is a shield to those who take refuge in him. Do not add to his words, lest he rebuke you and you be found a liar" (Prov 30:5–6). The same emphasis on the truthfulness of revelation can be seen in the words of the prophet Habakkuk: "For still the vision awaits its appointed time; it hastens to the end—it will not lie. If it seems slow, wait for it; it will surely come; it will not delay" (Hab 2:3).

Moreover, the prophets were amazed by the *perfection* of Holy Scripture. For example, King David boldly stated, "The law of the LORD is perfect, reviving the soul" (Ps 19:7a). It seems quite apparent that the Old Testament writers did not recognize such notions as "bibliolatry"[75] and felt no need to distinguish carefully

---

[73] It is also important to define the concept of "truthfulness." Lewis and Demarest write: "By 'true' content we mean propositions that correspond to the thought of God and created reality because they are logically non-contradictory, factually reliable, and experientially viable" (Gordon R. Lewis and Bruce A. Demarest, *Integrative Theology: Historical, Biblical, Systematic, Apologetic, Practical*, in 3 vols. (Grand Rapids: Zondervan Publishing, 1996), 1:160.

[74] Grudem, *Systematic Theology*, 83; Frame, *The Doctrine of the Word of God*, 112–17; McCune, *A Systematic Theology*, 1:91–92; Robert L. Reymond, *A New Systematic Theology of the Christian Faith*, 2nd ed. (Nashville, TN: Thomas Nelson, 1998), 28–29; Grudem, "Scripture's Self-Attestation," 29–35; Feinberg, "The Meaning of Inerrancy," 294.

[75] The term "bibliolatry" is used by some to accuse others of having a view of the Bible that is *too high* (cf. Frame, *The Doctrine of the Word of God*, 116). Moisés Silva writes: "Now this charge of 'bibliolatry,' in spite of its popularity, is really quite disconcerting. . . .

between the word of God and God Himself—as many theologians attempt to do so strongly today. Once again, the psalmist proclaimed, "I bow down toward your holy temple and give thanks to your name for your steadfast love and your faithfulness, for you have exalted above all things your name and your word" (138:2).

The Testimony of Jesus Christ

The Lord Jesus Christ regarded the verbal revelation of God as not only truthful, but as the very standard of truth itself: "Sanctify them in the truth; your word is truth" (John 17:17). In light of this text Wayne Grudem writes,

> The difference is significant, for this statement encourages us to think of the Bible not simply as being "true" in the sense that it conforms to some higher standard of truth, but rather to think of the Bible as being itself the final standard of truth. The Bible is God's Word, and God's Word is the ultimate definition of what is true and what is not true: God's Word is itself *truth*.[76]

Moreover, Jesus did not restrict the truthfulness of divine revelation to only oral or written forms, but equated the authority of the written Word of God with the authority of His own words. One example of this can be seen in John 5:46–47 where Jesus states, "If you believed Moses, you would believe me; for he wrote of me. But if you do not believe his writings, how will you believe my words?" John Frame remarks, "No passage suggests that these written words are of less authority than the oral prophetic word or the divine voice itself. There is not suggestion that the influence of the human writer injects any falsehood or inadequacy into the sacred texts."[77]

Such a dichotomy between a person's authority and the authority of what that person says is both false and meaningless" (Moisés Silva, *God, Language, and Scripture: Reading the Bible in the Light of General Linguistics* [Grand Rapids: Zondervan Publishing, 1990], 38).

[76] Grudem, *Systematic Theology*, 83; cf. also Feinberg, "The Meaning of Inerrancy," 294.

[77] Frame, *The Doctrine of the Word of God*, 116–17; cf. also 112.

Finally, Jesus did not treat any portion of Scripture He referred to as unimportant or its factual details as antiquated. For example, quoting the Old Testament, Jesus not only directed His audience's attention to the main teachings of each respective passage, but again and again reminds His listeners of the text's historical facts, recognizing their truthfulness—that is, the correspondence of these historical facts to reality (Matt 12:40, 41; 19:3–6; Luke 4:25, 27; 17:26–27, 28–29, 31–32; 20:37; John 3:14; 6:49; etc.).[78]

The Testimony of New Testament Writers

The apostles, standing in the same line of the Old Testament prophets and of Jesus Himself, expressed the same view regarding the truthfulness of God's Word. As their own Teacher exemplified, the apostles also associated the Word of God with absolute truth. For example, James speaks of regeneration as by "the word *of truth*" (James 1:18), and Paul encourages Timothy to "Do your best to present yourself to God as one approved, a worker who has no need to be ashamed, rightly handling the word *of truth*" (2 Tim 2:15). The New Testament writers also quoted various historical details from the Old Testament without a hint of doubt in the truthfulness and accuracy of such details (Acts 13:17–23; James 2:25; 1 Pet 3:20; 2 Pet 2:5, 6–7, 16; Rom 4:10, 19; 9:10–12; 11:2–4; 1 Cor 10:11; Heb 7:2; 9:1–5, 19–21; 11:1–40; 12:16–17).[79]

Thus, the complete inerrancy of Scripture is not only deductively formulated as a logical consequence of the plenary verbal inspiration of the entire biblical text, but also inductively formulated on the basis of the witness of individual biblical texts to the absolute truthfulness of God's Word. In other words, the doctrine of inerrancy rests on a solid biblical foundation in the form of innumerable evidences of the inspiration, truthfulness and authority of the Sacred Scriptures.

---

[78] McCune, *A Systematic Theology*, 1:67; Grudem, "Scripture's Self-Attestation," 41–43.

[79] Grudem, "Scripture's Self-Attestation," 41–43.

The Influence of Western Theology on the Bibliology of Russian Evangelical Christians

Returning to the concern of Australian theologian Michael Bird about the supposed intent of American evangelicals "to colonize the world with a proper doctrine of Scripture that reflects the American inerrancy tradition,"[80] and evaluating that concern in the light of the history of the evangelical movement in Russia, one comes quickly to the conclusion that Bird's concern is expressed in an entirely wrong direction. Since the concept of a perfect and inerrant Bible has always been in the minds of Russian evangelical Christians, conservative influences coming from any source—including the United States—are not the real concern. A far greater concern—which Bird appears to minimize and hide—is the impact of Western Protestant liberal theology on the bibliology of evangelical believers in Russia today. This impact—hand-in-hand with the spread of liberal Russian Orthodox teaching—is undertaking a major effort to dismantle the foundations of evangelical Christianity in Russia.

In response to Bird, Kevin Vanhoozer admitted the inevitability of liberal influence spreading from the West to the whole world when he wrote,

> it may be only a matter of time, given globalization and patterns of higher education, until the rest of the world is faced with similar challenges to biblical authority posed by biblical criticism, naturalistic scientism, and skeptical historicism. If you can find McDonald's or Starbucks in Taiwan and Timbuktu, can Richard Dawkins or Bart Ehrman be far behind?"[81]

Indeed, the erosion of evangelical Christianity in Russia is already being actively accomplished by means of translated literature from the West and by publications of Russian authors as well,

---

[80] Bird, "Inerrancy Is Not Necessary for Evangelicalism Outside the USA," 156.

[81] Kevin J. Vanhoozer, "Response to Michael F. Bird," in *Five Views on Biblical Inerrancy*, 190.

some of whom—having received training in Western theological institutions—are actually hostile to the supposed "American inerrancy tradition."[82]

An example of the destructive influence of translated Western literature can be seen in the influence of the writings of Bart Ehrman, whose books are being actively translated into Russian and promoted among liberal Orthodox and Protestant evangelicals alike. Already, seven of his books have appeared in the Russian language and are promoted to Christians as "bestsellers" of the West and received with eagerness in certain circles. In Bird's assault on the so-called "American inerrancy tradition," he fails to give adequate attention to this opposite influence of the American church on global evangelicalism.

In the second category of destructive influences, there can be found a growing number of Russian theological liberals who often lead aggressive attacks on the straw horse named "fundamentalism."[83] Each critic gives "fundamentalism" his own description, ascribes this label to his opponents, and then proceeds to cast dispersion on this straw enemy.

The problem in all of this is that such disingenuous attacks, which lack careful understanding and discernment, are directed not only against a specific expression of the American evangelical movement, but also serve a greater intent in destroying "the fundamentals" in general—those essential doctrines of the faith which were indispensable in the Christian church for centuries and which also characterized Russian evangelical Christians and have distinguished them from the modernistic, critical theological community.[84]

---

[82] See Егоров и Прокопенко, "О безошибочности Писания: российский контекст," 9–13; Коломийцев, *Библейская принципиальность в служении*, 48.

[83] Regarding the same problem in the West, see Gregory K. Beale, *The Erosion of Inerrancy in Evangelicalism: Responding to New Challenges to Biblical Authority* (Wheaton, IL: Crossway, 2008), 21. The history of the American fundamentalist movement and of the attempt to reform it is well documented in George M. Marsden's *Reforming Fundamentalism: Fuller Seminary and the New Evangelicalism* (Grand Rapids: Eerdmans Publishing, 1995).

[84] An example of such an attack can be found in the special appendix included in the Russian edition of James D. G. Dunn's *A New Perspective on Jesus: What the Quest for the Historical Jesus Missed* (see Дж. Данн, Новый взгляд на Иисуса: Что упустил поиск исторического Иисуса, пер. с англ. [М.: ББИ, 2009], 187–94). See also A.

Ultimately, the concerns of Western anti-inerrancy evangelicals such as Michael Bird do not help but actually hinder the efforts of Russian evangelical believers. Russian evangelicals must preserve and defend their legacy of a high view of Scripture from the growing erosion of the doctrines related to the revelation of God in written form. Bird—and others who share his views regarding the issue of inerrancy—clearly add their weight to such erosion taking place, not only in Russia, but on a global scale.

Conclusion

Michael Bird was right in his contention that confessions of faith of other peoples and languages—in our case, the confessions of faith of Russian evangelical Christians—often do not employ the specific terms of "inerrancy" and "infallibility," nor include the detailed arguments to support these ideas. However, Bird simply fails to consider that evangelicals—such as those of the evangelical movement in Russia—have firmly believed in the authority, trustworthiness, and absolute truthfulness of the Word of God simply on the basis of the teachings of Scripture about itself. The absence of terminology or argumentation is not a proof of their apathy towards it or rejection of it. As the historical documentation indicates, the positive terms and expressions they did use—however brief and simple—expressed clearly their highest respect for the nature of the revelation of God given to them in the written form of the Bible.

Moreover, contrary to Bird, it appears safe to conclude that the "American inerrancy tradition" was not responsible for the formation of Russian evangelicalism's high view of Scripture in its early stages, but only subsequently came to play a role in Russian evangelicalism's development. It appears that such a relationship developed most likely because of shared convictions between

---

Дубровский, "Фундаментализм как тормозящий фактор в развитии евангельских церквей постсоветского пространства," http://www.mbchurch.ru/publications/articles/15/6058/ (accessed November 2, 2014); В. Шленкин, "Богодухновенность," http://www.mbchurch.ru/publications/articles/15/7920/ (accessed January 3, 2014); Пузынин, Традиция, 411. Even Russian Orthodox biblical scholars today discuss the existence of "fundamentalism" and express their dissatisfaction with "literal inerrancy"—i.e., the inerrancy of the literal meaning of the biblical text (e.g., А. Десницкий, "Фундаментализм: выход или вызов для православной библеистики?" http://www.bogoslov.ru/text/1240183 (accessed January 3, 2014).

American and Russian evangelicalism in this crucial doctrinal area. We can thus conclude that the concept of Scripture's absolute truthfulness was not introduced to Russia nor forced upon it by the West in some questionable colonial effort.

Finally, the real need of the day for the Russian evangelical church is not protection from such conservative Western influences, but from the theological efforts to erode the very foundations of the evangelical faith in Russia. [Valci]

THE IMPORTANCE OF INERRANCY AND ITS IMPLICATION FOR THE CHURCH IN CHINA

by Roger Ng, John Zheng and Andrew Choo
(Singapore/China)

McDonald's Killing

Christians in China affirm the inerrancy of the Bible; however, on a closer look, what they practice and how they preach betray their theology. The surfacing of many Christian cults in China highlights the seriousness of the situation. Recently, members of the cult, Church of Almighty God, shocked the world by killing an innocent woman at a McDonald's restaurant.[1] Five members of the group tried to recruit a woman in the restaurant. When she refused, they beat her to death. A video of the attack went viral on the Internet. This cult, founded by Zhao Weishan, is known as the Church of the Almighty God or as Eastern Lightning. It derives its name from a passage in Matthew that refers to the lightning in the east and the second coming of Christ. Zhao believes that Jesus has returned and is a woman who now lives in China as Zhao's

---

[1] Richard Hartley-Parkinson, "Shocking Moment Mother is murdered in McDonalds." Mirror UK News, June 1, 2014. http://www.mirror.co.uk/news/world-news/shocking-moment-mother-murdered-mcdonalds-3632987

wife, Yang Xiangbin, according to official Xinhua News Agency in China. Eastern Lightning was started in the early 1990's in China's central Henan province. Today Eastern Lightning claims to have millions of members. In the wake of the McDonald's killing, the Daily Mirror newspaper from Guangdong, China released a list of cults operating in China which included: the Unification Church, the Shout, the Disciples' Society, the Bloody Holy Spirit, the All Ranges Church, Three Grades of Servants Church and, of course, the Church of the Almighty God.

China is plagued with "Christian" cults. What is interesting is that generally these cults were not imported from the West but are home grown. Why have the Christian cults burgeoned when the churches in China believe in the doctrine of the inerrancy of the Scriptures? If the Chinese churches believe in the inerrancy of the Bible and preach the Word of God, they would have the Truth to guard against cults. Just as the Lord intended, the pastors and teachers are to equip the saints for the work of ministry, for building up the body of Christ, until we all attain to the unity of the faith . . . so that we may no longer be children, tossed to and fro by the waves and carried about by every wind of doctrine, by human cunning, by craftiness in deceitful schemes (Eph. 4:12-14). Although churches in China affirm the inerrancy of the Scriptures, their practices deny it. Their erroneous bibliology as well as their bizarre hermeneutics have caused havoc in the life of the church.

Largest Christian Nation in the World Plagued with Cult Beliefs

China is officially an atheist country; however, *The Telegraph* reported on 19 April 2014 that China is on course to become "the world's most Christian nation" within 15 years.[2] Dr. Fenggang Yang, professor at Purdue University and author of *Religion in China: Survival and Revival under Communist Rule*, predicts that China, which had over 58 million Protestants in 2010 (Pew Research

---

[2]   1 Tom Phillips, "China on Course to Become World's Most Christian Nation." *The Telegraph*, April 19, 2014 http://www.telegraph.co.uk/news/worldnews/asia/ china/10776023/ China-on-course-to-become-worlds-most-Christian-nation-within-15-years.html

Center), will rocket to approximately 160 million by 2025. This number surpasses the 85 million members of the Communist Party in China. Tom Phillips of *The Telegraph* noted that "More Chinese are attending Sunday services each week than do Christians across the whole of Europe." One study found more searches on the internet for "Christian Congregation" and "Jesus" than "The Communist Party" and the president of China, "Xi Jinping." Yang went on to say that China's total professing Christian population, including Catholics, would be over 247 million by 2030. China would then become the largest Christian nation in the world.

It would be disastrous for the largest Christian nation in the world to be plagued with cults. It is imperative that the leadership in the Chinese churches be grounded firmly on the inerrant and infallible Word of God. To this end, Grace Bible Seminary, a member of TMAI, is working against time to train Chinese Christian leadership to return to the Bible and to expository preaching because lives, indeed, depend on it. Of the multiple complications and adversity faced in the battle for the souls of China, this paper will highlight one of the key problems in training leaders–the refusal to accept the doctrine of inerrancy in practice and, as a result, the refusal to preach the inerrant Word in an expository and systematical manner. This paper will highlight the problem, discuss the cause, and propose a solution.

Inerrancy of the Word

It is the Bible's own testimony and the testimony of our Lord Jesus Christ that the Bible is inerrant. The Bible says, "The words of the LORD are pure words, like silver refined in a furnace on the ground, purified seven times" (Ps. 12:6). God is light and in Him there is no darkness (1 John 1:5); therefore, he cannot lie (Heb. 6:18). The Bible says, "Every word of God proves true; he is a shield to those who take refuge in him" (Ps. 18:30; Prov. 30:5; 2 Sam. 22:31). The Word of God is not only true but eternal (Ps.119:89) and it endures forever (Is. 40:8 and 1 Pet. 1:25). Again the Bible says, "The grass withers, the flower fades, but the word of our God will stand forever" (Isa 40:8). The Word of the Lord is not only pure but all Scripture is inspired or breathed out by God

Psalm 119:89

(2 Tim. 3:16). Jesus said that God's Word is truth (John 17:17) and the Scripture cannot be broken (John 10:35). He also said, "Heaven and earth will pass away, but my words will not pass away" (Luke 21:33). Since the Lord said so, we believe it to be so.

The Word of God is the highest authority for our faith and our lives. We do not and cannot appeal to higher authority because there is no higher authority. Since the Word of God is inerrant and infallible, we are commanded by the Scripture to preach the Word (2 Tim 4:2). We are not only commanded to preach the Word but we are to preach *the whole counsel of God* (Acts 20:27; Col 1:25). How are we to ensure we preach the whole counsel of God unless we preach it with expository and systematic methods? and with emphasis on its inerrancy

The Problem: "Inspired Preaching"

One of the major problems in China is that most church leaders are not willing to teach the Bible in a consecutive and expository manner. For such leaders and pastors, the written Bible becomes the Word of God when they are "moved" by the Holy Spirit while they read their Bible. However, such a view of how to teach the Word favors existentialism and Karl Barth's neo-orthodoxy. Naturally they will not be "moved" by all the Scriptures in the same manner. As a result, they preach only portions of the Bible. According to 2 Timothy 3:16, all Scripture, not some Scripture, is breathed out by God and profitable for teaching, for reproof, for correction and for training in righteousness; therefore, all Scripture must be preached. The whole counsel of God must be declared, not just a portion of it (Acts 20:27).

This misguided view of how to teach from the Bible has also affected the hermeneutics of preachers and listeners alike. Christians in Chinese churches often fail to recognize the importance of taking into consideration the context of a passage when interpreting the Bible. They rely too heavily on a personal and subjective concept of being "moved" by the Holy Spirit in order to determine the meaning of a passage, instead of objectively deriving the purpose of a text through contextual, grammatical-historical hermeneutics. The subjective hermeneutics often lead to erroneous and dangerous interpretations. Worse yet, these interpretations are publicly broadcasted in pulpits every week.

David Helm labels the aforementioned approach "inspired preaching." Such an approach occurs when preachers read the Bible devotionally and whatever "moves" the preachers' spirit in their private reading of the Bible must be what God has desired for them to preach. Helm states that this kind of reading has a long history and is called Lectio Divina. Helm describes the process as such:

> It favors a view of biblical texts as "the Living Word" rather than as written words to be studied. Traditional forms of this practice include four steps for private Bible reading: reading, meditating, praying, and contemplating. You begin by quieting your heart with a simple reading of the text. Then you meditate, perhaps on a single word or phrase from the text, and in so doing intentionally avoid what might be considered an "analytical" approach. In essence, the goal here is to wait for the Spirit's illumination so that you will arrive at meaning. You wait for Jesus to come calling. Once the word is given, you go on to pray. After all, prayer is dialogue with God. God speaks through his Word and the person speaks through prayer. Eventually, this prayer becomes contemplative prayer, and it gives to us the ability to comprehend deeper theological truths.[3]

Such a manner of reading sounds pious, but it can be exceedingly subjective and definitely dangerous. Helm states, "It substitutes intuition for investigation. It prefers mood and emotion to methodical and reasoned inquiry. It equates your spirit to the Holy Spirit."[4] Of course, this is not to claim that we are not in need of prayer to ask the Holy Spirit to illuminate us. The Spirit must work in us, but the Spirit does not work independently of His inspired Word; it must be analyzed by objective grammatical-historical

---

[3] David Helm. *Expositional Preaching: How We Speak God's Word Today*. (Wheaton, IL: Crossway Books, 2014), 30.

[4] Ibid, 30-31.

hermeneutics, the natural human means of discovering the intent
and purpose of any written book.

There are various influences that contribute to this manner of
reading and preaching the Bible in the Chinese church. However,
the remainder of this essay will focus specifically on the impact
of Karl Barth's view of the inspiration of the Bible on the Chinese
churches and their method of preaching.

The Cause: "Inspired Reading"

Karl Barth's theology has had a great impact upon American
evangelicalism.[5] Barth's greatest convert was Bernard Ramm, a
man who whole-heartedly embraced Barth's theology, including
Barth's view that the Bible is not inerrant.[6] The American church,
being the center of evangelicalism in the world, naturally exports
its theology to China, where many often blindly accept it. There
is no doubt that Barthian theology has impacted the Chinese
church. In fact, Barth's commentary on Romans is popular among
the Chinese community. In order to combat this influence, one
must understand Barth's view of the Bible, expose his errors, and
subsequently explain the meaning of inerrancy and its importance.
Below, we will detail Barth's view of the Bible primarily through
his magnum opus, *Church Dogmatics*. We will mainly focus on
Barth's views on the human authorship of the Bible and on the
Bible as an errant witness of God.

Human Authorship

Barth believed that the Bible was written by men and, consequently, thoroughly human yet divine. He emphasized the human
aspect of the Bible to the point that he believed the Bible must
contain errors because it was written by humans. After all, to err
is human. Barth wrote, "The prophets and apostles as such, even
in their office, even in their function as witnesses, even in the act

---

5   John P Lewis. *Karl Barth in North America: The Influence of Karl Barth in the Making
    of a New North American Evangelicalism.* (Eugene, OR: Resource Publications, 2009)

6   Bernard L. Ramm. *After Fundamentalism: The Future of Evangelical Theology.* (San
    Francisco: Harper and Row, 1983)

of writing down their witness, were real, historical men as we are, and therefore sinful in their action, and capable and actually guilty of error in their spoken and written word."[7]

Barth emphasized the "historical" aspect of the Bible, which means the Bible is "uttered by specific men at specific times in a specific situation, in a specific language and with a specific intention."[8] When he used "historical", he did not refer to the actual historical settings of the Bible but rather to the human author's own perspectives, confined in a specific cultural, language, and historical context. Due to this, the authors will inevitably add their own culturally influenced input which might contain erroneous historical facts, thus rendering the Bible errant. However, God can still speak through these transient and imperfect human mediums. Barth lists various seeming contradictions and errors in the Bible in order to support his view of an errant Bible. He comments, "There are obvious overlappings and contradictions—e.g., between the Law and the prophets, between John and the Synoptists, between Paul and James."[9] Barth believes that the purported errors of the Bible were not just limited to words but he goes on to state that "the vulnerability of the Bible, i.e., its capacity for error, also extends to its religious or theological content."[10]

What is more disturbing is the fact that to Barth, the Bible was a timeless, human record of longing and seeking for the unconditioned. Since it was just a human record, the Bible can be read alongside similar writings that contain such longing and seeking. In fact, Barth claims that writings from other religions were sometimes more fitting and edifying than the Bible. For instance, He comments:

> As a timeless document of the human longing and seeking for the unconditioned, the Bible can, if we like, be read alongside documents of a similar kind. And we shall find that fundamentally at any rate it

---

[7]   Barth, Vol. 1. Bk. 2, 528-29.

[8]   Ibid, 464.

[9]   Barth, Vol. 1. Bk. 2, 509.

[10]   Ibid, 509.

is not different from other documents of this kind. Therefore we need not be surprised if we have to say that in other documents of this kind we may perhaps find more edification, i.e., a stronger impulse to this longing and seeking, that in Goethe's *Faust* or even in the sacred books of other religions we can better attain this end. On our own account and at our own risk we can go further and widen the concept of man of God, or prophet, or perhaps even apostle. And on all sorts of pretexts (not without approximation to the Catholic principle of tradition, and even perhaps assimilation to it) we can extend the concept of the witness of revelation to all the realities in which we think we can see an actual mediation of Christ, or more generally a divine impulse from man to man.[11]

Upon understanding Barth's view of Scripture, it would be logical to conclude that if the Scripture is only human and errant, then it should have no significance or authority! But Barth proposed that God is so powerful that He is able to speak to readers even through errant words. He stated, "For God once spoke as Lord to Moses and the prophets, to the Evangelists and apostles. And now through their written word He speaks as the same Lord to His Church. Scripture is holy and the Word of God, because by the Holy Spirit it became and will become to the Church a witness to divine revelation."[12]

Bible as a Witness of God

For Barth, the Bible is not the Word of God, but rather, it is tied to the Word of God. He stated, "The statement that the Bible is the Word of God cannot therefore say that the Word of God is tied to the Bible. On the contrary, what it must say is that the Bible is tied to the Word of God."[13] He believed that the Bible "Only

---

[11] Ibid, 496.

[12] Ibid, 457.

[13] Barth, Vol. 1. Bk. 2, 513.

'holds,' encloses, limits and surrounds it: that is the indirectness of the identity of revelation and the Bible."[14] To Barth, the Bible is only a witness of God. Since a witness can never fully represent the subject being witnessed, the Bible can never fully represent God and must contain errors.

Barth resisted the idea that the Bible is inerrant and that its truths are static and settled once and for all. He called this concept of the Bible a "paper pope" that limits the freedom and power of God. He thought it was even dangerous because this "paper pope" can be manipulated and abused by any human being who has a Bible in his hand.[15] *Then as they use to manipulate they are not true to God. (The truth shall make you free)*

To Barth, God revealed Himself not in words, but in acts. He stated, "To say 'the Word of God' is to say the work of God. It is not to contemplate a state or fact but to watch an event, and an event which is relevant to us, an event which is an act of God, an act of God which rests on a free decision."[16] He said this in order to make the Bible dynamic, not static and to give God freedom and power. He thought that God would otherwise be enslaved and limited in an inerrant, static Bible. *(The Power is in the Love)*

Ironically enough, Barth accused those who believe in inerrancy of imposing an alien view on the Bible,[17] but he himself was guilty of imposing an alien view on the Bible. This is clearly demonstrated by the fact that Barth hardly used the Bible to support his view of inspiration. His theologizing was almost completely based upon human wisdom, theories, and logic. Barth did not seriously interact with the Bible's own claims about inspiration and the nature of the Bible.

Interestingly, Barth believed that for the Bible to be truly miraculous, it must contain errors. Despite its errors, God is powerful enough to communicate His intended meaning to the readers when He chooses to. Barth stated, "That the lame walk, that the blind see, that the dead are raised, that sinful and erring men as such speak the Word of God: that is the miracle of which we speak when

---

[14] Ibid, 492.

[15] Ibid, 525.

[16] Ibid, 527.

[17] Ibid, 525.

we say that the Bible is the Word of God."[18] He even insisted that to call the Bible inerrant is to deny the divine miracle of revelation:

> For that reason every time we turn the Word of God into an infallible biblical word of man or the biblical word of man into an infallible Word of God we resist that which we ought never to resist, i.e., the truth of the miracle that here fallible men speak the Word of God in fallible human words—and we therefore resist the sovereignty of grace. . .If the prophets and apostles are not real and therefore fallible men, even in their office, even when they speak and write of God's revelation, then it is not a miracle that they speak the Word of God.[19]

Second Inspiration by God on the Readers

For Barth, revelation is not propositional but personal. Because it is personal in that sense, God is able to manifest His sovereign power, grace and freedom. This personal encounter occurs when the readers encounter the text and are moved by the Holy Spirit to discover fresh and intended meaning of the Bible. In other words, according to Barth, it is a second inspiration by God on the readers. However, if the Bible is inerrant, Barth argues, then the readers no longer need the Holy Spirit to help him understand the truth. The reader can simply rely on himself to discover the truth of the Bible, thus making the Bible into a human endeavor, with no divine help. The miracle of divine revelation and the sovereign power, grace, and freedom of God are manifested when God encounters the readers in his reading and is able to speak truth to the reader through errant words when He chooses to. According to Barth an inerrant Bible does not allow this personal and powerful encounter.

Karl Barth's subjective bibliology leads to subjective preaching. Just as Barth believed that the Bible subjectively becomes the Word

---

[18] Ibid, 529.

[19] Karl Barth, *Church Dogmatics*, vol.1 bk. 2, translated by G. T. Thomsen, (Edinburgh, Scotland: T & T Clark, 1936), 529.

of God when God chooses to reveal Himself to the reader, so Barth believed the preached Word only becomes the Word of God when God chooses to reveal Himself to the listener. Barth stated,

> Real proclamation, then, means God's Word preached, and in this second circle God's Word preached means human talk about God on the basis of the self-objectification of God which is not just there, which cannot be predicted, which does not fit into any plan, which is real only in the freedom of His grace, and in virtue of which He wills at specific times to be the object of this talk, and is so according to His good-pleasure.[20]

This subjective bibliology also allows for the listeners of a sermon to subjectively pick and choose what they want. They are justified in their subjectivity by the "moving" of the Holy Spirit. This bibliology eviscerates all authority from preaching, even when the sermon is completely based upon the Bible (Titus 2:15). This is extremely dangerous to the health of the church.

The Solution: Inerrancy and Infallibility of the Word of God

The above critique of Barthian bibliology shows that his view is clearly flawed and should not be embraced by Christians. To combat the influence of Barth, the church must not only expose his errors, but also declare the truth about the inspiration of the Bible. The Bible is the perfect Word of God because that is what it claims for itself (2 Peter 1:19-21, 2 Timothy 3:16-17, Matthew 5:18, and John 10:35). On first glance, there are apparent contradictions in the Bible, but in actuality, they are not real. For example, Barth listed contradictions between James and Paul. Undoubtedly he is referring to James 2:24, "You see that a person is justified by works and not by faith alone," which apparently contradicts Paul. But there is no contradiction; for James, his subject is the difference between true faith and false faith, which is why he asks

---

[20] Ibid, 92.

in James 2:14, "Can that faith save him?" True faith works, but works do not save us. True faith produces works, but work can never produce faith that saves. However, in Galatians and Romans, Paul is focusing on the difference between faith and works, not the difference between truth faith and false faith. This is why Paul emphasizes that sinners are saved by faith alone, not by works. Paul understands the importance of works when he said he was bringing the "obedience of faith" to the Gentiles in Romans 1:5 and 16:26. There is no contradiction between James and Paul.

The church needs to actively explain these apparent contradictions and show that they are not contradictions at all. Preachers should not hide these apparent contradictions but must expose them and show the congregation that they are not contradictions if they are interpreted correctly in context.

The Bible contains propositional statements. It states truths. These truths are not to be discerned through feelings and mood, but through objective and thorough investigation of the Bible via grammatical-historical hermeneutics with the illumination of the Holy Spirit. Since the Bible makes propositional statements, we can determine the inspiration of the Bible based upon its own propositional statements about its own inspiration. We must go to texts such as 2 Peter 1:19-21, 2 Timothy 3:16-17, Matthew 5:18, and John 10:35 to determine the inspiration of the Bible, not human reasoning, which is faulty. God alone—not human logic—is the source of truth. Logic is only a means to truth and is a God-given tool by which we come to conclusions. Preachers must endeavor to explain these key biblical passages on inspiration in order to ground the congregation on the inerrancy of the Bible.

Although we cannot know everything about God in the Bible, and our knowledge of Him is partial, we can revel in the fact that what we do know is the absolute truth. The Bible is not a witness to God; it is God's self-revelation. Its revelation is not exhaustive, but it is sufficient and true. We must preach the Bible, not about the Bible. We do not know everything about inspiration, but we do know that the Bible is inspired by God and the Bible itself claims to be inerrant in its original manuscript; therefore, we believe in the inerrancy of the Bible.

It is our hope that more and more Chinese believers will understand and accept that the Bible is fully inerrant and infallible and that all Scripture is inspired by God and profitable for the church. We pray that every pastor will make his best effort in studying all of Scripture and to preach all of Scripture for the edification of the church. We want the Chinese church to understand that the meaning of the passage is in the text. Pastors should not try to seek another "inspiration" of the text or a "moving" of the Holy Spirit in order to understand the text. They must endeavor to understand the text carefully by using grammatical-historical hermeneutics. They should demonstrate this method in their own preaching and also teach it to their congregation. They should make every effort to preach consecutive, expository messages as they preach through the Bible. We pray that the Chinese church will adopt a correct view of the Bible and preach the entire counsel of God truthfully, thoroughly, and wholly. In so doing, the churches in China will be equipped for the work of ministry, for building up the body of Christ, and will attain the unity of the faith. . .so that they may no longer be children, tossed to and fro by the waves and carried about by every wind of doctrine, by human cunning, and by craftiness (Eph. 4:12-14) seen in such groups as the Christian cults which plague China today.

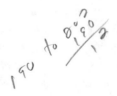

Influence and Authority in an Oral-Oriented Culture

By David Beakley and Nathan Odede (South Africa)

The evangelical church in the West has defended the authority of the Bible for generations against the advancing "creep" of liberalism. This evangelical movement was victorious. Earlier battles with modernity, such as the historicism and rationalism of liberal theology, were won. Those movements lost momentum and drifted onto the shores of irrelevancy.[1]

A new battle then arose concerning the doctrine of inerrancy. The emergence of a post-modern and skeptical culture in the church created a fertile ground for those who viewed the Bible as errant and fallible.[2] Coming out of seminary, I was well prepared for this battle. However, the Lord led me to serve as a professor and pastor in South Africa where, to my surprise, I found an entirely different battle raging around the Bible. The battle in South Africa is not concerning inerrancy directly. In this paper we present the primary challenge to scriptural authority common throughout Africa. This challenge is presented and illustrated as originating from traditional African beliefs. Finally, the paper concludes with

---

[1] Kenneth S. Kantzer, "Evangelicals and the Doctrine of Inerrancy" in *The Foundation of Biblical Authority* (London & Glasgow: Pickering & Inglis, 1979), 147.

[2] Ibid., 148. Also see J. Merrick and Stephen Garret, "Introduction: On Debating Inerrancy" in *Five Views on Biblical Inerrancy* edited by Stanley M. Gundry (Grand Rapids, Mich.: Zondervan, 2013) 9.

an improved methodology in missions and an example of Christ Seminary in training pastors who will have a high view of the authority of Scripture.

The African Mindset

The challenge of authority facing the African church is based in the dilemma of two competing views regarding the source of authority. Within the traditional African church, a historic reliance upon oral tradition, passed generationally among illiterate tribal groups, continues to create a challenge to biblical authority not experienced in the West. In Africa, authority has been more associated with a tribal leader than with the content of the message itself. Tribal leaders communicate "truth" and are themselves considered the source of authority. Not accustomed to examining an actual written text as a reliable and authoritative source of "truth", Africans most often place their confidence in the bearer of the message rather than the written text. Expectations for reliability and inerrancy are thereby circumvented. Contemporary Africans must be encouraged to reconsider their assumptions regarding the authority of Scripture and examine whether they are derived from the Bible's inerrancy and self-attested authority.

In the West, authority is the product of inerrancy, but in South Africa, it is more typical for inerrancy to be the product of authority. This is not meant to confuse or to be clever. This statement has real meaning for those not in the West. In the battle for the doctrine of inerrancy, Western evangelicals defending this doctrine hold to the former (authority is a product of inerrancy) as a foundational premise for objective truth, and that source of objective truth is seen as the adjudicator for all disputes. And, again in the West, that source must be non-human (sourced in documents or concepts). Every Western preacher, scholar, or theologian is countered by older and more preferred writings by other scholars. A person's position or qualification is not the kernel of their authority. Rather, authority is derived from one's skillful argument in dealing with words and concepts. In Africa, this is all a foreign concept. In Africa, all truth is derived from indisputable authority.

There is much to be said about the generic African worldview, and there are many foreign concepts that present no insignificant obstacle to the gospel and receiving God's written Word. This article is not concerned with the unregenerate or pagan African worldview, but rather the African "Christian" and their mindset—particularly with regard to the area of authority, from which inerrancy is derived.

The African mindset does not ask, "What is inerrant or absolute truth?" In fact, the idea of truth that is disconnected with an individual is like a Möbius strip[3]—a one-sided impossibility because it is an effect without a cause. In the West, authority resides in a law code; in Africa in a person. However, in both contexts, truth is still valid when it originates from an authoritative source. The African mindset seeks to identify truth with an individual, as the culture is one in which all rules, regulations, standards, cultures, and customs are given by the chief, elders in a community, or the previous (deceased) elders of a community. In a Christian setting, it is always the supposed "man of God." Whatever this anointed man claims to be true (including what he claims he can accomplish in matters spiritual) is regarded as authoritative, because he is God's man.

But this does not necessarily mean that inerrancy within the African context is non-existent or should be redefined as compared to the Western definition and experience. The battle remains the same; it is the field that is different. The African context does not fight a hermeneutical battle on the literary field, but rather in the area of personal testimony by "recognized" authoritative voices. Once this authoritative person is established and recognized, all proclamations, sermons, and "prophesies" by that person are considered to be inerrant.

In essence, the African man and woman is looking for an authority figure, because without this figure there is no truth in which to take comfort. Simultaneous with this is the African concept of "community", where not only goods and services are shared, but values, beliefs, and behaviors are shared and valued

---

[3]   A Möbius strip is a surface with only one side, and can be modeled by taking a strip of paper and giving it a half-twist and then taping or gluing the ends together. The result is a circular strip that will only have one surface.

as well. Because of a culture of "shame" (or rather "no shame") which breaks community, confrontation with the recognized authoritative person is not only not allowed, it leads to rejection by the community itself. Truth is what the recognized authority says. Since truth and authority should never contradict or oppose one another, this is not necessarily a bad concept—unless the authority is not an absolute authority and is proven wrong. This weakness (of identifying authority without any objective verification of "truth") was inadvertently exploited by something that is inherently good—missions.

Missions and the Problem of Authority

Though Christianity came to Africa before it came to the Western world (Acts 8:27-39), Christianity has traditionally been viewed by the African as a modern and white man's religion. One of the main reasons for this is that the missionaries largely ignored the cross-cultural context. Wilbur O'Donovan accurately points out:

"A major problem in the period before 1960 was that very few efforts were made to relate Christian theology to the African context. Many Africans found that the presentation of Western issues in theology did not answer their inmost questions or solve some of the spiritual problems related to African culture. Western methods of thinking and learning were often unsuited to African ways."[4]

O'Donovan concludes that as a result, Christian theology was thought by many Africans as Western instead of universal to mankind.

In addition, this misunderstanding was compounded by the fact that many missionary activities sprung up during the colonial era. In South Africa, rivalry between black and white communities was evident from the late eighteenth century on. White settlers viewed the "different" indigenous black people as inferior. For example, early European settlers were dismissive of the people whom they called "Bushmen," and regarded them as simple and childlike,

---

4   W. O'Donovan, *Biblical Christianity in African Perspective*. (Carlisle: The Paternoster Press, 1996), 5.

incapable of religious thought.[5] This brought much appropriate criticism to missionaries as being among those undermining the life and culture of the nationals. Various other factors, including wars and a governmental system of apartheid, would later arise and further affect missionary efforts, though the work would continue.

Thus the question arose within the African Christian community: "How can we be Christian and African?"[6] Pluralism and syncretism was the result. For the African, this brought one of two choices. The first choice (pluralism) is to see the gospel as intrinsically connected to the culture of the missionary. To have the gospel is to adopt the Western culture. There is no real spiritual transformation, just a transformation of authority. When one wanted to be "Christian" they must be as the colonial because the authority of the gospel is the authority of the colonial. This is evident in the wide acceptance of the "successful" and "authoritative" Charismatic churches from the West. There is no real gospel, but rather a serious effort to duplicate the cultural and ritualistic formulas that exercise "power."

The second choice (syncretism) is to reject the separatist and critical instructions and teaching that was given (the African people were instructed to "rise up" from their pagan and backward ways and to accept the "right" way of living from the missionary) and to take the gospel and form their own religion. This is seen in the Zion Christian Church of South Africa, which has a mixture of Old Testament teachings combined with pagan rituals and in which the recognized authority (the grandson of the founder) is the mediator between God and man.

In either case, the gospel is partially received, but there is no demand for rejection of their African pagan beliefs. In the first case, they associated the gospel with a culture, and in the second, they combined the gospel to share a place of worship with other gods. In every case, the authority was never transferred from the missionary to the actual message itself coming from the authoritative book—the Word of God. Instead, the authority rested on the missionary

---

[5]   J. W. Hofmeyr and G. J. Pillay, eds., *A History of Christianity in South Africa Vol. 1* (Pretoria: HAUM Tertiary, 1994), xvi.

[6]   Timothy Training Institute, *The Church in African Context: with Emphasis on African Independent Churches* (Johannesburg: Timothy Training Institute, 1997)

or missionary family that ministered to a specific people, and that authority left as they either left the continent, moved to another mission opportunity, or died.

A Case Study—The Zion Christian Church

The largest denominational church in South Africa is the Zion Christian Church with a membership of between four to six million.[7] The Zionist movement in South Africa actually had its roots in the US through the Christian Catholic Apostolic Church in Zion City, Illinois near Chicago, founded in 1896 by John A. Dowie.[8] Among the many things that Dowie taught, the main emphasis was on divine healing. Dowie merged an interpretation of holiness with divine healing, which played well into the African mindset of authority.[9]

A few years later, in 1906, two missionary families went to South Africa and joined with a former Dutch Reformed theologian to work with Dowie to continue the work. By 1905, the Zion Church had five thousand members, the majority of whom were African.[10] During this entire time, there was no priority or effort put into expository preaching or serious Bible teaching. At the end of Dowie's life, he was thought to be quite deluded and claimed to be Elijah the Restorer.

Over time, the Zionist churches began to acquire more of an African flavor. They would feature a blend of the old (African traditional religion) and the new (Christianity).[11] Along these lines, Engenas Lekganyane founded the Zion Christian Church (ZCC) in 1925, with its headquarters in Moriah[12], after converting to Zionism in 1913. Lekganyane was educated by Scottish Presbyterian

---

[7] The actual number is difficult to ascertain.

[8] Hoffmeyer and Pillay, 214.

[9] Ibid., 189.

[10] Ibid., 189.

[11] Ibid., 214-215.

[12] Moriah is a small village located about thirty kilometers East of Polokwane, the small town which is home to Christ Seminary and 250 kilometers North of Pretoria. Every Easter, several million pilgrims make their way to the small mountain at Moriah for three days to receive the blessing from their leader.

missionaries, and he was a former member of the Free Church of Scotland, along with the Apostolic Faith Mission (Pentecostal) church. He was the perfect syncretistic leader.

Over time, the ZCC became more isolated, as they desired to escape from colonialism and the idea of a "White Christianity." Lekganyane welcomed polygamy, which was acceptable in the African culture. Upon his death in 1948, his two sons, Edward and Joseph, fought over control of the church causing a church split. Each faction identified themselves with a special insignia. Edward's followers wear a silver star while Joseph's church wears a silver dove. The two churches continue today, and the leadership of each church was passed down to their respective sons.

With no theological or biblical training, the churches maintain gospel language, while following mostly African Traditional Religion (ATR) practices. Church members must wear special clothes, and purchase relics from the church for special miracles and power. The leaders of each church purport to be mediators between God and the people, and each one claims deity in some form. Each rules his people with fear by his claims of omnipresence. Church members believe that the leader can "see" them through their badge that they wear and through a portrait of the leader in their homes. They also believe that he will "hear" their prayers through the portrait.

In South Africa, the ZCC is a great hindrance to the spread of the gospel. All of the members would say they are "saved" and can say that their leader uses the Bible. All, however, are enslaved in a system ruled by fear and the need for works. There is no need to know Scripture or the God of the Bible, because the authority rests in the leader—their mediator between God and them. Evangelization continually falls on deaf ears.

What is more amazing is that the Zion Church in the USA is still willing to work with the ZCC in South Africa. The Zion Church in the USA is a broad-band evangelical church and they are working to send missionaries to train the pastors of the ZCC in order to "help" them preach more accurately. This would be identical to a Baptist Church sending men to train Mormon pastors to help them in expository preaching.

The point here is that Africans come to Scripture first with a view to authority. Inerrancy naturally follows. Since the mission effort to start the ZCC began and continued with the authority remaining with the leader, this naturally fit the understanding of the African mindset that theology and truth rest in an authoritative leader. It would have been much better if there had been no missionary activity to these people for the past century, and that there would be a blank slate relative to Christianity. There will most likely never be a debate on inerrancy in the African culture, as the understanding is that inerrancy flows from authority. It is the authority of the Scriptures themselves that must be established and then lived out by preachers.

The Biblical Solution—Expository Preaching in Missions

The thrust of missions in Africa has been that of a social gospel (to alleviate third-world suffering) and evangelizing. The methodology often comprised going from village to village preaching a message of salvation, while providing more "Western" methodologies of worship, dress, behavior, farming and subsistence, and living standards. The preaching was often clear and compelling on the person and work of Jesus Christ, but there was no real sustained teaching on the need to turn completely and renounce their African Traditional Religion and all its practices (1 Thess. 1:9).

The result of this effort yielded the expected fruit. Confusion, syncretism, and a sense of commercializing the gospel divided regional dynasties as each tribal group adopted different parts of the gospel and kept different parts of their own pagan religious beliefs and practices. If this is the result of over two centuries of variegated approaches by sincere mission-minded men and women, what new approaches could be offered?

For this, we look to one of the oldest mission endeavors recorded in history, found in Nehemiah 8. The return of the Babylonian captives to their home country of Israel was one of the greatest acts of God's faithfulness found in Scripture, but it is also a situation that created a need for a Jewish missionary. After living in Babylon for a generation, and then returning to a land dominated by foreigners, the Israelites were complete strangers to their new surroundings. Most all of the younger generation could not even speak Hebrew (Neh. 13:24). In many ways, this was identical to the current African context. The people were a closed community (tribal), syncretistic (in that they followed many of the customs and spoke the language of the surrounding nations) and had either forgotten or not been taught the laws and ordinances of Israelite behavior and worship, much less the teaching of the character of their God (Neh. 13). When Ezra the scribe came to stay, he was very much a missionary.

The success of Ezra's approach is very clear. Although he was seen as their spiritual authority, he made sure that their attention was on the Word of God and not on Ezra himself. He had the people make a pulpit (Neh. 8:4) and opened the Book of the Law in the sight of all the people (v. 5). When Ezra preached, no doubt he had implied authority, as the people did not even understand the meaning of his words (v. 8). Ezra took the time to assign capable "interpreters" to provide the meaning of the text and its application to the hearers (v. 8). The effect was phenomenal. The people wept uncontrollably because they understood clearly that they were accountable to know and obey the instructions of Moses, but had been totally deficient. They were convicted of their sin.

Specifically, as the people listened for much of the day, they went home with much to consider. They were exhorted to return the next day, when they heard a second reading and interpretation of Scripture. Specifically, they heard and understood that they were required to carefully observe the Feast of Tabernacles as written in the book of Leviticus. God had so carefully worked out the details of their lives that it was the exact month and day (Neh. 7:73) on which to observe the Feast of Tabernacles, they read Moses' instruction on this and they were convicted because they were not even remotely thinking of observing this feast. And it is not as if they had not heard of the Feast of Tabernacles because it had been observed in the earliest part of Israel's return to the land (Ezra 4:4).

Needless to say, after the second sermon by Ezra, the people saw that they must obey God, not Ezra. They followed the instructions of Moses, made all the necessary preparations, and observed the Feast of Tabernacles in a way that had not been done since the time of Joshua almost a thousand years earlier!

Expository preaching yields results—and this preaching is not the "hit and run" type of preaching that is done by some missionaries. Ezra preached, and then preached again. Ezra's ministry was one of teaching the Law to the people, and he did so continually. What Ezra showed here is that, while he had authority as a scribe, and was a recognized "man of God" to be obeyed, he dutifully demonstrated through careful and bold preaching that God must be obeyed. This act is accomplished through reading, understanding, and applying God's objective truth given in His written Word. Any other methodology will have the fulfillment of cotton candy—sweet to the taste initially, but vanishing in a moment.

The Biblical Solution—Discipleship-Based Missions

Undoubtedly, the model missionary for the New Testament Church is the Apostle Paul. He was noted as a minister to the Gentiles (Gal. 3:8). Discipleship was critical to Paul's ministry. Without hesitation, Paul knew about the final command of his Lord to "make disciples," and he knew that Jesus Himself spent over two years with twelve men to prepare them for ministry. He knew that there were no "quick fixes" in ministry.

Paul began his first mission journey with Barnabas, who was a proven and worthy associate. Together, they accompanied Mark, who was Barnabas' cousin and possibly one of Jesus' early converts (Mark 14:51). Mark's immaturity and lack of perseverance caused Paul considerable concern (Acts 15:37-40), and Paul refused to work with Mark again.[13] Paul also saw the falling away of another disciple, Demas, who was a convert from Thessalonica (2 Tim. 4:10). But, not everyone failed the Apostle in his missionary activity.

When Paul began his second missionary journey, on his first stop in Derbe, he picked up a young man named Timothy, who was of mixed descent (Acts 16:1). Paul saw that this man was

---

[13] We do know, however, that Paul kept up with Mark's spiritual progress, as Paul and Mark continued on in the ministry and crossed paths again (Col. 4:10; 2 Tim. 4:11).

committed and had a good theological foundation (2 Tim. 1:5; 3:15). Therefore, Paul and Timothy agreed that Timothy needed to be circumcised so that he would not be an offence to any Jews (Acts 16:3).[14]

As Timothy accompanied Paul on his perilous journeys, he began to learn the required discipline needed for ministry. He was often Paul's trusted messenger to the churches (1 Cor. 4:17; Phil. 2:19; 1 Thess. 3:2) and he was included as a co-author in many letters to the churches as he was involved in their creation from the beginning (Phil. 1:1; Col. 1:1; 1 Thess. 1:1; 2 Thess. 1:1). While many men were helpful in the ministry, none was more critical than Timothy. As a result, Paul entrusts the leadership and pastoral care of the church of Ephesus entirely to this young disciple.

Timothy was a young man, but able to handle the pulpit (1 Tim. 1:3-4). Over the years, Timothy had seen the effect of Paul's preaching, and had seen *lived out* what Paul taught in his expository preaching. Timothy knew the difference between sound doctrine and pragmatic preaching (2 Tim. 4:2-3). He also knew how to persevere under persecution with joy in order to strengthen other believers (Heb. 13:23).

No doubt, Timothy had a great effect on the growth of the church in the first century. Paul knew that his own time was limited. Three long journeys, two imprisonments, shipwrecks and snakebite all impressed on this aging Apostle the rigors of ministry. Whom could he trust? He had seen so many fail and others fade away back into the pleasures of the pagan world. He saw the traumatic effects of legalistic Jews, who sought to take over every young church like a virus. How could the church survive? Who could carry on with the work?

Fortunately, this was not a question that Paul had to wrestle with as he saw his end coming. The seasoned missionary did not rely on his work, and he did not rely on his popularity. For this, Paul had something much more reassuring. In his last days, when discouragement abounded, and the church began to face extreme persecution—even attempted annihilation from both pagans and

---

[14] Although Paul's ministry was to the Gentiles, in every city he began preaching in the Jewish synagogues. These were mostly occupied by Gentiles since they were in Gentile territory, but the Jewish faith is where the preaching began.

Jewish religionists—Paul had seen this day coming. For this, Paul relied on his trusted disciple Timothy, the man whom he invested in for decades. It is this man whom Paul called in his final days in prison (2 Tim. 4:9) to provide instructions on how to stand firm and provide a lasting ministry that would not succumb to syncretism, pluralism, and "every wind of doctrine."

Christ Seminary—A Twenty-first Century Solution

The seemingly asymptotic goal of missions is to create such a strong spiritual maturity among the nationals that they themselves become disciple makers and missionaries (1 Thess. 1:8-9). In Africa, this is rarely the case, as missionaries often believe that the mission cannot survive beyond their leadership, since their leaving will result in a defenseless flock that is devoured by syncretism, politics, and the culture. This points out the clear need for trained national pastors.

Since 1997, Christ Seminary has channeled all its efforts into training national pastors in South Africa. The initiative began as a church-based seminary (more like a Bible Institute) that offered a Diploma of Theology to local pastors. No real academic entrance requirements were enforced. In 2005, the program was elevated to a Bachelor's Degree of Theology (BTH) when the seminary was accredited by the Department of Education of South Africa. Currently, there are over one hundred and fifty graduates of Christ Seminary from over twenty African countries (including pastors in Europe and the US) and the ministry is growing in strength and focus.

The full-time faculty of Christ Seminary is now completely indigenous (meaning that every full-time faculty member is an African). The Seminary is a ministry of a local church (Christ Baptist Church) pastored by a Master's Seminary graduate. There is one PhD professor, and every other faculty member is pursuing a Masters or Doctoral degree. The method used by Christ Seminary is that which was highlighted above—expository preaching and discipleship. In addition, a very strong emphasis is placed on shepherding the flock.

The role that this institution plays in the inerrancy debate in Southern Africa is crucial. The seminary is known for its absolute trust in the authority and sufficiency of Scripture, and the commitment to inerrancy is resolute. The seminary stands out amongst a sea of training institutions that range from Covenantal Reformed to Pentecostal and broad-band evangelicals (who allow for varying hermeneutics in the area of women in ministry, additional revelation, and a Bible with errors). Christ Seminary is the one institution that focuses on graduating expository preachers.

One of the many examples of this impact involves a 2014 graduate named Joseph. When he interviewed, Joseph was a complete Charismatic. He came to Christ Seminary because one of the graduates was his friend, and they had preached together many times. Joseph noted that this friend now preached and lived differently. In fact, this friend (who was a former Charismatic) was diagnosed with a deadly disease with no cure. Instead of pursuing "healing" and "miracles," this friend faithfully preached the Word of God with increasing power, conviction, and joy. Joseph wanted what this friend had.

As Joseph came to the Seminary, he himself began to change, along with his preaching. In his third year, Joseph was afforded ten lucrative invitations to preach during the semester break, yet he turned down every one. This decision was not taken lightly, as Joseph's life is difficult, and by most Western standards would be considered as living slightly above a "third world" situation.

The reason for the rejection? Joseph said he must turn down these invitations because he knew it was setting up the man of God (himself as the Lord's anointed) against the Word of God to preach the agenda of man. Despite the monetary gain these opportunities would have provided, he saw none of them as an "opportunity." Joseph neither saw himself nor the messages he used to preach before seminary as authoritative or inerrant, because those messages were outside of Scripture and its proper interpretation.

Although Joseph is now ridiculed in the Charismatic community, he is known as a compassionate and knowledgeable man of God in the local community. He is a man who now stands by his convictions, and has "the conviction to lead."[15] Like Timothy, Joseph is just one of many who now have the conviction to demonstrate the authority of Scripture to Africans. His commitment to Scripture will carry all the weight involved with biblical inerrancy. While this anecdote does not weigh in on the "Western" debate about biblical inerrancy, it does provide an excellent illustration of the "African" debate on the same issue. A discussion about inerrancy without settling the question of biblical authority is futile.

Is the Bible authoritative because it is inerrant? Or, is the Bible inerrant because it is authoritative? On different sides of the ocean, the cause and result might appear reversed, but the relationship between the two is identical. One cannot say the biblical text is fully authoritative without also agreeing with a rigorous and unbending definition of inerrancy. Likewise, a biblical text with errors is hardly authoritative. In Africa, the path to inerrancy cannot be trod without first lodging at the inn of authority. Since authority in the African mind rests in an individual (the perceived "man of God"), there must be a wresting of the mantle of authority from a spiritual man to a spiritual text. This can only come through committed preaching, and continuous discipleship. Only after a long stay at this lodging is the short path to inerrancy reached. Christ Seminary is such a haven.

---

[15] Al Mohler, *The Conviction to Lead* (Minneapolis, Minn.: Bethany House Publishers, 2012).

Catholicism, Postmodernism, and Inerrancy in Southern Europe

By Ruben Videira (Spain)

Inerrancy in Europe: What is at Stake

The written Word of God has stood at the center of Christianity as long as there have been followers of the Living Word of God. In fact, absolute confidence in the authority of Scripture as God-breathed truth led to the Reformation in the sixteenth century. This movement sparked a religious fire, which the Roman Catholic Church (RCC)[1] could not put out.[2] The focus of the Reformation was the so-called fourfold *solas*: *sola gratia, solus Christus, sola fide* and *sola Scriptura*.[3] The problem was that the RCC believed, according to Sinclair Ferguson, that to speak of *sola Scriptura* would lead unconditionally to spiritual anarchy.[4] Therefore they

---

[1]   Henceforth referred to as RCC.

[2]   Sinclair Ferguson. "Scripture and Tradition: The Bible and Tradition in Roman Catholicism," in *Sola Scriptura! The Protestant Position on the Bible*, ed., Don Kistler (Morgan, PA: Soli Deo Gloria Publications, 1995), 184.

[3]   Salvation is by grace alone, in Christ alone, by faith alone and everything that is needed for salvation is contained in Scripture alone. See Ferguson, "Scripture and Tradition," 184–85.

[4]   Ibid.

battled for tradition—an alternative channel of divine revelation, as the safeguard against this. The purpose of the Reformation principle of *Sola Scriptura*, however, was to call the church to turn toward the Scripture itself in the midst of all human traditions,[5] contradicting the RCC, which claimed that the revelation of God was also contained in oral tradition.[6]

The impact of the Scripture is because it is God-breathed, finding its origin in God. In other words, Scripture is the result of God's own activity and is based upon His character. This establishes the foundation of the Bible's reliability, as stated by B.B. Warfield when he writes, "It is on this foundation of Divine origin that all the high attributes of Scripture are built."[7] Therefore, if God is true (Rom 3:4), then His written revelation must also be true (John 17:17). The inspiration of the Scriptures (2 Tim 2:16) necessitates its inerrancy, which according to Paul D. Feinberg means that "when all facts are known, the Scriptures in their original autographs and properly interpreted will be shown to be wholly true in everything they teach, whether that teaching has to do with doctrine, history, science, geography, geology, or other disciplines or knowledge."[8] Article IX of the *Chicago Statement on Biblical*

---

[5] G. C Berkouwer. *Holy Scripture* (Studies in Dogmatics), (Grand Rapids: W. B. Eerdmans Pub. Co., 1975), 313.

[6] During the Council of Trent in the sixteenth century, the RCC declared that: "This [Gospel], of old promised through the Prophets in the Holy Scriptures, our Lord Jesus Christ, the Son of God, promulgated first with His own mouth, and then commanded it to be preached by His Apostles to every creature as the source at once of all saving truth and rules of conduct. It also clearly perceives that these truths and rules are contained in the written books and in the unwritten traditions, which, received by the Apostles from the mouth of Christ Himself, or from the Apostles themselves, the Holy Ghost dictating, have come down to us, transmitted as it were from hand to hand. Following then the example of the orthodox Fathers, it receives and venerates with a feeling of piety and reverence all the books both of the Old and New Testaments, since one God is the author of both; also the traditions, whether they relate to faith or morals, as having been dictated either orally by Christ or by the Holy Ghost, and preserved in the Catholic Church in unbroken succession" (*Creeds of the Churches: A Reader in Christian Doctrine, from the Bible to the Present,* ed., John H. Leith, 3rd., ed., [Lousiville, KY.: John Knox Press, 1982], 402). This assertion contradicts Jesus Himself, who always used the Scriptures and not Tradition, to bring any argument to an end. The Word of God was the judge of Tradition. In fact, Jesus often criticized Tradition (see Mat 4:4; 15:2–9, 17–19; 22:29–32).

[7] B.B. Warfield. *Revelation and Inspiration* (Grand Rapids: Baker Book House Company, 2000), 280.

[8] Paul D. Feinberg, "The Meaning of Inerrancy", in *Inerrancy*, ed. Normal L Geisler (Grand Rapids: Zondervan, 1980), 294.

Inerrancy defines inerrancy similarly, "We affirm that inspiration, though not conferring omniscience, guaranteed true and trustworthy utterance on all matters of which the Biblical authors were moved to speak and write. We deny that the finitude or fallenness of these writers, by necessity or otherwise, introduced distortion or falsehood into God's Word."[9] Since God cannot lie (Heb 6:18, 1 Pet 2:22), and Scripture originated in Him, the key component to inerrancy must be truthfulness.[10] As Michael Canham writes, "Positively this means that the Bible is entirely true. Negatively, it means that the Bible is never false."[11] In other words, the Scripture's infallibility demands its inerrancy.[12] No lower ground than this can be held.[13] Augustine explains it as it follows:

> Most disastrous consequences must follow upon our believing that anything false is found in the sacred

---

[9] R.C. Sproul. *Can I Trust the Bible?* The Crucial Questions Series (Lake Mary, FL.: Reformation Trust, 2009), 28.

[10] Several biblical texts affirm inerrancy. In the Old Testament the mark of a true prophet of God was that he spoke the truth, that is, his message was inerrant (Deut 13:1–5, 18:22). The Psalms speak of the Word of God as pure words (Ps 12:6), perfect, sure (Ps 19:7), right, pure (Ps 19:8), and true (Ps 19:9). See also Psalm 119:142, 151, and 160. The book of Proverbs describes the Scripture as certain and true (Pro 22:10–21). Those who add to His Word will be proved liars, so by implication it is understood that God's Word is inerrant (Pro 30:6). The New Testament also states that the Scripture is inerrant. Jesus spoke of His Words as eternal (Mat 25:35), and only pure words—true inerrant words will pass the test of time. He also affirmed that Scripture is true (John 8:31–32; 16:13; 17:17). The apostles also understood and accepted the inerrancy of the Holy Writings (see 1 Tim 1:15; Titus 3:8 [trustworthy statement]; James 1:25; 1 Pet 1:23; Rev 21:5). For more passages and a further explanation see Wayne Grudem, *Systematic Theology: An Introduction to Biblical Doctrine* (Grand Rapids: Zondervan, 2004), 90–92.

[11] "The Inerrancy of the Bible," Exalting Christ Pastor's Conference Notes (September 2014), 2.

[12] Though the terms inerrancy and infallibility are often used as synonyms there is a distinction between them. R. C. Sproul explains it as follows, "The distinction is that of the potential and the actual, the hypothetical and the real. Infallibility has to do with the question of ability or potential; that which is infallible is said to be unable to make mistakes or to err. By contrast, that which is inerrant is that which, in fact, does not err. Theoretically, something may be fallible and at the same time inerrant. That is, it is possible for someone who errs to not err. However, the reverse is not true. If someone is infallible, that means he cannot err, and if he cannot err, then he does not err. If he does err, that proves that he is capable of erring and therefore is not infallible. Thus, to assert that something is infallible yet at the same time errant is to distort the meaning of *infallible* and/or *errant*, or to be in a state of confusion. Infallibility and inerrancy in this sense cannot be separated, though they may be distinguished in terms of meaning" (*Can I Trust the Bible?*, 36).

[13] Bernard Ramm. *Protestant Biblical Interpretation: A Textbook of Hermeneutics,* 3rd rev., ed., (Grand Rapids: Baker Book House, 1970), 201–202.

books: that is to say that the men by whom the Scripture has been given to us and committed to writing, did not put down in these books anything false. If you once admit into such a high sanctuary of authority one false statement, there will not be left a single sentence of those books, which, if appearing to any one difficult in practice or hard to believe, may not by the same fatal rule be explained away as a statement, in which, intentionally, the author declared what was not true.[14]

As a result of the Scriptures being inspired, inerrant, and infallible,[15] they are by their very nature materially sufficient for the Church in all matters related to what they teach. This reliability extends to matters not only of the faith, but also to that which relates to moral, historical, factual, scientific and numerical facts.[16] Consequently, the Bible is sufficient as God's revelation to man. This means that there is no external truth to the Scriptures necessary for the believer's salvation and sanctification that has been preserved or revealed outside of the Holy Writings. Since Scripture has a unique relationship to God Himself, to deny the sufficiency[17] of the Written Word has direct implications upon God's truthfulness.

In short, when inerrancy is attacked, much is at stake—God's character is distorted and His Word caricatured. This results in the spiritual starvation of believers, which is a sad reality in Southern Europe. Those who deny the Scriptures' inerrancy would not necessarily and openly make such a claim, but they would rather reject the sufficiency of God's Word on a pragmatic level.[18] The problem,

---

14 Augustine, *Letters of St. Augustine* 28.3.3, in *The Confessions and Letters of St. Augustine with a Sketch of His Life and Work: A Select Library of the Nicene and Post-Nicene Fathers of the Christian Church, First Series*, edited by Philip Schaff, translated by J. G. Cunningham (Buffalo, NY: Christian Literature Company, 1886), 251–52.

15 See footnote 14 for an explanation on the distinction between inerrancy and infallibility.

16 William Webster. *Roman Catholic Tradition: Claims and Contradictions* (Battle Ground, WA: Christian Resources, 1994), 8.

17 This concept flows out of several biblical passages: Deut 4:2; 12:32; Psal 19:7–11; 119:1; Prov 30:5–6; Isa 8:19–20; John 17:17; 2 Tim 3:15–17, James 1:18; 1 Pet 1:23; Rev 22:18–19.

18 Wayne A. Mack, Program Director and Professor of Biblical Counseling at The Master's College, says: "Many in our day and previously have affirmed the inerrancy and authority

however, is that sufficiency is dependent upon infallibility,[19] which flows out of the Scriptures' inerrancy, and emerges from their inspiration.[20] So as one may see, to question the sufficiency of God's Word in all matters related to what they teach, is positively detrimental to their inerrancy, and by extension, to God's veracity and trustworthiness. For this reason, the affirmation of the Bible's inerrancy has never been more crucial for the evangelical movement in Southern Europe. Without inerrancy, Christianity will become dissolute and indifferent in its faith and doctrines, and confused about its message.[21] Inerrancy in Southern Europe, however, is challenged from two fronts: religiosity and postmodernism.

and Conute realition

Inerrancy and Religiosity: An Errant Bible but an Inerrant Magisterium

Roman Catholicism has had a great religious influence in Southern Europe for centuries,[22] shaping the understanding of biblical inerrancy, especially during the last two centuries when it sought to "wed together contemporary historical-critical methods of biblical interpretation with the ancient dogmas of the Church."[23] This resulted in the ratification of an inerrant historical Tradition that takes priority over Scriptures.[24]

of Scripture in matters of faith and practice, but have not affirmed the sufficiency of Scripture for understanding and resolving the spiritual (non- physical) problems of man. They believe that we need the insights of psychology to understand and help people. In essence, they believe that when it comes to these matters, the Bible is fundamentally deficient. They believe that God did not design the Bible for this purpose and so we must rely on extrabiblical, psychological theories and insights. For many Christians, the Bible has titular (given a title and respected in name) rather than functional (actual, practical, real, respected in practice) authority in the area of counseling. They acknowledge it to be the Word of God and therefore worthy of our respect, but when it comes to understanding and resolving many of the real issues of life, they give it limited value" ("The Sufficiency of Scripture in Counseling," *The Master's Seminary Journal* 9, no. 1 [Spring 1998]: 64).

[19] See footnote 14.

[20] See footnote 1.

[21] R. Albert Mohler. "When the Bible Speaks God Speaks: The Classic Doctrine of Biblical Inerrancy," in *Five Views on Biblical Inerrancy*, eds., J. Merrick and Stephen M. Garrett (Grand Rapids: Zondervan, 2013), 2930.

[22] Jose Graw. *Catolicismo Romano: Origenes y Desarrollo,* 2a ed., de Concilios (Barcelona: Ediciones Evangélicas Europeas, 1965), 2:1275–277.

[23] Ferguson, "Scripture and Tradition," 186.

[24] See footnote 7.

The Roman Catholic Church (RCC), however, affirms the inerrancy of the Scriptures. At the beginning of the twentieth century, Pope Pius X wrote: "We, Venerable Brethren, for whom there is but one and only truth, and who hold that the Sacred Books, written under the inspiration of the Holy Ghost, have God for their author, declare that this [Modernism] is equivalent to attributing to God Himself the lie of expediency or the officious lie."[25] Despite the soundness of this affirmation, the RCC stresses the human aspects of the Bible rather than the divine,[26] to the extent that the human authors had the flexibility to exaggerate and distort the historical events in order to highlight what God did.[27] The biblical writers could only enunciate the reality about God through their understanding of their own culture, society and history.[28] This means that they took their materials from the tradition and mythology of pagan nations around them. The miracles became literary devices to portray a theological truth but not a historical event.[29] For

---

[25] Dean Bechard.*The Scripture Documents: An Anthology of Official Catholic Teachings* (Collegeville, MI.: Liturgical Press, 2002), 74.

[26] Jean Levie. *The Bible, Word of God in Words of Men,* trans., S. H. Treman (New York: P. J. Kenedy, 1961), 216–29. This emphasis on exploring the Scripture's humanity and ignoring its divinity was the result of significant developments that took place within the RCC due to worldwide events such as WWI and WWII. These wars, especially the latter, exposed the emptiness of the optimistic, modernist idea of God's global Fatherhood and human brotherhood. These developments highlighted the importance of other natural sciences taking precedence over the literal meaning of the Sacred Text and making a clear distinction between the original meaning of Scriptures and their significance (see Ferguson, "Scripture and Tradition,"187–92).

[27] R.A. MacKenzie. *Faith and History in the Old Testament,* (New York, NY.: Macmillan, 1963), 80–81.

[28] John L. McKenzie. *Myths and Realities: Studies in Biblical Theology* (Milwaukee: Bruce Publishing Co., 1963), 200.

[29] Vatican II affirms: "The Bible was not written in order to teach the natural sciences, or to give information on merely political history. It treats of these (and all other subjects) only insofar as they are involved in matters concerning salvation. It is only in this respect that the veracity of God and the inerrancy of the inspired writers are engaged. This is not a quantitative distinction as though some sections treated of salvation (and were inerrant), while others gave merely natural knowledge (and were fallible). It is formal, and applies to the whole text. The latter is authoritative and inerrant in what it affirms about the revelation of God and the history of salvation. According to the intentions of its authors, divine and human, it makes no other affirmations" (Walter M. Abbott, ed., *The Documents of Vatican II with Notes and Comments by Catholic, Protestant and Orthodox Authorities* trans., Joseph Gallagher [Boston, MA: The America Press, 1996], 119). This declaration denies the veracity of the claim that the Bible is inerrant because it is inspired by a God who cannot lie. According to the RCC, the Bible speaks of truth but not necessarily historical truth.

example, the purpose of the Creation account in Genesis 1–2 is not to narrate how God created the universe but that He is the Creator. The author simply described Creation in those terms because he imitated other creation accounts with similar structure and vocabulary. This approach to the Scriptures allowed Catholics to doubt the inerrancy of the Word of God and remain in full fellowship with the RCC, as long as they affirmed the Virgin Birth and the Resurrection.[30] However, on what basis are these two miracles now historical? Could it not be that the Gospel authors wanted to emphasize the significance of the divinity of Jesus, so they invented the Virgin Birth and the Resurrection miracles? If one questions the inerrancy of the Scripture, what guideline is he supposed to follow to determine whether a miracle was historical or not? In the end, this becomes mere subjectivism, because of the enthronement of the human elements of the biblical text over the divine. Therefore, the Scriptures become errant, fallible, insufficient, in essence, man-breathed.

The RCC's ultimate standard of biblical truth is the RCC itself. This emphasis on the human element transformed the RCC from a static structure into a dynamic organism.[31] In other words, they no longer use history and past creeds as checkpoints for their present interpretation, but rather "truth" is reshaped capriciously under the rule of the Magisterium of the Church. When this takes place, every previous teaching changes according to the reinterpretation of the Magisterium. This poses a serious epistemological challenge: every catholic generation that preceded the new reinterpretation of the Magisterium believed an insufficient truth that needed to be reshaped. So why is the RCC so confident in its Tradition? How can they trust the "true gospel"? A future Magisterium might reshape the "salvific" message of Catholic tradition, showing that it was a lie all along. This dynamic approach to truth makes it impossible for the RCC to legitimately claim that it knows the truth.

---

[30] John Warwick Montgomery. "The Approach Of New Shape Roman Catholicism To Scriptural Inerrancy: A Case Study For Evangelicals," *Bulletin of the Evangelical Theological Society* 10, no. 4 (Fall 1967): 215.

[31] Karl Adam. *The Spirit of Catholicism*, trans. Justin McCann, rev., ed. (Garden City, NY: Doubleday Image Books, 1954), 62–63.

Since the Church existed before the books of the New Testament were written, the RCC claims that her early traditions are just as authoritative as the Word of God. The RCC's belief in apostolic succession is manifested in the infallibility of the Magisterium and the Pope. As the Vicar of Christ, it is the Pope who determines the true meaning of the Tradition, including the Holy Writings.[32] Catholic tradition, in the true sense, is not merely what it is thought to be, it is what the RCC decides that it is,[33] as illustrated by the words of Pope Pius IX:

> They [fomenters of heresy and schism] recognize in Scripture and Tradition the source of Divine Revelation, but they refuse to listen to the ever-living magisterium of the Church, although this clearly springs from Scripture and Tradition, and was instituted by God as the perpetual guardian of the infallible exposition and explanation of the dogmas transmitted by these two sources.[34]

The Magisterium is responsible for the explanation of the Sacred Tradition and Text. Therefore persons outside this group ought not to interpret Scripture. Thus, the RCC through the Magisterium and the Pope is the ultimate judge and interpreter of the Word of God.[35] In short, they believe that the Bible is errant because of their acceptance of form criticism, but the Church itself is considered to be inerrant and infallible—the ultimate authority of truth—a role that belongs to God alone.

---

[32] See footnote 24.

[33] James Likoudis and K. D. Whitehead, *The Pope, the Council and the Mass,* rev., ed., (Steubenville, OH: Emmaus Road Pub., 2006), 72.

[34] Ibid.

[35] Vatican II claims, "A written record is a dead letter, needing constant interpretation and commentary in succeeding ages. It cannot of itself answer new questions, or explain what was once clear and has now become obscure. But the writings transmitted in a living community, from one generation to another, are accompanied by a continuous tradition of understanding and explanation which preserves and re-expresses their meaning, and which applies them, from time to time, to the solving of new problems. If this tradition were only human, it would be liable to grave error. But such a consequence is avoided by the Church's magisterium" (*The Documents of Vatican II,* 119).

The RCC has also reinterpreted the concept of inspiration. According to Catholicism, the Word of God is Church-breathed, and thus, inerrancy has also been redefined to such a point that it means little or nothing. In other words, Catholic doctrines have been shaped to harmonize with everything, and consequently, the Bible loses the spotlight—to affirm, on the one hand, biblical inerrancy, and then, on the other, to allow for inconsistencies and contradictions because of Tradition, implies an errant definition of inerrancy.

How is this relevant for Protestant Evangelicalism in Southern Europe? Catholicism allows for a general affirmation of biblical truth without a full commitment to the particulars. Likewise, contemporary evangelicals have created a false dichotomy between theological and secular truth.[36] Thus, any discrepancy in the Bible does not affect its inerrancy as long as it is not related to faith and morals. Whenever evangelicals affirm the infallibility of Scriptures and yet admit historical contradictions and inaccuracies, they not only promote confusion but also deny plenary inspiration. As John Montgomery said, "I must—if only on the basis of common sense—protest the idea that 'error can't affect inerrancy.' This is like saying that the presence of corners can't affect a circle."[37]

---

[36] According to John Warwick Montgomery, it is held by some evangelicals that Scripture is inspired, but only as God's authoritative message in matters spiritual. In matters historical and scientific they recognize the human, fallible element in the biblical witness (see "Inspiration And Inerrancy: A New Departure," Bulletin of the Evangelical Theological Society 8, no. 2 [Spring 1965]: 46). As an example of this false dichotomy, Roy A. Harrisville writes, "we admit to the discrepancies and the broken connections in Scripture, we let them stand just as they are—this is part of what it means that faith has its sphere in this world and not in some cloud cuckoo-land" ("A Theology of Rediscovery," Dialog 2, no. 3 [1963]: 190). This means that Scripture is authoritative and authorized fundamental witness to revelation as long as no attempt is made to apply such inspiration to the historical and scientific parts of the text. In other words, there is an alleged distinction between spiritual truth and earthly truth. The problem is that you cannot have one without the other. Charles Joseph Costello explains, "Inerrancy is so intimately bound up with inspiration that an inspired book cannot assert what is not true" (*St. Augustine's Doctrine on the Inspiration and Canonicity of Scripture* [Washington, D.C.: Catholic University of America, 1930], 30). Jesus speaks of theological and secular truths as one of the same truth, "If I told you earthly things and you do not believe, how will you believe if I tell you heavenly things?" (John 3:12). Jesus saw a correspondence between the earthly and the heavenly. If Nicodemus did not understand that which was earthly, or secular, how could he understand the heavenly truths? For a more detailed explanation see Montgomery, "Inspiration And Inerrancy," 45–75.

[37] James Warwick Montgomery, "The Approach of New Shape Roman Catholicism To Scriptural Inerrancy," 222.

The Magisterium has turned the truth into an always-changing phenomenon that changes according to social, historical, cultural and scientific pressures that it encounters. The Scriptures, however, do not portray truth as a reality that is shaped by social coercion. The veracity of Jesus' person and message depended on objective facts that must not be reinterpreted according to the mutating standards of society.[38]

The influence of the RCC in Southern Europe has led evangelicals to impose on the Bible a definition of inspiration determined by sources outside the Bible. Inspiration and inerrancy are concepts that must be defined from the Scriptures themselves. Evangelicals do not believe in the Magisterium, and yet, at times, they function like the RCC by allowing for the inerrant truth of the Word of God to be reshaped according to a new scientific or supposed historical tradition. The RCC has converted truth into a subjective matter, an approach that found its way into Southern European Protestantism.

Because of the divine origin of Scripture, there is no need for other writings or human traditions which pass judgment on it. There is the Bible and then everything else. Whenever one limits the meaning of inerrancy based on external sources, it is like comparing apples to oranges. Inerrancy is affirmed, not because it is presupposed, but because the Scripture itself declares it. If the revelation of God shows contradictions, such as occurs in the Magisterium, then it cannot be trusted. A contradiction in the Word of God would force one to wonder whether or not other biblical assertions are in fact true. Then, where is the line drawn? Why is the Scripture true in matters for salvation and not in historical and scientific issues? If the Bible contains even one error then it would have a domino effect on the trustworthiness of the whole Written Revelation. Contrary to what the RCC has done, evangelicals cannot and must not redefine inerrancy, which automatically

---

[38] When the apostle Paul summarizes the gospel, he refers to historical events as facts: "For I delivered to you as of first importance what I also received, that Christ died for our sins according to the Scriptures, and that He was buried, and that He was raised on the third day according to the Scriptures, and that He appeared to Cephas, then to the twelve. After that He appeared to more than five hundred brethren at one time, most of whom remain until now, but some have fallen asleep; then He appeared to James, then to all the apostles; and last of all, as to one untimely born, He appeared to me also" (1 Cor 15:3–8). A reshaping of this historical account would result in a different gospel that would not result in salvation.

would change the origin of the Scriptures from God-breathed to man-breathed. Thus, they would become the revelation of man and not God.

Inerrancy and Postmodernism: A Relative Bible but an Absolute Worldview

The present postmodern denial of inerrancy in Southern Europe began with Modernism years ago. Modernism originally referred to something recent, present or contemporary, showing the desire to express its distinctiveness from its predecessors. Today, however, such a term expresses obsoleteness.[39] René Descartes along with others laid the theoretical foundation for Modernism. He was a radical Reconstructionist,[40] so he took the method of the doubt almost to the limit. For Descartes, according to James W. Sire, "doubting equaled thinking."[41] This summarizes the essence of this philosophy,[42] which worshipped the autonomy of human reason, leaving God out of the equation. It *liberated* man from religious

---

[39]   Albert Borgmann. *Crossing the Postmodern Divide* (Chicago: Chicago Press, 1992), 20.

[40]   Beginning with the truth that men doubt and are therefore not perfect, Descartes reasoned to the existence of God as the Perfect Being. Since a Perfect Being would not deceive lesser beings, whatever it can be deduced by means of reasoning must be true (see Gary R. Habermas "Skepticism: Hume," in *Biblical Errancy: An Analysis of Its Philosophical Roots*, ed., Norman L. Geisler [Eugene, OR: Wipf and Stock Publishers, 1981], 26). Descartes was not only philosophically disinterested in special revelation, but also ambiguous about the origin of innate ideas, and about their relation to the sphere of supernatural and ultimate Reason. For him, the idea of God was detached from grace and personhood, becoming a mathematical inflexible idea. God was merely a force that bridged matter and mind together, a force that later was going to be defined by the evolutionary naturalist as simple energy. For more information, see Henry, *God, Revelation, and Authority*, 301–307.

[41]   James W Sire. *The Universe Next Door* (Downers Grove: IVP Academic, 2004), Kindle Electronic Edition: location 2109. The following paragraph written by Descartes illustrates Sire's assertion: "I do not now admit anything which is not necessarily true: to speak accurately, I am not more than a thing which thinks, that is to say a mind or a soul, or an understanding, or a reason, which are terms whose significance was formerly unknown to me. I am, however, a real thing and really exist; what thing? I have answered: a thing which thinks" (René Descartes, *Meditations on First Philosophy* [Sioux Falls, SD: NuVision Publications, 2007], 29).

[42]   Habermas explains that Modernism was based on the "theory that reality is essentially rational and that by making the proper deductions, an individual could achieve knowledge of self, others, and the world. Reason and particularly deductive logic were emphasized. Even God could be known, at least to some extent, by the exercise of reason." (Habermas, "Skepticism", 26)

oppression. The new appeal was the authority of the individual human mind apart from other authority structures such as the RCC and tradition. According to Borgmann, "Modernism subverted the authority of the Word of God, leading to the erosion of truth and realism."[43] Society became characterized by the deconstruction of historical facts, which later reconstructed according to people's subjective desires.[44] In the end, it was a celebration of the autonomous human being without inhibitions. This new enthronement of the human mind often ignored God's written revelation. Thus, biblical inerrancy became irrelevant.

Modernism nurtured two movements that to some extent found their way through different manifestations into Postmodernism: Deism and Existentialism. The former sought to devise a rational religion that did not depend upon divine revelation.[45] Its founder is considered to be Herbert of Cherbury,[46] who identified the basic tenets of Deism as the existence of a supreme God, moralism, repentance, and eternal life. These became the foundation for human reason.[47] According to Deism, the design of nature proves the existence of a God,[48] although he is no longer involved in creation. In short, God was only necessary to get everything started, but now he is unable to act supernaturally therefore miracles were denied,[49] and by implication, the Bible could not be inspired or inerrant.[50]

Existentialism was the major philosophical movement in the late nineteenth and early twentieth century, significantly paving

---

[43] Borgmann, Crossing the Postmodern Divide, 24–25.

[44] Rick C Shrader. "Postmodernism," Journal of Ministry and Theology 3, no. 1 (Spring 1999): 25.

[45] See Habermas, "Skepticism," 27.

[46] Ibid.

[47] Edward Lord Herbert of Cherbury, De Veritate, trans. Meyrick H. Carre (Bristol: J. W. Arrowsmith Ltd., 1937), 289–307.

[48] Charles Darwin and his Evolution theory, however, argued that God was not even necessary to explain the origin and design of creation.

[49] Matthew Tindal considered natural religion as true Christianity. Therefore, everything contrary to reason was rejected. Hence, he dismissed miracles. John Toland also believed that reason overrides the Bible. So, he explained miracles by natural processes (see Habermas, "Skepticism," 27).

[50] Norman L. Geisler, and William C. Roach, *Affirming the Accuracy of Scripture for a New Generation* (Grand Rapids: Baker Books, 2011), Chapter 12, Kindle edition.

the way for Postmodernism.[51] For many existentialists, the movement attempted to define truth in a context where universals and absolutes did not exist, reshaping the truth according to subjective standards.[52] Sören Kierkegaard, considered the first important existentialist, maintained a high regard for Scripture,[53] and yet he believed that uncertainty lay at the root of each historical fact. So, the biblical historical accounts were only approximations to what truly happened.[54] Thus, doubt plagued his reading of the Bible, leading him to renounce the objectiveness of the Christian faith founded on accurate historical accounts. Kierkegaard gave little importance to the original documents of the Word of God, dismissing textual criticism.[55] As a result, truth turns out to be what the individual feels it needs to be. Concepts of right or wrong could no longer be known. People only experience the world as it is.[56] Biblical inerrancy became a relative notion that was redefined according to the individual's experience.

Jim Holt, in a review of *Fashionable Nonsense* for the *New York Times*, defines Postmodernism as "the notion that physical

---

[51] Gene Edward Veith, *Postmodern Times*, (Wheaton: Crossway Books, 1994), 28.

[52] Existentialism presupposes the possibility of a mindset not influenced by history and culture. No individual, however, can think from a blank slate. This presupposition is a contra-response to the Modern worldview. The existential mind is the result of his environment, determined by its culture and its history. If Existentialism is taken to its logical conclusion, epistemology and language also need to be rejected. Consequently, the question would then be, how could Existentialism know?

[53] Sören Kierkegaard wrote about the books of the Bible: "These books, no others, belong to the canon, they are authentic, they are complete, their authors are trustworthy – it can well be said that it is as though every letter were inspired. . . Furthermore, there is no trace of contradiction in the sacred books" (Sören Kierkegaard, *Concluding Unscientific Postscript*, Cambridge Texts in the History of Philosophy, ed., Alastair Hannay [Cambridge: Cambridge University Press, 2009], 25).

[54] Kierkegaard said, "If Christianity is looked on as a historical document, the important thing is to obtain completely reliable reports of what the Christian doctrine really is. Here, if the investigating subject were infinitely interested in his relation to this truth, he would despair straight away, because nothing is easier to see than that with regard to history the greatest certainty is after all only an approximation, and an approximation is too little to base his happiness on, and incongruent to such a degree with an eternal happiness that no ready solution can emerge" (Ibid., 21).

[55] E. Herbert Nygren. "Existentialism: Kierkegaard," in *Biblical Errancy: An Analysis of Its Philosophical Roots*, ed., Norman L. Geisler (Eugene, OR: Wipf and Stock Publishers, 1981), 117–19.

[56] Robert C Greer. *Mapping Postmodernism, a Survey of Christian Options* (Downers Grove: InterVarsity Press, 2003), 224–25.

reality is nothing but a social construct and that science, despite its pretensions to truth, is just another 'narrative' that encodes the dominant ideology of the culture that produced it."[57] This means that Postmodernism results in multiple realities created by individualistic perspectives and the lack of critical consensus (pluralism) that place the emphasis on the community—truth is defined by groups of people. Thus, the only truth is change.[58] Postmodernism is "deconstructionist literary criticism and relativistic nihilism."[59] To put it briefly, it is more than a worldview and less than a philosophy. It is a social reaction to Modernism, which is the reason why it cannot escape the influence of the philosophical tenets of Deism and Existentialism. Therefore, in the postmodern worldview, inerrancy, due to the influence of the former, has become experiential, and of the latter irrelevant.

Deconstructionism[60] is the driving force of Postmodernism and affirms that all human constructions are a flux of indetermination, denying access to the original truth about self. For example, in regards to language, there is nothing else but the flow of linguistic constructs. In other words, since language is in constant change, it is impossible to know what it communicated in the past.[61] Deconstructionism changed the nature of truth, affecting the understanding of biblical inerrancy. Truth is objective, but Postmodernism opened the door to subjective elements that deny

---

[57] Jim Holt. "Is Paris Kidding?" *New York Times*, November 15, 1998, under "Books." http://www.nytimes.com/1998/11/15/books/is-paris-kidding.html?ref=bookreviews (accessed November 3, 2014).

[58] Harold Johnson. "The Research and Development of a Storying Model to Address The Postmodern Worldview with the Biblical Worldview," (Doctoral Thesis, New Orleans Baptist Seminary, March 2000), 6–7; William Edgard,"No News Is Good News: Modernity, The Postmodern, and Apologetics." *Westminster Theological Journal* 52, no. 2 (1995): 371; Sire, *The Universe Next Door,* Kindle Electronic Edition: location 2076; and Shrader, 24.

[59] Oden, "The Death of Modernity," 26.

[60] For more information, see Marika Enwald, "Displacements of Deconstruction," (Academic Dissertation, University of Tampere, 2004), 46–61; Phillips, 299, and Greer, 227.

[61] Gotthold Ephraim Lessing illustrates this as he sees a large unknowable abyss between the historical and the eternal truths: "the ugly ditch which I cannot get across, however often and however earnestly I have tried to make the leap" (Lessing's Theological Writings. Selection in translation with an Introductory Essay by Henry Chadwick [Stanford: Stanford University, 1957] 55).

propositional truth. This false worldview claims that people read the past through their personal lenses, thus, reshaping it according to their present experience. In the end the person imposes his own understanding of reality.

This claim is diametrically opposed to what the apostle Paul implies in 2 Corinthians 10:5. In this verse, he explains that the fight for the truth—the knowledge of God, is based on objective, logical, linguistic and cognitive arguments, rooted on the confidence that it is possible to know what has been previously communicated through language.[62] This is why those speculations against God need to be destroyed. The problem does not lie within the nature of truth, but the sinfulness of men who in their pride rose against the truth of God. God, because of their rebellion, gave them over to a depraved mind (Rom 1:28), becoming fools (Rom 1:22) without understanding (Rom 1:31). Deconstructionism is nothing more than deadly deception, and the manifestation of a fool and depraved mind that exchanged the truth of God for the fiction of men.

Regardless of what a postmodern world is trying to make people believe, in theory postmodernists live their lives much differently in practice. This is the reason why postmodernists express phrases like, "that is not true," or "tell the truth." When a person says such things he is implying that there is a correspondence between truth and reality. Intentionality or potentiality are not qualifiers of truth. For example, what would happen with the judicial system if a person was judged on the basis of his intentions, regardless of whether these correspond with reality? In that case, everybody would be guilty.[63] As Geisler and Roach write, "true justice depends on the right view of truth. Otherwise the innocent would be punished, and the guilty would go free."[64] Even at a practical and logical level it is easy to see the absurdity of Deconstructionism. Truth is factual precision in correspondence with reality.[65]

---

[62] The Greek word for speculation is λογισμός and refers to "the product of a cognitive process, calculation, reasoning, reflection, thought" (BDAG, "λογισμός," 598).

[63] Geisler and Roach, *Defending Inerrancy,* Kindle Electronic Edition: Chapter 13, Location 5562.

[64] Ibid.

[65] The command in Exodus 20:16 implies that any fact that does not correspond to reality is false. Satan is called a liar (John 8:44) because he asserts things contrary to facts

Postmodernism not only makes inerrancy irrelevant, but also denies it, which makes men fall into one error after another. Postmodern theologians have been telling the people of God that He can make His truth known through untruths. To deny inerrancy on the basis of Deconstructionism is the same thing as affirming that truth does not exist, and even if it did, the Church has no access to it. The proof of how this false view has found its way into the Church is the undermining of biblical preaching. Churches have replaced preaching with social programs and events. As soon as inerrancy is removed from the picture, the Scriptures lose their inherent divine authority in the mind of men, and so preaching is no longer deemed necessary or helpful for the growth of the church.

Today's hermeneutical approach to the Word of God is infested with postmodern ideas. Instead of asking the right question, "What did this passage mean to the original audience?" people often say, "What does it mean to you?" This is the doing of none other than Deconstructionism. The person imposes his subjective meaning according to his own experiences. Due to this approach, biblical truth is an ongoing, changing entity, impossible to correspond with reality. When the wrong questions are asked, the true original meaning of the text cannot be understood, so one may read the Bible but not have the inerrant Word of God—indispensable truth for the sanctification of the believer (John 17:17). In a nutshell, Postmodernism's redefinition of inerrancy has made the Scripture obsolete, incomprehensible, and irrelevant for today. Consequently, Postmodernists conclude that the Church of God *needs* to abandon the Word of God.

Conclusion

Inerrancy is under attack. Both the RCC and Postmodernism pose the same challenge—the reshaping of inerrancy by sources outside of the Bible. The RCC makes inerrancy dependent on the Magisterium, while Postmodernism gives authority to the autonomy of the individual. Evangelicalism in Southern Europe

---

(cf., Gen 2:17; 3:4). Acts 5:1–4 illustrates how misrepresenting reality is not truthful. Scriptures clearly declare that truth corresponds with reality.

has fallen victim to believing that the Word of God is unimportant as long as the truth behind it is revealed. At this point, subjectivism becomes the ruling agent; so the issue is more philosophical than factual. It is not that new evidences or facts have been discovered to undermine biblical inerrancy, rather, just the opposite is true. If new evidence is found, it will confirm once again that the Sacred Text contains no error. The confusion created by the RCC and Postmodernism is manifested in that different evangelical circles have embraced new philosophies which are incompatible with the biblical understanding of inerrancy. The church must act firmly in order to eliminate the unbelief which threatens to engulf it in a dark era. In the words of Jason Sexton, "The Bible is God's Word. As such, the church must look for ways to hold it and its message out as God's steadfast truth in a time of great error. It is a rock because the God who attributes to it His very own authority is a solid rock in an age where every other ground is sinking sand."[66]

In conclusion, the concept of the Word of God is twofold. On the one hand, it refers to the Scriptures, but on the other hand, to Christ Himself. Therefore, to claim that the Word of God is errant, has a negative effect against the testimony of Christ contained in Scripture. It is a direct attack to God's character and truthfulness. Inerrancy is a necessary doctrine for the integrity of God's own veracity. If the Bible is not inerrant God reported a *true* faulty testimony. Then, why should the Church trust his declaration about his Son? Why should some historical facts be trusted and others not? If inerrancy is redefined, the Bible—and by extension, the account of the life of Christ—must also be redefined. The possibility of a historical error in the narrative of Jesus will be devastating for the trustworthiness of the gospel and God, resulting in a Church fearful of becoming a gospel-less church.

---

[66] Jason Sexton, "How Far Beyond Chicago? Assessing Recent Attempts to Reframe the Inerrancy Debate," *Themelios, An International Journal for Students of Theological & Religious Studies*, 35, no. 1 (April 2009),: 48–49.

INERRANCY AND THE TRANSMISSION OF THE NEW TESTAMENT

By Mykola Leliovskiy (Ukraine)

B iblical inerrancy is of crucial importance to those whose sole rule of faith and practice is the Bible. However, some prominent scholars in the English-speaking academia portray inerrancy as an embarrassing vestige of early American Fundamentalism.[67] Moreover, many who hold to inerrancy struggle with the preservation and the transmission of the text of the New Testament. After all, what value is there to holding to inspired and inerrant autographs, if what most Christians today call the Bible is a translation of handwritten manuscripts? One of the most prominent spokesmen against the reliability of the New Testament, Bart Ehrman, articulates this position in the following way: "The fact that we don't have the words [of the original text] surely must show. . .that [God] did not preserve them for us. And if he didn't perform that miracle, there [seems] to be no reason to think that he performed the earlier miracle of inspiring those words."[68]

The reliability of the text of the New Testament is an issue directly related to inerrancy. The matter of reliability is also one of the primary

---

[67] As clearly evidenced by the recent volume in the Zondervan Counterpoints series, *Five Views on Biblical Inerrancy.*

[68] Bart D. Ehrman. *Misquoting Jesus: The Story Behind Who Changed the Bible and Why* (New York: Harper, 2005), 11.

fronts of attack on the Christian faith from all directions. Those who insist we simply cannot know what was initially written since we lack the autographs, as James R. White explains, can base their arguments on very different foundations and have very different goals:

> The atheist or skeptic may seek to overthrow the entirety of biblical revelation by alleging an inability to know the text of the originals. On the other hand, most of those who promote this particular argument do so from a religious foundation: They are either members of outside religions (e.g., Muslims) who use this argument to deny the validity of the Christian faith or they are members of groups that claim fidelity to Christianity yet seek to establish an extra-biblical source of authority. This is a common approach, for if you can instill doubt concerning the text itself, then you can seek to assert the authority of your leader/group/organization and thereby subjugate Scripture to your group's interpretations, deletions, additions, traditions, etc.[1]

The purpose of this article is to defend the concept of inerrancy by showing that the textual transmission of the New Testament is trustworthy. This article will show that the New Testament is unique among the documents of antiquity that still exist.

Analyzing Manuscripts and Variants

Prior to Johannes Gutenberg's introduction of the printing press to Europe in the middle of the 15th century, all documents were written and copied by hand. Variation in the copying process was unavoidable and in fact, "of the approximately five thousand Greek manuscripts of all or part of the New Testament that are known today, no two agree exactly in all particulars."[2]

---

[1]   James R. White. *Scripture Alone: Exploring the Bible's Accuracy, Authority and Authenticity* (Bloomington: Bethany House Publishers), 136-137.

[2]   Bruce Metzer. United Bible Societies, *A Textual Commentary on the Greek New Testament, Second Edition a Companion Volume to the United Bible Societies' Greek New Testament (4th Rev. Ed.)* (London; New York: United Bible Societies, 1994), xxiv.

It is interesting to note how this natural and expected phenomenon is presented by those who stand against Christianity and the reliability of the text of the New Testament. Bart Ehrman's assessment of the current situation, for instance, concludes with this,

> . . .what can we say about the total number of variants known today? Scholars differ significantly in their estimates—some say there are 200,000 variants known, some say 300,000, some say 400,000 or more! We do not know for sure because, despite impressive developments in computer technology, no one has yet been able to count them all. Perhaps, as I indicated earlier, it is best simply to leave the matter in comparative terms. *There are more variations among our manuscripts than there are words in the New Testament* (italics added).[3]

Hence, if there are 138,162 words in the New Testament (in the NA27 Greek text) and 400,000 variants, which results in approximately three variants per word, the case against the reliability of the New Testament is airtight. John Frame writes:

> People sometimes say it doesn't make sense for God to inspire a book and then require us to determine its original content by textual criticism, by human means. When you think of transmission as a process carrying the word from God's lips to our hearts, eventually there will have to be a role for human thought, reason, even science. God might have made it so that whenever he spoke a word, we would all understand it instantly. Clearly that didn't happen. God evidently intended some human teaching and thought to go on before his people would be able to appropriate the Word completely. He wanted this to be a communal process, so that we would depend on one another. The business of figuring out the original text is part

---

[3] Ehrman, *Misquoting Jesus*, 89-90.

> of that. Since God has not promised to preserve these
> processes from error, we will sometimes make mis-
> takes. *So, although the autographic text of Scripture
> is infallible, the transmission of that text to our hearts
> is not* (italics added).[4]

Some Christians feel uncomfortable with that fact. It seems that many would prefer a single copy with zero variants than thousands of copies with thousands of variants. Some are even willing to exchange truth for certainty. Unfortunately, they fail to grasp that herein lies one of the most assuring truths about the reliability of the text of the New Testament. Possession of a single copy eliminates the problem of textual variants; however, it substantially reduces confidence in whether or not that copy got it exactly right.

It is important to note that the abundance of manuscripts and their relative proximity to the original date of writing in relation to other works of antiquity is remarkable, as the following diagram demonstrates:[5]

THE RELIABILITY OF THE NEW TESTAMENT COMPARED TO OTHER ANCIENT TEXTS

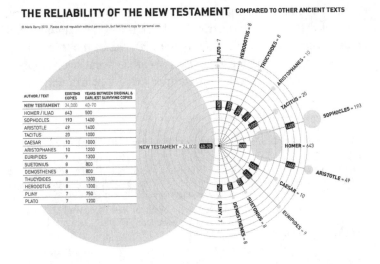

AUTHOR / TEXT	EXISTING COPIES	YEARS BETWEEN ORIGINAL & EARLIEST SURVIVING COPIES
NEW TESTAMENT	24,000	40-70
HOMER / ILIAD	643	500
SOPHOCLES	193	1400
ARISTOTLE	49	1400
TACITUS	20	1000
CAESAR	10	1000
ARISTOPHANES	10	1200
EURIPIDES	9	1300
SUETONIUS	8	800
DEMOSTHENES	8	800
THUCYDIDES	8	1300
HERODOTUS	8	1300
PLINY	7	750
PLATO	7	1200

---

4   John M Frame. *Salvation Belongs to the Lord: An Introduction to Systematic Theology* (Phillipsburg, NJ: P&R Publishing, 2006), 67.

5   Mark Barry (http://visualunit.me). Used by permission.

What about the issue of 400,000 variants? While there are numerous variants, it is far from being an airtight argument against reliability and, ultimately, inerrancy. First, 99% of all the variants do not affect the meaning of the text, as "the great majority of these variants are spelling differences, transpositions of words or letters, or synonyms."[6] In other words, they are not relevant to either translation or interpretation of the text. This means that there are about 4,000 meaningful variants for 138,162 words, or a variant for every 3 pages. Second, only half of these variants are viable, that is, have the possibility of being original. This limits the range of variation in the manuscript tradition to about 1,500 to 2,000 viable textual variants.[7]

Currently there are 5,839 catalogued Greek manuscripts.[8] They are mostly incomplete, not containing the entire New Testament, yet are about 200 pages on average, which makes for 1.3 million pages of text.[9]

The reality is that 1,500 to 2,000 viable textual variants found in 1.3 million handwritten pages over the period of 1,500 years accounts for an amazingly small percentage of the text and an amazingly accurate history transmission. As Wallace concludes, "The fact that no major doctrine is affected by any viable textual variant surely speaks of God's providential care of the text."[10]

The vast majority of these variations arose because of unintentional scribal errors arising from faulty eyesight, hearing, memory,

---

6   Daniel B Wallace. "Textual Criticism of the New Testament," ed. John D. Barry and Lazarus Wentz, *The Lexham Bible Dictionary* (Bellingham, WA: Lexham Press, 2012).

7   For a detailed discussion of the nature of the textual variants see Ed Komoszewski, M. James Sawyer, and Daniel B. Wallace *Reinventing Jesus: What* The Da Vinci Code *and Other Novel Speculations Don't Tell You* (Grand Rapids: Kregel, 2006). Especially, Part 2: Politically Corrupt? The Tainting of Ancient New Testament Texts (pp. 53-120).

8   This number was given by The Center for the Study of New Testament Manuscripts' executive director Dan Wallace in a recent presentation at Bethel Church of Houston's Robert A. Tolson Bible Lectureship Series on September 21, 2014.

9   For a detailed description of Greek New Testament manuscripts, their date, content and characteristics see the section titled "The Manuscripts Of The Greek New Testament" in Kurt Aland and Barbara Aland, *The Text of the New Testament: an Introduction to the Critical Editions and to the Theory and Practice of Modern Textual Criticism*, 2 ed. (Grand Rapids: Wm. B. Eerdmans Publishing Co., 1995), 72-184.

10   Daniel B. Wallace. "Inspiration, Preservation, and New Testament Textual Criticism," *Grace Theological Journal*, 12, (1991): 43.

and judgment.[11] These errors are discerned by the principles and practice of textual criticism involving *external evidence*, having to do with the manuscripts themselves, and *internal evidence*, having to do with two kinds of considerations, those concerned with transcriptional probabilities (i.e. relating to the habits of scribes) and those concerned with intrinsic probabilities (i.e. relating to the style of the author).[12] For the great majority of textual problems, the evidence is clear as to which reading is authentic and which is not.[13]

In recent debates with Daniel Wallace and James White, Bart Ehrman was seemingly forced to concede that the modern textual critic was able to have a very high degree of certainty as to which readings in the extant manuscripts are not original. This, however, has forced him and many others to shift their argument. Ehrman writes,

> What is unsettling for those who want to know what the original text said is not the number of New Testament manuscripts but the dates of these manuscripts and the differences among them. Of course, we would expect the New Testament to be copied in the Middle Ages more frequently than Homer or Euripides or Tacitus; the trained copyists throughout the western world at the time were Christian scribes, frequently monks, who for the most part were preparing copies of texts for religious purposes. But the fact that we have thousands of New Testament manuscripts does not in itself mean that we can rest assured that we know what the original text said. If we have very few early copies—in fact, scarcely any—how can we know that the text was not changed significantly *before* the New Testament began to be reproduced in such large quantities (italics original)?[14]

[11] Bruce M. Metzger. and Bart D. Ehrman, *The Text of the New Testament: Its Transmission, Corruption, and Restoration*, 4th ed. (New York: Oxford University Press, 2005), 250-271.

[12] Bruce Metzger. *A Textual Commentary on the Greek New Testament*, xxv.

[13] Wallace, "Textual Criticism."

[14] Bart Ehrmann. *Lost Christianities: Battles for Scripture and the Faiths We Never Knew* (New York: Oxford University Press, 2005), 219.

Multifocality of New Testament's Textual Transmission

Multifocality of the textual transmission of the New Testament is the reason we can have a very high degree of certainty that the text was not changed significantly before the production of the manuscripts in our possession today. Some scholars at times speak of the "Dark Age" in the transmission of the text of the New Testament, which refers to the period of time between the autographs and the first extant copies. Ehrman and others posit that we are absolutely ignorant of the vast theological alterations that the text has undergone from the moment of its original writing to the time the first copies begin to emerge in the textual tradition.[15]

Before explaining what is meant by "multifocality," it seems reasonable to set the record straight in terms of the duration of this so-called "dark period." Currently we possess more than 124 Greek manuscript witnesses within the first 300 years after the writing of the New Testament.[16] We have twelve manuscripts from the second century, i.e., within 100 years of the writing of the New Testament. These manuscripts contain portions of all four Gospels, nine books of Paul, Acts, Hebrews, and Revelation, comprising a majority of the books of the New Testament we possess today.[17] Hence, this dark period is relatively short since no work of antiquity even comes close to this early attestation as shown on the chart below.

---

[15]   Ibid.

[16]   Philip Wesley Comfort and David P. Barrett. *The Text of the Earliest New Testament Greek Manuscripts* (Wheaton: Tyndale House, 2001). A useful volume that provides the Greek text, along with many paleographical annotations, of sixty-five papyrus and four parchment fragments dated prior to A.D. 300.

[17]   Ibid.

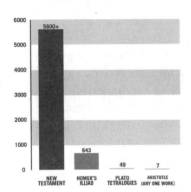

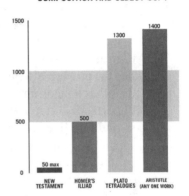

Note: Homer's *Illiad* is the best attested ancient work after the New Testament. Plato and Aristotle are used in the graph for how well known they are.

Bibliography: Josh McDowell, *Evidence that Demands a Verdict*, (San Bernadino, CA: Here's Life, 1972, 1992).

Manuscript Authority of the New Testament Compared to Other Classical Works[18]

Multifocality is a term coined by James R. White.[19] It refers to the fact that the New Testament has multiple lines of transmission. In other words, the New Testament was written by multiple authors, from multiple locations, directed to multiple audiences, during multiple timeframes.[20] White has since used the concept in numerous apologetic encounters to successfully defend the reliability of text of the New Testament. Matthew, Mark, Luke, John, Paul, Peter, James, and Jude all wrote from different locations at different dates to audiences found all throughout the ancient Mediterranean such as Asia Minor, Galatia, Macedonia, Achaia, Rome, etc. The relevance of this fact could be described as follows:

> ... due to the widespread distribution of the originals as well as copies, individual or small-scale attempts at alteration would produce clear evidence upon

---

[18] Ted Cabet et al., *The Apologetics Study Bible: Real Questions, Straight Answers, Stronger Faith* (Nashville, TN: Holman Bible Publishers, 2007), 2008.

[19] *The King James Only Controversy*, 2nd ed. (Minneapolis: Bethany House, 2009), 82.

[20] Ibid.

comparison with other transmission streams during the same period. . . If individuals without control over the entirety of the text would make major alterations to individual manuscripts, the copying of those manuscripts would produce a text that would stand out like the proverbial sore thumb when compared against the other noncorrupted transmission lines. Hence the importance, once again, of multifocality resulting in multiple lines of transmission. We do not have a single line of transmission, or two, or three, but many, coming from different places, crossing with each other, producing new lines, compilations of books (the collection of Paul's writings into manuscript P^{46}, for example), and so forth. While these multiple lines create difficulties for textual scholars who seek to unscramble them so as to identify the relationship of one manuscript to another, on the positive side they make the real danger—wholesale corruption—an impossibility. [21]

In other words, if, as Ehrman and others posit, purposeful and theologically-motivated alterations were made, one can expect to discover drastically different portrayals of Christ in one version of Matthew or Luke as compared to other versions akin to the "stark contrast to the bizarre picture of Jesus portrayed in the Gnostic Gospels."[22] However, as Holmes notes,

> In view of the circumstance that Romans certainly and other letters probably circulated independently prior to the formation of the corpus, the essential uniformity of the existing tradition is remarkable. This means that since the manuscript tradition began, the letters always have had the same form they now exhibit. (The one letter which does exist in multiple forms,

---

[21]   Ibid, 82, 87.

[22]   Richard G Howe. "The New Testament, Jesus Christ, and the Da Vinci Code," in *Reasons for Faith: Making a Case for the Christian Faith*, ed. Norman L. Geisler and Chad V. Meister (Wheaton, IL: Crossway Books, 2007), 277.

Romans, is the exception which proves the rule, since clear traces of later editorial activity are visible in the tradition.) Therefore any editorial activity, such as that proposed by partition or interpolation hypotheses, must have occurred prior to a letter's entrance into the textual tradition. *The burden of proof lies on those who suggest otherwise, and any proposal regarding post-publication textual alterations which is unsupported by evidence of disruption of the textual tradition is inherently implausible* (italics added).[23]

Another implication of multifocality of the transmission of the text can be expressed as follows:

First, wholesale *purposeful* corruption of the text would require a centralized controlling body or group to produce the consistent New Testament we see appearing in the historical record in the second century... wholesale changes to the entire manuscript tradition during this time would require a centralized controlling authority. If the largest portion of the copies could not be collected and edited simultaneously, with an authoritative recension then being produced and distributed, then we would have a widely divergent manuscript tradition appearing in the second century, not the united one we have today. The only way to explain the consistency of the historical manuscript tradition is to assume the existence of such a controlling body that could produce this harmony (italics original)[24]

Perhaps this point can be illustrated by the comparison of the New Testament's textual history with the history of the Qur'an. As evidenced from the Islamic sources, shortly after the text of the

---

[23] Michael W Holmes. "Textual Criticism," in *Dictionary of Paul and His Letters*, Gerald F. Hawthorne, Ralph P. Martin, and Daniel G. Reid, eds. (Downers Grove, IL: InterVarsity Press, 1993), 930.

[24] Ibid., 83.

Qur'an had been committed to writing it underwent a revision by the Caliph Uthman.[25] As White explains,

> The Uthmanic Revision places the Qur'an in a completely different classification than the New Testament. The latter had multiple smaller books by multiple authors from multiple locations, each starting out with its own transmission history, first brought together into smaller collections (like the Gospels or Pauline Epistles), and finally coming together as a single body in free, uncontrolled transmission. There is never a Christian Uthman, never a Zaid bin Thabit. *The Qur'an had one author (according to Islamic orthodoxy), one compilation, then two decades later, a revision, followed by the concerted central-government effort to destroy any competing textual form.* With revision and a controlled transmission, one would expect a much "cleaner," more unanimous text. Combine governmental propagation with the Qur'an being shorter than the New Testament and undergoing around six hundred years less time in pre-modern transcription, and the result should be obvious: a very stable text with few textual variants. And by and large, this is what we find with the Qur'an. Muslims see this as a great advantage, even an example of divine inspiration and preservation. In reality, just the opposite is the case.
>
> When a text has a major interruption in transmission—as with Uthman, his committee, and the effort to suppress competing versions—one's certainty of being able to obtain the original text becomes limited to the materials that escape the revisionist pen. For the Muslim, Uthman had to get it right, because if he was wrong, there is little hope of ever undoing his work... *So if Uthman was at all biased, at all influenced by*

---

25 F.L. Cross and Elizabeth A. Livingstone, eds., *The Oxford Dictionary of the Christian Church* (Oxford; New York: Oxford University Press, 2005), 940.

> *the debates and struggles of his times, the resulting
> text could be altered forever. And how would anyone
> know? This is the danger of a controlled transmission:
> You have to have ultimate trust in the controller. If
> there is any reason to distrust those who control the
> form and content, the resultant trust you can place
> in the text is commensurately reduced. . .* Unlike the
> New Testament, the Qur'an had no wide variety of
> freely reproduced texts from all over the Islamic state
> to draw upon to determine the earliest text. With every
> one of those early manuscripts destroyed at Uthman's
> command, the light dims on the original Qur'anic text.
> (italics added).[26]

Despite the fact that many critics of the Christian faith use
the history of the transmission of the text of the New Testament
as an argument against its reliability and, ultimately, its inerrancy,
a careful consideration of the facts yields a contrary conclusion.
Thousands of manuscripts and a relatively minuscule number of
variants contained in them serve only to bolster our confidence
in the text. As one of the foremost New Testament textual
scholars explains,

> The transmission of the New Testament textual
> tradition is characterized *by an extremely impressive
> degree of tenacity. Once a reading occurs it will per-
> sist with obstinacy.* It is precisely the overwhelming
> mass of the New Testament textual tradition, assuming
> the ὑγιαίνουσα διδασκαλία of New Testament textual
> criticism (we trust the reader will not be offended by
> this application of 1 Tim. 1:10), which provides an
> assurance of certainty in establishing the original text.[27]

---

[26] James R White. *What Every Christian Needs to Know About the Qur'an* (Minneapolis: Bethany House, 2013), 262-63.

[27] Aland, Kurt and Barbara. *The Text of the New Testament*, 291-92.

This means that one can conceive of New Testament textual criticism as a puzzle game that consists of 1000 pieces but has 1010 in the box. A skilled player can confidently eliminate the extra pieces or, as Daniel Wallace put it,

> ...when one looks at the Nestle-Aland Novum Testamentum Graece, he or she is looking at the original text—either in the text or in the apparatus. The argument, then, that inerrancy is an unsupportable doctrine because the autographs are gone is moot: we have the original somewhere on the page of the Greek New Testament.[28]

The history of the transmission of the text of the New Testament is a remarkable testimony of God's providential work of preserving His Word. The reliability of the New Testament should strengthen our commitment to biblical inerrancy.

---

[28] Wallace, "Textual Criticism."

THE INERRANCY OF SCRIPTURE AND BIBLICAL AUTHORITY IN EASTERN ORTHODOXY

by Alexey Kolomiytsev (US-Russian Language)

The doctrine of biblical inerrancy is directly related to the authority of Scripture. There is a significant difference in interpretation between those who hold to the doctrine of inerrancy and those who do not. Only an inerrant and infallible Scripture can be a source and a channel of God's authoritative revelation. Any other alternative will inevitably contaminate it with human authority. While God's authority is being subverted by man's autonomous reason and secular science in the Western world, the East has its own problems. This article focuses on one of the key areas of Eastern Orthodox mentality—its approach to authority in general and the authority of Scripture in particular. This mentality plays a fundamental role in the Eastern understanding of the inerrancy of Scripture.

The Church as a Source of Authority

The two largest Christian sects in the world, Roman Catholicism and Eastern Orthodox, are proponents of the idea that the Church is a significant authority in Christian faith and practice. Their theology is built upon the belief that the authority of God and His Word are tightly related to the authority of the Church. Both these churches view the body of Christ as an active participant in the process of communicating God's authoritative revelation. Rejecting the Protestant Reformation principle "*Sola Scriptura*," Roman Catholics and Eastern Orthodox believers make the Scripture dependent upon the Church for its origin and interpretation.

Theologians of both churches claim that for the first several centuries the Church existed in a situation where the canon was not established, and therefore, the Scripture in its entirety did not exist as the only source of authority.[1] This is being used to argue that the life of believers was directed by an authoritative source other than the Bible. Eastern Orthodox theologian Sergey Bulgakov writes, "The Church was able to exist in the best of her times without a written Word. In the same way, to a certain degree, it continues today in some of its circles."[2] Another well-known contemporary Russian Orthodox theologian, Andrey Kuraev, in his lecture *Conflict of Interpretations*, attacks the doctrine of inerrancy by pointing to textual difficulties of the Bible such as problems of translation, the late formation of the canon, claims that the Bible was not intended to be treated as a book, and precision in minute details. He argues that when the Bible was translated into different languages, translators had to change words to be faithful to the meaning of the text, and therefore, inerrancy and authority connected to the text are meaningless.[3] All of this evidence, according to Eastern Orthodox theologians, proves that the Bible was not written to be sufficient by itself. It needs an authoritative approval, and an interpreter which can be found only within the Orthodox Church.[4] Bulgakov goes even farther: "But the Bible, taken as a

---

[1] Андрей Кураев, Конфликт интерпретаций, *http://www.kuraev.ru/konflict.html* (1 Nov, 2004).

[2] Сергей Булгаков, Православие (Москва: Издательство АСТ, 2003), 41.

[3] Андрей Кураев, Конфликт интерпретаций, *http://www.kuraev.ru/konflict.html* (1 Nov, 2004).

[4] 4 Alexander Schmemann, "The Missionary Imperative in the Orthodox Tradition" in *Eastern Orthodox Theology. Contemporary Reader*, ed. by Daniel Clendenin, (Grand Rapids: Baker Books, 1995),197. The same claim is made by Bulgakov in, Булгаков, Православие, 3.

book, ceases to be the Bible, which it can become only in the Church."[5]

According to the Orthodox position, the Church as the body of Christ is filled with the Holy Spirit and actively cooperates with God, becoming the co-author of revelation, and therefore, sharer of God's ultimate authority. The authority of church tradition, such as church councils and church hierarchy, plays a major role in this approach. Both Roman Catholic and Orthodox churches have ways to introduce and legitimize new principles to biblical teaching. Sergey Bulgakov plainly states that the Orthodox Church does introduce new doctrinal rulings. The source of authority of such rulings, in his opinion, is in the Church and the Church's hierarchy. He writes, "Newly established doctrinal rulings after being accepted are protected by hierarchy."[6]

Both Roman Catholic and Eastern Orthodox churches believe that Scripture was established with the authority of the Church. While they claim that the authority of tradition cannot be opposed to the authority of Scripture, they often make statements about the primacy of tradition. Russian Orthodox theologian Vladimir Losskiy notes,

> This approach affirms the primacy of tradition over Scripture, since the oral transmission of the apostles' preaching preceded its recording in written form in the canon of the New Testament. It even might be said that the church could dispense with the Scriptures, but she could not exist without tradition.[7]

Additionally, Bulgakov agrees that the very existence of Scripture would not be possible without the Church: "The Holy Scriptures are given to us by the Church and in the Church."[8]

---

[5] Булгаков, Православие, 41

[6] Сергей Булгаков, *Православие* (М.: ООО «Издательство АСТ», 2003), 48.

[7] Vladimir Losskiy, "Tradition and Traditions" in *Eastern Orthodox Theology. A Contemporary Reader*. ed by Daniel B. Clendenin (Grand Rapids, Michigan: Baker Books, 1995), 128

[8] Ibid, 110.

Within this group, which generally accepts the high role of the church as a source of authority, there are several subgroups that view the authority of the church in different ways. For example, Roman Catholics, having been influenced by philosophical positions of Thomas Aquinas, see the expression of authority in a more rational way as being presented by the Pope, committees and other authoritative officials within the Church. Eastern Orthodoxy, on the other hand, is mystically oriented and claims that authority belongs to the Church body, meaning that it is expressed within and by the "collective conscience of the body of Christ."[9] This is called *sobornost*, which basically means that the truth is being generated, protected and interpreted in a mystical way by the Holy Spirit within the entire Church as a whole. Eastern Orthodox theologians believe that while Church councils can be mistaken at times, and Church hierarchy can misinterpret the Scripture or tradition, eventually the truth, which is being kept in a mystical way within the "collective conscience" of the Church body, will overcome wrong decisions and interpretations. Donald Fairbairn, a recent Western student of Eastern Orthodoxy, explains the difference between the Roman Catholic idea of the authority of the Church and that of Eastern Orthodoxy:

> In the Orthodox understanding, groups of bishops do not gather in a council in order to determine what is true; they gather to listen to the truth and to proclaim it. No council's decision is valid simply because a gathered group of bishops made that decision. Rather,

---

9. The word *sobornost* is a Russian translation of the Greek word kaqolikhn. The use of this term in Orthodox theology was popularized by famous anti-western Russian theologian, Alexey Khomyakov in 19th century. Since, during the last couple of centuries Russia had become a major player in the Eastern Orthodox world, the use of this term by Russian Orthodox theologians turned it into a technical term referring to the idea of collective agreement, or internal mystical unity within the body of the Church. Usually the term *sobornost* is used in the context when theologians refer to internal unity of all individual members of the Church with its saints, councils, traditions, etc. The Russian word *sobornost* comes from the word «собирать» (sobirat), which means, "to gather together." The Eastern Orthodox Church used this word to emphasize the inner mystical and lively connection, consensus and agreement between all Orthodox believers.

> the community of faith, the Church as a whole, accepts
> or rejects a decision of its bishops.[10]

Having studied Orthodoxy exhaustively, Fairbairn concludes that Orthodox believers view the very idea of authority differently. The Western idea of direct, positional, and individual authority is substituted in the East with shared, relational authority of the group. However, despite the fact that Orthodoxy places very little emphasis on authority, and despite the fact that this authority is of a different kind than authority in the Western sense of this term, there is still certain authority on which the Orthodox Church and Orthodox people practically function. In this case, the authority is some sort of collective religious experience. To a large degree, this difference is based not so much upon the theological positions, but more on the difference between the eastern and western mindset. While the western mind is able to achieve a rational understanding of all things, people in the east need to feel and experience before they accept validation. Archbishop Sergiy Starogorodskiy, in his book *Православное учение о спасении* (*Orthodox Doctrine of Salvation*), emphasizes that the validity of any worldview can and should be confirmed only by its practical results and not by theoretic reasoning. According to Starogorodskiy, life is the highest authority, which pronounces its approval or disapproval on any theological or philosophical system. He writes, "Life serves as the best tool for determining and clarifying man's real worldview, certain philosophical system as well as for the evaluation of this worldview."[11]

Speaking about the practical way of expressing this authority of the group, or *sobornost*, most often it comes to oral tradition and opinions that live within the church and exist around its people. In a practical way, the works of the church fathers,[12] or oral tradition,

---

[10] Donald Fairbairn, *Eastern Orthodoxy through Western Eyes* (Louisville: Westminster John Knox Press, 2002), 12.

[11] Архиепископ Сергий Старогородский, Православное учение о спасении. (Москва: Издательство «Просветитель», 1991), 4.

[12] When Orthodox priests and saints speak practically to parishioners on the issue of authority, they often regard the church fathers and councils as the final authority. Thus, Father Ioann, the Orthodox saint from Balaam Monastery in Northern Russia, who lived in late 19th and early 20th century, in his letter directly states this, "In Orthodoxy authority is in Church Fathers and Councils" http://www.ccel.org/contrib/ru/Letioann/Let7.htm 27 Nov. 2004.

take the place of functional authority.[13] Starogorodskiy regards oral tradition as a more accurate witness to real Christianity than any propositional statements about Christian doctrine.

> We know that Jesus Christ brought to us not just doctrine, and that ministry of apostles and the Church was not just in careful listening of Jesus' words in order to pass it along to the next generations: for this purpose some sort of stone tablets would serve better than oral tradition.[14]

It is true that Jesus Christ has not brought a dead letter of some sort of speculative teaching unrelated to real life. However, to say that the words of Jesus did not express the fullness of God's revelation to humanity, that there was something else which accompanied His words and constituted the reality of true Christianity, is to create several serious problems. First, such an approach directly contradicts the clear teaching of Scripture, which unapologetically states that God's written Word is the only sufficient source of authority for true Christian life (John 17:17; 2 Tim 3:16-17; 1 Pet 1:23-25;). Second, oral tradition that was generated by the church fathers also comes from written sources (which are not inspired and do not claim to be inspired as is the biblical text). This raises an obvious question: if certain things could not be written down by the Apostles of Christ early on, why did it become possible to write them down later by the church fathers? This is a significant flaw in the author's argument concerning the superiority of oral tradition in the process of determining correct theology.

Eastern Orthodoxy and Roman Catholicism have another common argument to prove the authority of the Church over the Scriptures. They claim that the Church was the one that established the canon. In other words, the Church was the authority that

---

[13] Although in these cases Orthodox theologians tend to speak about "limited authority," i.e. authority that is checked by the other forms of tradition, etc. An example of it can be seen in the article by George Florovskiy, "The Authority of the Ancient Councils and the Tradition of the Fathers" in *Eastern Orthodox Theology. Contemporary Reader* ed. by Daniel Clendenin (Grand Rapids: Baker Books, 1995), 115-124.

[14] Православное учение, 8.

validated certain books and disqualified others. This argument is also without ground. John Calvin, in his *Institutes of the Christian Religion*, spoke against such an idea with full force:

> Nothing, therefore, can be more absurd than the fiction that the power of judging Scripture is in the Church, and that on her nod its certainty depends. When the church receives it, and gives it the stamp of her authority, she does not make that authentic which was otherwise doubtful or controverted, but acknowledging it as the truth of God, she as in duty bound, shows her reverence by an unhesitating assent.[15]

Nowhere in Scripture is it said that the Church will have authority over the Word of God. To the contrary, there is clear testimony that God is the one who established His Word in heaven and takes care to preserve it on the earth (Ps. 119:89) All the Church does is recognize God's authoritative Word, and even this is done by the Holy Spirit, living in each true believer, and not by any kind of human authority. God gives His children the ability to understand and accept things that come from Him, and their work and responsibility is just to be faithful in receiving this authoritative revelation. R.C. Sproul elaborates on Calvin's view of the Church and canon by saying,

> The Church is indeed active in the historical process of canon formation. But the crucial point is that the church neither *creates or validates* the canon. The canon has prior authority and validity. What the church does in the historical process of canon development is to receive it, acknowledge it to be the truth of God, show reverence to it, and give *unhesitating assent* to it.[16]

---

[15] trans. Henry Beveridge, Vol - I. (Grand Rapids: Eerdmans, 1964), 69.

[16] R.C. Sproul, "Internal Testimony of the Holy Spirit" in *Inerrancy,* ed. by Norman Geisler (Grand Rapids: Zondervan, 1980), 339

It is clear that ecclesiastical authority in Eastern Orthodoxy as well as in Roman Catholicism comes down to their view of man and his role in the universe. Roman Catholic and Eastern Orthodox theologians express their belief in the greater role of man in the formative process of revelation. Man in this case has some authority, and actually all God's authority becomes dependent upon the authoritative interpretation of the Church (which is a certain group of men). In Orthodox theological writing, the phrase, "the church believes," is one of the most frequently used phrases.[17] Appeals to the authority of the Church greatly outnumber appeals to the Scripture in Orthodox texts. In a similar way, Catholicism holds its hierarchy and Pope as a practical final authority in their matters of faith and life. Cornelius Van Til described this problem in Roman Catholicism:

> The hierarchy of the church in general and of the Pope in particular is not to be thought of as itself subject to the final and comprehensive revelation of God. There is no place anywhere in the whole of Roman Catholic thought for the ideas that any human being should be wholly subject to God. On the contrary, the position of Rome requires the rejection of the counsel of God as all-determinative.[18]

God is the Only Source of Authority

The Bible presents God as the only absolute source of authority. Recognition of the unequivocal authority of God is vital to man's relationship with his Creator and the necessary condition for a successful and blessed life. This authority of God is the framework and structure without which true Christianity is not possible.

One of the fundamental problems of man's fall in the Garden of Eden was loss of the centrality of God as absolute authority. From

---

[17] One example of this can be seen in another work of Sergius Bulgakov, "The Virgin and Saints in Orthodoxy" in *Eastern Orthodox Theology. A Contemporary Reader,* ed. by Daniel Clendenin (Grand Rapids: Baker Books, 1995), 65-75.

[18] Cornelius Van Til, *The Defense of the Faith*. (Phillipsburg, NJ: Presbyterian and Reformed Publishing, 1955), 138.

the very first pages of the Bible, God presents the world based upon His unquestioned authority. The Lord's authority is so superior that He literally speaks the world into being (Gen 1). The Bible is clear that nothing in the world is comparable to the authority of God. Anyone or anything which has any level of authority has it only because God has allowed it (Rom 13). God delegated to man authority and dominion over the creatures of the earth (Gen 1:28).

The book of Job also points to God's complete authority over Satan (Job 1-2). Additionally, the Apostle Paul, in his epistle to the Romans, emphasizes that the absolute authority of God is the heart and beauty of the gospel:

> Oh, the depth of the riches both of the wisdom and knowledge of God! How unsearchable *are* His judgments and His ways past finding out! "For, who has known the mind of the LORD? Or who has become His counselor?" "Or who has first given to Him and it shall be repaid to him?" For of Him and through Him and to Him *are* all things, to whom *be* glory forever. Amen. (11:33-36).

The total authority of God is categorically the central point of a biblical worldview. Satan, in his approach to Eve in the Garden of Eden, precisely directed his attack on the absolute authority of God. His goal was to plant within the minds of God's first people the possibility that God might be wrong. This then would prompt them to take authority into their own hands. Van Til explains that Satan talked Eve into taking a look at things from an "independent position," which in reality was an attempt to make herself the final authority. Van Til describes this event:

> He said that she should be neutral with respect to his interpretation and God's interpretation of what would take place if she ate of the forbidden tree. Eve did ignore the question of being in answering the question of knowledge. She said she would gather the opinions of as many as she could find with a reputation for having knowledge and then give the various views

> presented a fair hearing . . . She denied God's Being as ultimate being. She affirmed therewith in effect that all being is essentially on one level . . . She said we know independently of God. She said that God's authority was to be tested by herself. Thus she came to take the place of ultimate authority. She was no doubt going to test God's authority by experience and reflection upon experience. Yet it would be she, herself, who should be the final authority.[19]

Adam and Eve fell when they attempted to make themselves an authority equal or comparable to the authority of God. Because of this, salvation is presented in the Bible as the restoration of God's absolute authority into man's worldview. In his presentation of the gospel to the Romans, Paul clearly and concisely states that all the problems of fallen humanity originate from its rejection of God's authority. He writes, "Because, although they knew God, they did not glorify *Him* as God, nor were thankful, but became futile in their thoughts, and their foolish hearts were darkened. Professing to be wise, they became fools" (Rom 1:21-22). Speaking to the Greek philosophers in Athens, Paul again points to the need of beginning with the recognition of God's absolute authority, and on the basis of that, he charged that they must reject their own ways and submit to God's lordship in repentance (Acts 17:24-31).

Recognition of the absolute authority of God is the foundational principle upon which theology must be built. Martin Lloyd-Jones, in discussing the theological problems of the contemporary church, emphasizes that one of the most significant problems is the attempt to reduce God's truth from an authoritative proposition to a mere personal experience. He cites the argument of those who advance this position:

"Just as you cannot analyze the aroma of a rose, so you cannot reduce their great and glorious truth to a number of statements and propositions. In other words, it is something which can only be experienced, something you can feel. You might dance to it.

---

[19]   Van Til, *Defense*, 34.

You might sing to it. But you cannot state it in propositions. You cannot define it." [20]

This is the precise position held by Russian Orthodoxy. Its central problem lies in the fact that it downplays the authority of God and mixes it with the authority of man's subjective experience. Orthodox theologian John Meyendorff defends this approach in more detail:

> Direct communion with God rather than external authority, sanctification rather than justification, personal experience rather than intellectual proof, consensus rather than passive obedience—these are some important Orthodox intuitions about the nature of the Christian faith.[21]

Unfortunately, this Eastern Orthodox view of the authority of God has been carried over into Russian evangelicalism in recent years. Being influenced by the Eastern mentality, Russian evangelicalism concentrates heavily upon the experiential side of the faith. This permits religious experience to define what is authoritative and what is not. Man and his personal experience in some way becomes a part of the revelation. With this as the benchmark, God's Word is regarded only as a source of inspiration and not the source of authority which demands absolute submission. The Baptist theologian from Moscow, Nikolay Kornilov, is one who advocates this approach. Speaking in Barthian terms, he insists that the Bible should be taken as a narrative that creates a certain experience for its readers: "In spite of the fact that the Bible does not belong to our reality, understanding it as a narrative or a story which enhances our imagination allows us access into a different world, a world in which we can experience the here and now."[22]

Eastern Orthodoxy does not view the fall of man in as radical terms as the Reformers. They do not believe that man is by nature a rebel against God and His authority. Rather, they consider man

---

[20] D. Martin Lloyd-Jones, *Authority* (Carlisle, PA: The Banner of Truth Trust, 1997), 9..

[21] John Meyendorff, "Doing Theology in an Eastern Orthodox Perspective" in *Eastern Orthodox Theology* ed. by Daniel Clendenin (Grand Rapids: Baker Books, 1995), 93.

[22] Корнилов, Какое Богословие нам нужно, 15.

to be essentially good; one who was merely duped by Satan. Being humanistic in nature, Orthodox theologians cannot agree with God's right to determine man's salvation. Such a position leads Sergiy Starogorodskiy to numerous unresolved questions:

> Indeed, if justifying grace is God's action within man which does not depend upon man, then how can one explain its existence in him? Why does God renew one and deny this mercy to another?. . .it makes it necessary to recognize that all people are undeserving of salvation and justification is exclusively God's work. . . But, in this case, why does God justify those and not these?[23]

The misunderstanding of God's justice displayed here by Starogorodskiy is, once again, rooted in a wrong understanding of the authority of God. <u>Man is viewed here as deserving good, and God is obligated to present a certain minimum of equal rights to all people.</u> In reality, this is an assault against the complete authority of God. Many contemporary Russian evangelicals approach the issue of salvation from exactly the same point of view. In one of his articles, Gennadiy Gololob argues for an Arminian theology by advancing the same idea, almost word for word in agreement with Starogorodskiy,

> Do all people deserve to be condemned to perish? If this is so, why is the Gospel call still directed to them? Arminian doctrine differentiates the level of guilt in different people. All people sin, but not equally. This gives God a basis upon which to express his mercy toward those who are able to condemn their behavior and turn to Him for help.[24]

---

[23] Старогородский, Православное учение, 43.

[24] Геннадий Гололоб, «Предопределяет ли Бог зло?» *Луч Евангелия* 8:117 (Август, 2004):4.

This position thrusts man's role and his authority into one of the most important areas of theology: soteriology. In their refusal to see man as utterly rebellious against God, and to believe that salvation is rooted in God's absolute authority, many Russian evangelicals lay the foundation for the human-centered theology in all its other aspects.

The Dangers of Mixing Human Authority with the Authority of God

The Bible says fallen man wages a war against God's authority. In different ways and forms, unredeemed man attempts to elevate himself instead of submitting to God. This problem becomes especially problematic and serious in the area of theology. Here humanistic authority often appears in disguise, not as directly opposing God, but rather as mixed with His authority. The root of such a problem lies in human pride and the desire to elevate personal opinions to the level of God's authority. Despite man's unceasing effort to elevate himself to a position of equality with God, in reality man does not become more authoritative. In the end, man is blinded, more deceived, and has further invoked the anger of a Holy God.

The more different religions, denominations and churches allow human authority into their theology, the more they become susceptible to the dangers of idolatry and its related issues. In his epistle to the Romans, Paul warned of the danger of human authority in religion:

> Because, although they knew God, they did not glorify *Him* as God, nor were thankful, but became futile in their thoughts, and their foolish hearts were darkened. Professing to be wise, they became fools, and changed the glory of the incorruptible God into an image made like corruptible man (Rom 1:21-23).

The result of an unwillingness to submit to God is that one becomes a fool while at the same time thinking of himself as wise. Later in this chapter, Paul states yet other consequences of spiritual pride,

> . . . who exchanged the truth of God for the lie, and worshiped and served the creature rather than the Creator, who is blessed forever. Amen. For this reason God gave them up to vile passions . . . And even as they did not like to retain God in *their* knowledge, God gave them over to a debased mind, to do those things which are not fitting. (Rom 1:25-26, 28).

God cannot tolerate any rivalry that challenges His absolute status and position in the universe. Since man does not have parity with God, it is impossible to mix the absolute authority of God with the assumed authority of man. If that fusion does occur, God's perfect authority ceases to be an authority at all. John Frame describes this in his critique of the Barthian attempts to integrate the authority of God with the authority of man:

> To Barth, the eminence of God implies that words of merely human authority, words which are fallible, may from time to time "become" the word of God. Thus the only authority we have, in the final analysis, is a fallible one. The only "word of God" we have is a fallible human word. God does not make authoritative demands which require unconditional belief; he does not determine the presuppositions of our thought; he does not resist all falsification—rather he endorses falsehood and sanctifies it.[25]

The exact same result occurs when Eastern Orthodox and Roman Catholic churches attempt to mix the authority of God with the authority of church tradition. Introducing the biblically unwarranted doctrine of *sobornost,* Eastern Orthodox theologians attempt to find ground to substantiate their inflated view of man.

---

[25] John M. Frame, "God and Biblical Languages: Transcendence and Immanence." In *God's Inerrant Word*, ed. J.W. Montgomery (Minneapolis, MN: Bethany Fellowship, 1974), 173.

As a result of such attempts, the church is elevated to a position of authority and the Bible is relegated to a position with little authority at all. Bulgakov in his book on Orthodoxy presents the Bible as a production of the church that is still being developed by church tradition:

> The Bible has neither an external system, nor an external completeness. While the canon of the Holy books has been closed by church decree, this completeness for the human eye is just external, which has the power of fact and not an internal self-evidence. The fullness of the Word of God is not in external closeness of its contours, which does not exist, but in its inner fullness, which it reveals in inseparable connection with the church tradition.[26]

As soon as the Bible is stripped of its status as the absolute and exclusive authority, the door is flung wide open to doctrinal errors of all kinds. Another chapter of Bulgakov's work reveals his stand on having dogmatic regulations within the church. He asks rhetorically: "Is it possible to have dogmatic regulations in the church if the church itself, as a pillar and foundation of the truth, is the foundation of all dogmatic regulations?"[27]

When attempts are made to mix the Word of God with the word of man, it is impossible to differentiate between the authoritative and non-authoritative part of the mix. Losing the clearly defined and direct connection between God's authority and the biblical text makes all moral demands of the Bible relative. Frame states:

> God's lordship, transcendence, demands unconditional belief in and obedience to the words of revelation; it *never* relativizes or softens the authority of these words . . . To obey God's word is to obey *Him*; to disobey God's word is to disobey *Him* . . . Dishonoring the divine is just as sinful as idolizing the creature.

---

[26] Булгаков, Православие, 38.

[27] Ibid, 124.

> The two are inseparable. To disobey God is to obey
> something less than God.[28]

Hiding behind the shadow of mystical *sobornost*, Eastern Orthodoxy elevates man to the level of authority, which belongs only to God. Instead of resting on the authoritative, inerrant Scriptures to determine what is good for any particular situation, the Orthodox Church turns to an expert, hierarch, or saint with his wisdom or mystical experience. This creates a dangerous trend: it makes the Bible relative in a practical sense. Eastern Orthodox theologians openly admit such relativity of the Bible.

If the inerrant Scriptures are not being held in a position of absolute authority, then people do not see the absolute necessity of obedience to it. Culture and various religions offer such authorities as a mystical "church," hierarchy and tradition, psychology, science, etc., but they cannot hold ground. People know that they are not real, and therefore they obey God's Word only to a certain degree. As a result of these things, it is incumbent upon the church of Jesus Christ to uphold the authority of the inerrant Scriptures to speak truth to our culture, to build up the Body of Christ, and to convert the lost.

---

[28] Frame, "God and Biblical Languages," 175.

SANCTIFIED BY TRUTH NOT ERROR: INERRANCY IN THE SPANISH-SPEAKING WORLD

By Josiah Grauman (US-Spanish Language)

The purpose of this article is to trace the unbreakable connection between inerrancy, expository preaching, and Christ-likeness. Believers will become most like Christ when they are exposed to every word of God's inerrant revelation. Specific examples and illustrations will be presented from the perspective of a missionary to the Spanish-speaking world.

God commands Christians to seek holiness in all areas of their lives (Heb 12:14). Yet only those who believe in inerrancy expose themselves to the full sanctifying power of every word in the Bible. If a certain word of Scripture is considered false, that word is removed from the Spirit's arsenal to transform the believer because the truth is what He uses to sanctify (John 17:17). In addition, when the truthfulness of one of God's words is called into question, man's wisdom in that area necessarily replaces the transforming power of God's Word. Finally, the link between inerrancy and sanctification can also be observed in the responsibilities of teachers and preachers. Since the goal of every biblical discipler is to "present everyone perfect in Christ" (Col 1:28), the only way this can be accomplished is by exposing disciples to every word of the entire counsel of God.

What is Inerrancy?

The doctrine of inerrancy teaches that every word of Scripture, when interpreted correctly, is absolutely truthful. This simple definition is attacked at many different levels. Perhaps the easiest way to defend inerrancy on every front is to ground it into a robust, biblical understanding of inspiration. Many erroneously believe that God "inspired" human authors to write Scripture, but that human errors slipped in between God's "inspiration" of the author and the actual words that were written down. This is biblically impossible, since God places inspiration not only at the level of authorship (2 Pet 2:20-21), but also on the text itself. The apostle Paul writes, "All Scripture is breathed out by God" (2 Tim 3:16), not "All biblical authors were inspired by God." Therefore, every word of Scripture is just as "inspired" as the Ten Commandments—every word was directly authored by God. Since every word was directly authored by God, without human interference (2 Pet 1:20-21), any error would necessarily constitute a divine lie. God knew the truth; thus, any error would signify that He misrepresented that truth, which is impossible (Heb 6:18).

At the same time, it must be noted that inerrancy does not negate the human author's will, style, or vocabulary. For example, Paul wrote to a church because he had the desire to exhort and encourage them, and he did so with his own passion and terminology. Inerrantists do not dispute this. Rather, they insist that God superintended both the desire and writing of Paul that the end product—the words themselves—ended up exactly as God wanted to write them. The text could not be more "breathed out by God" even if God Himself had etched the words in stone. Therefore, it can be said that Scripture's words are one hundred percent divine and one hundred percent human.

Other biblical truths illustrate this same paradox. For example, the doctrine of the hypostatic union teaches that Jesus' deity never negated His humanity—nor did His humanity negate His deity. He was completely divine and completely human. In the same way, the divine nature of Scripture never negated the human authors' own will. God did not normally dictate to the biblical authors. Nor does the human nature of Scripture introduce error, negating the

Divine author's will. Another example relates to salvation. The Christian is responsible for deciding to believe the gospel from his own will (John 3:16-18). Yet when he/she believes, God insists that it is He who initiated (John 6:44; 1 John 4:19), both electing and regenerating the dead sinner (Eph 1:3-14). Finally, sanctification also illustrates a paradox. For example, if a believer decides to pray, it can be legitimately said that this desire came from the believer's will. It is one hundred percent human. Yet it is also one hundred percent divine because God is the one who accomplished both the desire to pray and the act of praying (Phil 2:13). Thus, God receives all the glory from the believer's obedience, because He is the one who worked both in and through the believer to fulfill His good purpose (Eph 2:10).

How is Inerrancy Attacked in the Spanish-Speaking World?

The doctrine of inerrancy is attacked when the truthfulness of any word of Scripture is considered false. It must also be noted that the inerrancy of Scripture is eroded when any word is considered less relevant today than it was when it was written. This devious way of denying inerrancy allows someone to outwardly claim that the Bible is inerrant while undermining its truth by elevating man's authority to the level of God's authority. In other words, if one claims that Paul's words were truthful 2,000 years ago, yet modern psychology demonstrates that his words are not as relevant today, those words are effectively eliminated from Scripture and human wisdom added in its place.

Macroevolution, the erroneous theory that man evolved from other species, is taught pervasively as truth in Latin-America, especially by the increasingly influential Argentinian Pope.[1] It is no surprise that its errors have crept into the Church. A literal understanding of six-day creation as narrated in Genesis 1 is often denied under the pretext that Moses did not understand modern science. This is devastating to the human conscience for a number

---

[1]   http://www.usatoday.com/story/news/world/2014/10/28/pope-francis-evolution-big-bang/18053509/

of reasons. First, the creature's sense of direct accountability to the One who made him is eroded. Second, the truth of Scripture is replaced with a lie, and lies do not sanctify. Third, the confidence in the rest of Scripture is diminished, since it contains words pertaining to both science and salvation.

If Genesis does not describe a real Adam who sinned (Gen 3) and brought a curse upon the earth, why should anyone believe that the second Adam really brought salvation to the earth? Paul presents Adam as a person just as real as Jesus in Romans 5:12–21. In fact, Romans 5:12 is especially fatal to the theistic evolutionary lie, because Paul explains that death only entered into the world after Adam sinned. If a single animal died in any evolutionary process before the Fall, then God would be the author of sin's consequences and the Christian faith a lie. Thanks be to God, though death came to all[2] born in Adam, salvation came to all born in Christ.

Worldly psychology is also a major enemy of inerrancy. Unfortunately, it is also taught extensively throughout Latin-America, even inside the evangelical church.[3] Worldly psychology is the lie that God's revelation is insufficient to care for the soul of man. The question revolves around the source of truth. Should the believer's life be lived in strict obedience to every word of God, which is true and sufficient for everything needed for life and godliness (2 Pet 1:3), or is the Scripture imperfect and in need of man's wisdom to provide him with the care his soul needs?

The Bible speaks to every one of man's needs. Those claims are either true or false. However, many run to psychology for help with sins like depression, eradicating their guilt and pain through medication and self-inflating words of human wisdom (self-esteem). These methods are sufficient only to sear the conscience and send a person to hell, not to save. In fact, if a pastor teaches a congregant how to deal with guilt apart from the cross, all is primed to be lost. Believers should not love themselves, thinking they are very important (as psychology would teach), but rather should

---

[2] Paul makes clear that death came only to those born in Adam after the Fall (Rom 5:17). If more humans were alive parallel to Adam, as many evolutionists claim, those humans would not have inherited Adam's fallen nature and not deserve death (Rom 6:23).

[3] http://iglesiametodistaarroyito.blogspot.com/p/recursos.html

love Christ, finding their worth in their own self-crucifixion so that Christ might live in them (Gal 2:20; Col 3:5).

In both evolution and psychology, the connection between a denial of inerrancy and the detriment to sanctification is notable. Once a person determines that the Bible contains errors of history, science or medicine, he/she necessarily begins to look to human wisdom instead of Scripture as the source of help and guidance. This has a serious effect upon sanctification, since sanctification is accomplished through the truth of Scripture, not the proposed truth of man.

The most predominant movement in Latin-American evangelicalism today could probably be described as a mystical search for an "encounter" with the Holy Spirit and His power.[4] The Holy Spirit is indeed powerful and believers certainly experience His work (1 Cor 2:9-16; Eph 1:13; Tit 3:5). Nevertheless, the question is whether the Holy Spirit exercises His power and speaks to the believer exclusively through His Word, as the Bible teaches, or whether He is to be experienced mystically. Said a different way, are the words of Scripture enough for believers, or should they seek something else? Sadly, many Latin-Americans look for unction, direction, and transformation from the Holy Spirit, but apart from His inerrant Word.

In their quest to "experience" the power of the Spirit, Latin-Americans often consider external signs and miracles as the pinnacle of the Christian faith. Unfortunately, even if the Holy Spirit was still working the same sort of miracles as He did through Jesus, the unbelieving masses would be healed and fed only to use their strengthened bodies to crucify their Healer, just as they did in Jesus' day. Man is an open tomb, spewing out his uncleanness at every level. The end goal is not for physical healing or spiritual encounters, but rather for full scale spiritual transformation.

In addition, external "encounters" with the Spirit's power, even if they were happening, would not be powerful enough to change man from the inside out. Jesus highlighted this very truth in the parable of the rich man and Lazarus. The rich man was convinced that if his family experienced a real resurrection from the dead,

---

4   Ministerios Cash Luna, http://www.cashluna.org/templates20/print.cfm?id=347

they would surely repent and be saved. Christ negated that claim by explaining that only hearing the words of Moses and the prophets could change the hearts of the rich man's family (Luke 16:31). The irony cannot be missed. Jesus cites the words of Moses as the solution, the very man whom modern critics claim was not wise enough to understand history and science!

These "encounters" may sound benign and non-offensive to biblical inerrancy, but they are not. In fact, since the "encounters" often contradict the truths of Scripture, those who seek them are necessarily put in the position of deciding whether it is their mystical experience or Scripture that is true. It is sad to say that the inerrancy of the Spirit's inspired truth is often sidelined under the pretext that the Spirit directed in a different way.

Another related area where inerrancy is attacked in Latin America is in the rise of personal prophecies.[5] Though many see these personal prophecies as a new outworking of the Holy Spirit not seen in ages past, the desire to hear and experience something "new" is, in fact, very old. Luke recorded that the Athenians "would spend their time in nothing except telling or hearing something new." They did not heed the words of Solomon, who wrote "there is nothing new under the sun" (Ecc 1:9). Instead of seeking something new, they ought to "fear God and keep his commandments, for this is the whole duty of man" (Ecc 12:13). Instead of seeking something new, man should diligently keep every word of God's commandments. They alone are everything the believer needs (Ps 19:7-9).

When the Scriptures are seen as old, containing obsolete information on history and science, a sinful desire for new and fresh "truth" naturally arises. In Latin-America, this has led to the unhealthy practice of seeking personal prophecy. The Scriptures are seen as general and basic truths that lead the believer to salvation; however, for daily life, personal prophecy is needed. In fact, one of the largest Spanish-speaking churches in Los Angeles says this in their doctrinal statement: "We believe that the Bible contains the word of God. . . it is the basics of what men need in this

---

[5]   http://coalicionapostolica.blog.com/files/2011/01/4-c%c3%93mo-responder-a-la-pro-fec%c3%8da-personal.pdf

generation."[6] However, the Bible does not simply contain the word of God; it *is* the word of God. If Scripture is just the basics, then the door is wide open for adding human prophecy to it. Scripture is not, however, just the basics; it is everything. And since it is sufficient and inerrant, personal prophecy is not an innocuous addition, but a replacement of divine truth.

Once a single word of Scripture is judged as outdated or false, God's words are reduced to merely helpful prophecies. Such a view puts Scripture on the same level as modern-day charlatans. These supposed apostles and prophets then profit from the promulgation of their own personal prophecies, which, in their estimation, are not old and stale like Scripture, but more living and active—as if that were possible! Only when Scripture is understood to be inerrant can it become the sole source and judge of all truth. Once a single error is found, it can no longer be the plumb line by which any other supposed prophecy can be judged. Consequently, modern-day false apostles and false prophets flourish among non-inerrantists, because only the pure and perfect truth can cast out error.

Although the proponents of personal prophecy may claim that the Bible is inerrant, their prophecies often contain material which contradicts the Scriptures. Thus, they are forced to either admit that their prophecies are false or deny the inerrancy of the Bible. All too often, the latter becomes reality.

A final example is seen in the heresy of the Oneness Pentecostal movement, a rapidly growing force among Spanish speakers.[7] Oneness Pentecostalism is, at heart, a modalistic heresy that denies the three persons of the Trinity, the dual natures of Christ, and other essential doctrines. The pride of man loves to limit the paradoxes of Scripture and bring God down to human comprehension (Psalm 50:21). This is another way to deny inerrancy, as its proponents claim that certain texts are true, such as the ones that affirm that God is one. However, they refuse to embrace the truth of texts they believe to be contrary, such as the ones that affirm the deity of Father, Son, and Spirit. In summary, if human logic goes against

---

[6]   http://www.llamadafinal.com/ministerio/credo.html, translation mine).

[7]   http://www.pentecostalesdelnombre.com; http://www.iafcj.org

Scripture, God's words are judged false and man places himself on the judge's seat.

What is Sanctification?

Sanctification refers to the setting apart of a believer for the purpose of being transformed into the image of Christ. God has sanctified believers positionally; they are set apart for Christ (1 Cor 1:2). He also promises to fully sanctify them in the future; they will be Christ-like in heaven, having their sin completely eradicated (1 Thess. 3:13; Rom 8:29). In the meantime, He also promises to progressively transform all believers into the image of His Son (2 Cor 3:18). This process of transformation is accomplished by the Holy Spirit through the application of His Word (John 17:17). Progressive sanctification then occurs as believers renew their minds (Rom 12:2) through the truth that God has revealed.

It must be emphasized that progressive sanctification is dependent upon the believer's exposure to truth. Paul clearly explains in 2 Corinthians 3:18 that believers are transformed from one degree of glory to another as they behold the glory of the Lord. Thus, believers are progressively transformed after the glory they observe. Like Moses at Sinai, the more Christians gaze upon Christ, the more their own lives reflect His glory.

Therefore, if a believer does not behold and meditate upon a certain facet of God's glory, the Holy Spirit will do little transformation in that area. For example, if a believer meditated for years upon the glory of God's love, there is no doubt that the Holy Spirit would make that believer more loving. But this also applies in reverse. If a believer never took time to meditate upon the justice of God, that area of their character would be affected negatively.

When Adam and Eve sinned in the garden, the image of God created was shattered to the point of being nearly unrecognizable (Cf. Gen 1:26 with Gen 5:3, but also James 3:9). The work of the Spirit in sanctification is not just to repair the image believers lost at the Fall, but to surpass it. The Spirit makes them even more Christ-like than Adam was in the garden, since they are exposed to salvation truths that not he, nor even angels, could have comprehended (1 Pet 1:12). The responsibility, then, is clear: Believers must seek after the full image of Christ so that they can be fully transformed into His image.

John explains in 1 John 3:2 that one day the Spirit will completely eradicate sin in believers' lives and make them like Christ. What is important to understand is how and why this will be the case. Fortunately, John does not leave this up to the reader's imagination. He explicitly states, "We shall be like him, because we shall see him as he is" (1 John 3:2b). One day the Christian will see Christ fully, and in that day, the Spirit will finish the work, because sanctification is linked with seeing God's glory. Therefore, until that day, it should be the desire of every follower of Christ to study His image as much as possible, gazing upon every one of His perfections with detail and determination so that they may be transformed as much like Him as possible.

How Does Inerrancy Affect a Believer's Sanctification?

Believers must work and labor according to the methods by which the Holy Spirit has promised to sanctify them. There can be no doubt that the Holy Spirit sanctifies Christians with the sword of His Word. What is unfortunate is how many believers deliberately avoid some of the sharpest edges of that sword.

The believer can be compared to an incomplete sculpture, being carved and shaped after the image of a living being, Christ Himself. If certain parts of His image are seen to be insignificant or false and are then covered up, the sculpture will not end up exactly as is intended. Unfortunately, non-inerrantists conceal certain parts of the revelation of Christ (the parts they believe contain errors). This is pride at its worse. It is tantamount to the fallen creature thinking that he has a better idea of what Christ looks like than Christ Himself. Non-inerrantists have fashioned an idolatrous image of Christ in their minds by altering the glorious image of Christ codified in Scripture.

Therefore, inerrancy affects sanctification because man becomes the judge concerning which portions of Scripture are true and which are false. As a failed judge, he necessarily denigrates the perfect pattern that God is using to sanctify the believer. God explicitly states that "All Scripture is breathed out by God and profitable. . . that the man of God may be complete" (2 Tim 3:16-17). Once inerrancy is denied, the man of God will be less complete, since Scripture is no longer deemed profitable in its entirety.

Furthermore, as has been observed above, when a certain portion of Scripture is considered false, the non-inerrantist necessarily replaces the truth of Scripture with a "truth" of his own, such as evolution, psychology, or any other worldly philosophy. Scripture is clear that Christians must trust in Christ alone (Col 2:8-23). By denying a truth of Scripture, the non-inerrantist not only subtracts from the image of Christ, but also adds heretical lies to that image, distorting and degrading His image, making it more like fallen man. Sadly, this subverts the sanctification process; sin's lies have no positive transforming power.

How Does Inerrancy Affect Preaching and Sanctification?

If a preacher does not trust a certain part of the Bible as true, it follows that he will not preach that portion with urgency and authority. This leads to sermons that contain parts of God's revelation (the parts the preacher deems truthful), instead of the whole counsel of God. Unfortunately, if only a portion of the truth is proclaimed, the Church will only be partially sanctified.

In addition to the necessity of preaching the entire truth of Scripture, the preacher must also confront the lies that attempt to replace it. The perfection of God's revelation must be preserved by teaching every truth contained therein, and in confronting any lie that could undermine its sanctifying power (Tit 1:9). This is a war, and one that must be waged diligently (2 Cor 10:3-6).

In Acts 20:26, Paul stood before the Ephesian elders and proclaimed, "I am innocent of the blood of all." His conscience was clear. The question is: How could he possibly reach such a blessed condition? Verse 27 explains his reason: "for I did not shrink from declaring to you the whole counsel of God" (Acts 20:27). What a challenge to the preacher! Could a non-inerrantist dare to speak such words? Could his conscience possibly find peace, having deliberately withheld certain words from God's people? May it never be! And may every preacher seek to stand before God, innocent of the blood of men, having sought to proclaim every word of the whole counsel of God so that every one of his hearers might be fully conformed after His perfect revelation.

Believers should long to become more like Christ in every way possible, understanding that God is glorified when they become more like His Son. There is no other image more beautiful or desirous than that of Christ. Believers also understand that they worship and exalt Christ when they esteem His image and work to follow His example. Therefore, believers ought to hate their sin and seek to eradicate any part of their being that does not reflect Christ's image. Using the illustration of a sculpture once again, if believers look at their own lives and observe that they have an extra piece of clay where Christ has none, they gladly pick up the knife to cut it off.

Believers have much sin in their lives to eradicate. The question the non-inerrantist must answer is: Why would someone be unwilling to wield the entire Sword of the Spirit in their fight against sin? What possible motivation would drive a believer to keep some of the sword from being exposed? What incentive would they have to replace the sharp steel of God's truth with the ineffective rubber of man's supposed wisdom, which has no value in stopping the indulgence of the flesh (Col 2:23)? Do they love themselves that much? If believers truly hate their sin and genuinely desire to be like Christ, would they not want the sharpest blade possible—the one that God fashioned Himself? The only answer that presents itself is that non-inerrantists love their pride too much and are unwilling to beg God to unsheathe His entire sword and cut it out.

The Scripture is a scalpel, perfectly sharp and exact in accomplishing its purposes. To alter or change a single word would be to dull its edge, diminishing its sanctifying effect. Those who long for God's glory through the sanctification of the body of Christ ought to relentlessly fight to keep God's word pure, knowing that only beholding the whole revelation of Christ's image will allow them to be transformed into the image they so love.

(*AMEN!*)

BIBLIOGRAPHY

Albania

Abdul-Haqq, Abdiyah Akbar. *Sharing Your Faith with a Muslim*. Minneapolis: Bethany House Publishers, 1980.

"Answering Islam – a Christian-Muslim Dialog and Apologetic." http://www. answering-islam.org/ (23 Feb. 2008).

Barbieri, Louis A., Jr. "Matthew." In *The Bible Knowledge Commentary: An Exposition of the Scriptures by Dallas Seminary Faculty, New Testament*. Edited by John F. Walvoord and Roy B. Zuck. Wheaton: Victor Books, 1985.

Barrick, William D. "Ancient Manuscripts and Biblical Exposition." *The Master's Seminary Journal* 9/1 (Spring 1998): 25-38.

"The Bible: What They Didn't Tell You." http://www.islamnewsroom.com/ content/view/292/52/ (08 Apr. 2008).

Blomberg, Craig L. *Matthew*. New American Commentary. Volume 22. Edited by David S. Dockery. Nashville: Broadman Press, 1992.

Combs, William W. "The Preservation of Scripture." *Detroit Baptist Seminary Journal* 5 (Fall 2000): 3-44.

"Contradictions and Proofs of Historical Corruptions in the Bible." http:// www.quransearch.com/contra.htm (23 Feb. 2008).

Deedat, Ahmed. "Is the Bible God's Word?" In *The Last Great Frontier: Essays on Evangelism*. Compiled by Phil Parshall. Philippines: Open Doors, 2000.

Deedat, Ahmed. "Is the Bible God's Word?" http://www.jamaat.net/bible/ Bible7-9.html (08 Apr. 2008).

Erickson, Millard J. *Christian Theology*. Grand Rapids: Baker Book House, 1993.

Estes, Yusuf and Gary Miller. "Bible Islam: Bible Compared to Quran." http://www.bibleislam.com/bible_vs_quran.php (07 Apr. 2008).

"Faqe Islamike Shqiptare." http://www.geocities.com/Athens/Delphi/6875/libra.html (01 Apr. 2008).

Geisler, Norman L. *Christian Apologetics*. Grand Rapids: Baker Book House, 1976.

———. *Systematic Theology*. 4 Volumes. Minneapolis: Bethany House, 2002.

———, ed. *Inerrancy*. Grand Rapids: Zondervan, 1980.

Geisler, Norman L, and William E. Nix. *A General Introduction to the Bible*. Revised and expanded. Chicago: Moody Press, 1986.

Gilchrist, John. "Christian Witness to the Muslim." *In The World of Islam: Resources for Understanding*. CD-ROM.

"Glorious Islam: Ask Yourself." http://www.muslimtents.com/gloriousislam/english.htm (09 Apr. 2008).

Grudem, Wayne. *Systematic Theology: An Introduction to Biblical Doctrine*. Grand Rapids: Zondervan, 1994.

"Islam in Albania – Albania: Freedom Undiscovered." http://members.tripod.com/worldupdates/islamintheworld/id22.htm (05 Apr. 2008).

"Islam and Christianity: A Comparative Analysis." http://www.jamaat.net/deedat.htm (12 Apr. 2008).

"Islam News Room." http://www.islamnewsroom.com/ (23 Feb. 2008).

Kateregga, Badru D. and David W. Shenk. "A Muslim and a Christian in Dialogue." *In The World of Islam: Resources for Understanding*. CD-ROM.

Lewis, Gordon R., and Bruce A. Demarest. *Integrative Theology*. Volume 1. Grand Rapids: Zondervan, 1996.

"Leximi i Biblave." http://www.albislam.com/pdf/albislam28.pdf (02 Apr. 2008).

"The Lie of 1 John 5:7." http://www.answering-christianity.com/1john5_7.htm (01 Apr. 2008).

Lightfoot, Neil R. *How We Got the Bible*. 3rd ed. Revised and expanded. Grand Rapids: Baker Books, 2003.

MacArthur, John. *Matthew*. The MacArthur New Testament Commentary. Chicago: Moody Press, 1989.

Mark, Brother. *A Perfect Qur'an*. n.p.: n.p., 2000.

Marmaduke Pickthall, Mohammed. *The Meaning of the Glorious Koran: An Explanatory Translation*. New York: Mentor and Penguin Books, n.d.

McDowell, Josh. *Evidence that Demands a Verdict: Historical Evidences for the Christian Faith.* Volume 1. San Bernardino, CA: Here's Life Publishers, 1979.

"Mere Islam." http://www.mereislam.info/ (23 Feb. 2008).

Morris, Henry M. *Many Infallible Proofs: Practical and Useful Evidences of Christianity.* El Cajon, CA: Master Books, 1974.

"Muslim-Answers.org." http://www.muslim-answers.org/ (23 Feb. 2008).

"The Quran Miracles Encyclopedia." http://www.55a.net/firas/english/ (07 Apr. 2008).

Unger, Merrill F. "The Inspiration of the Old Testament." *Bibliotheca Sacra* 107 (October 1950): 430-49.

U.S. Department of State. "Albania: International Religious Freedom Report." http://www.state.gov/g/drl/rls/irf/2005/51536.htm (05 Apr. 2008).

Wickwire, Daniel. *101 Questions About the Bible and the Qur'an.* Ankara: ABC Matbaacilik, 2002.

Zebiri, Kate. *Muslims and Christians Face to Face.* Oxford: Oneworld, 1997.

Croatia

Hyde, Daniel R. *God in Our Midst: The Tabernacle and Our Relationship with God.* Orlando: Reformation Trust, 2012.

Kaiser, Walter C. Jr. *Preaching and Teaching from the Old Testament.* Grand Rapids: Baker Academic, 2003.

Lawson, Steven J. "The Sufficiency of Scripture in Expository Preaching." *Expositor Magazine* 01. Dallas: OnePassion Ministries, 2014.

McCune, Rolland D. "The Doctrine of Scripture." In *A Systematic Theology of Biblical Christianity.*

Volume 1. Detroit: Detroit Baptist Theological Studies, 2005.

Maier, Gerhard. "Biblical Hermeneutics." Translated by Robert W. Yarbrough. Wheaton: Crossway Books, 1994.

Noll, Mark A. "Pietism." In *Evangelical Dictionary of Theology.* Edited by Walter A. Elwell. Grand Rapids: Baker Academic, 2006.

Zemek, George J. *Doing God's Business God's Way.* Grand Rapids: Wipf and Stock, 2004.

Czech Republic

"Ateismus po Česku." Ta naše povaha česká. Česká Televize: 2008. http://www.ceskatelevize.cz/porady/1100627928-ta-nase-povaha-ceska/308295350270004-ateismus-pocesku

Hitchens, Christopher and Doug Wilson. *Is Christianity Good for the World?* Moscow, ID: Canon Press, 2008.

Král, Jiří. "Ekumena mezi protestanty a katolíky – nejde to!" http://www.reformace.cz/zod/ekumena-mezi-protestanty-katoliky-nejde-cislo-121 (accessed November 11 2014).

MacArthur, John. "Preaching the Book God Wrote, Part 1." http://www.gty.org/Resources/Print/articles/4825 (accessed November 28, 2014).

Mohler, Albert. *Atheism Remix: A Christian Confronts the New Atheists.* Wheaton: Crossway, 2008.

Nash, Ronald. *Worldviews in Conflict: Choosing Christianity in the World of Ideas.* Grand Rapids: Zondervan, 1992.

Nespor, Zdeněk. *Religious Processes in Contemporary Czech Society.* Prague: Institute of Sociology, 2004.

Novak, David. "Ekumena mezi protestanty a katolíky – jde to?." http://www.krestandnes.cz/article/david-novak-ekumena-mezi-protestanty-a--katoliky-jde-to/22924.htm (accessed November 11, 2014).

Palmer, Jason. "Religion May Become Extinct in Nine Nations, Study Says." BBC News, March 21, 2011. http://www.bbc.com/news/science-environment-12811197 (accessed November 11, 2014).

"Population by Religious Belief and by Municipality." 2011. http://www.czso.cz/sldb2011/eng/redakce.nsf/i/tab_7_1_population_by_religious_belief_and_by_ municipality_size_groups/$File/PVCR071_ENG.pdf (accessed November 11, 2014).

Projekt Zet. "Basic Information About Evangelical Churches in the Czech Republic." http://projektzet.cz/en/resources/research/research/Research.pdf (accessed November 13, 2014).

Sánchez, José Mariano. Anticlericalism: A Brief History. Notre Dame: University of Notre Dame Press, 1972.

Sproul, R. C. *If There's a God Why Are There Atheists?* Orlando: Ligonier Ministries, 1997.

"The Chicago Statement on Biblical Inerrancy." http://library.dts.edu/Pages/TL/Special/ICBI_1.pdf (accessed November 11, 2014).

Ziebert, Hans G., and Ulrich Riegel. *How Teachers in Europe Teach Religion.* Munster: LIT Verlag, 2009.

Germany

Archer, Gleason Leonard. *A Survey of Old Testament Introduction.* Updated and revised. Chicago: Moody Press, 1994.

Armerding, Carl Edwin. *The Old Testament and Criticism*. Grand Rapids: Eerdmans Pub. Co, 1983.

Ascol, Tom. "Systematic Theology and Preaching." *The Founders Journal* 4 (Spring 1991): 5-9.

Barton, John. *The Nature of Biblical Criticism*. 1st ed. Louisville: Westminster John Knox Press, 2007.

Friedman, Richard Elliot and H. G. M. Williamson, eds. *The Future of Biblical Studies: The Hebrew Scriptures*. Atlanta, GA: Scholars Press, 1987.

Couch, Mal, ed. *An Introduction to Classical Evangelical Hemeneutics: A Guide to the History and Practice of Biblical Interpretation*. Grand Rapids: Kregel Publications, 2000.

―――. *The Fundamentals for the Twenty-First Century: Examining the Crucial Issues of the Christian Faith*. Grand Rapids: Kregel Publications, 2000.

Davidson, Samuel. *An Introduction to the Old Testament: Critical, Historical and Theological, Containing a Discussion of the Most Important Questions Belonging to the Several Books*. Edinburgh: Williams and Norgate, 1862.

Enns, Paul. *The Moody Handbook of Theology*. Chicago: Moody Press, 1989.

Free, Joseph P. "Archeology and Biblical Criticism. Archeology and Higher Criticism." *Bibliotheca Sacra* 114, no. 453 (January 1957): 23-39.

―――. "Archeology and Biblical Criticism. Archeology and Liberalism." *Bibliotheca Sacra* 113, no. 452 (October 1956): 322-338.

―――. "Archeology and Biblical Criticism. [1], Archeology and Neo-Orthodoxy." *Bibliotheca Sacra* 114, no. 454 (April 1957): 123-132.

Geisler, Norman L. *A General Introduction to the Bible*. Edited by William E Nix. Revised and expanded. Chicago: Moody Press, 1986.

Gray, Edward Dundas McQueen. *Old Testament Criticism: Its Rise and Progress from the Second Century to the End of the Eighteenth. A Historical Sketch*. 1st ed. New York: Harper, 1923.

Grier, James M. "The Apologetical Value of the Self-Witness of Scripture." *Grace Theological Journal* 1, no. 1 (Spring 1980): 71-76.

Harrington, Daniel J. "Biblical Hermeneutics in Recent Discussion: New Testament." *Religious Study Review* 10, no. 1 (January 1984): 7-10.

Hayes, John Haralson. *An Introduction to Old Testament Study*. Nashville: Abingdon, 1979.

Hoffecker, W. Andrew, ed. *Revolutions in Worldview: Understanding the Flow of Western Thought*. Phillipsburg, NJ: P&R Pub, 2007.

Horton, David, ed. *The Portable Seminary*. Minneapolis: Bethany House, 2006.

Johnson, Alan F. "The Historical-Critical Method: Egyptian Gold or Pagan Precipice." *Journal of the Evangelical Theological Society* 26, no. 1 (1983): 3-15.

Kaiser, Walter C. *Toward Rediscovering the Old Testament*. Grand Rapids: Zondervan, 1987.

Kaiser, Walter C., and Ronald Youngblood, eds. *A Tribute to Gleason Archer*. Chicago: Moody Press, 1986.

Linnemann, Eta. *Historical Criticism of the Bible: Methodology or Ideology?* Grand Rapids: Baker Book House, 1990.

Maier, Gerhard. *The End of the Historical-Critical Method*. Eugene, OR: Wipf and Stock Pub, 2001.

McCune, Rolland D. "The Formation of the New Evangelicalism: Historical and Theological Antecedents." *Detroit Baptist Seminary* 3 (Fall 1998): 3-34.

————. "The Formation of the New Evangelicalism: Historical and Theological Antecedents." *Detroit Baptist Seminary* 4 (1999): 109-150.

Möller, Wilhelm. *Are the Critics Right? Historical & Critical Considerations Against the Grof-Wellhausen Hypothesis*. 2nd ed. London: The Religious Tract Society, 1903.

Soulen, Richard N. *Handbook of Biblical Criticism*. 3rd ed. Louisville: Westminster John Knox Press, 2001.

Stearns, Miner Brodhead. "Biblical Archaeology and the Higher Criticism." *Bibliotheca Sacra* 96, no. 383 (Fall 1939): 307-318.

Traina, Robert A. *Methodical Bible Study*: A New Approach to Hermeneutics. Ridgefield Park, NJ: [distributed by] Biblical Seminary in New York, 1952.

Walker, Larry L. "Some Results and Reversals of the Higher Criticism of the Old Testament." *Criswell Theological Review* 1 (Spring 1987): 281-294.

Honduras

Boomsma, Clarence. *Male and Female, One in Christ: New Testament Teaching On Women in Office*. Grand Rapids: Baker Books, 1993. 2013 iBook edition for iPhone.

"Egalitarianism." *Theopedia*. http://www.theopedia.com/Egalitarianism (accessed on November 21, 2014).

Grudem, Wayne A. *Evangelical Feminism: A New Path to Liberalism?* Wheaton: Crossway Books, 2006.

———. *Evangelical Feminism and Biblical Truth: An Analysis of More Than One Hundred Disputed Questions*. Wheaton, IL: Crossway, 2012. Kindle edition.

Hughes, R. Kent. "Living out God's Order in the Church," *The Master's Seminary Journal* 10, no. 1 (Spring 1999).

Jewett, Paul King. *Man as Male and Female: A Study in Sexual Relationships from a Theological Point of View*. Grand Rapids: Eerdmans, 1975.

Knight, George W. *The Pastoral Epistles: A Commentary On the Greek Text*. The New International Greek Testament Commentary. Grand Rapids: W.B. Eerdmans, 1992.

Merrick, J., and Stephen M. Garrett, eds. *Five Views on Biblical Inerrancy*. Grand Rapids: Zondervan, 2013.

Myers, Michelle. Review of *Man as Male and Female: A Study in Sexual Relationships from a Theological Point of View*, by Paul K. Jewett. *Biblical Woman*, http://biblicalwoman.com/wp-content/uploads/Myers-reivew-of-Man-as-Male-and-Female.pdf (accessed on November 21, 2014).

"Our History," *The Council on Biblical Manhood and Womanhood*, http://cbmw.org/history (accessed on October 31, 2014).

Piper, John, and Wayne A. Grudem, eds. *Recovering Biblical Manhood and Womanhood: A Response to Evangelical Feminism*. Wheaton, IL: Crossway Books, 1991.

Terry, Milton Spenser. *Biblical Hermeneutics: A Treatise on the Interpretation of the Old and New Testaments*. Eugene, OR: Wipf and Stock, 1999.

India

Boyd, Robin. *Indian Christian Theology*. Delhi: ISPCK, 1969.

Carey, S. Pearce. *William Carey*. London: Wakeman Trust, 1923.

Engle, Richard W. "Contextualization in Missions: A Biblical and Theological Appraisal." *Grace Theological Journal*, 4:1 (Spring 1983).

Firth, C.B. *Indian Church History*, Delhi: ISPCK, 1976.

Hedlund, Roger E. *Christianity is Indian: The Emergence of an Indigenous Community*. Delhi: ISPCK, 2000.

Lee, Moonjang. "Identifying an Asian Theology: A Methodological Quest." *Common Ground Journal* (Spring 2009).

Moreau, A. Scott. *Contextualization in World Missions: Mapping and Assessing Evangelical Models.* Grand Rapids: Kregel, 2012.

Nida, Eugene A. *Toward a Science of Translating: With Special Reference to Principles and Procedures Involved in Bible Translating.* Lieden: Brill, 1964.

Satyaranjan, Dandapati Samuel. *The Preaching of Daniel Thambirajah Niles: Homiletical Criticism.* Delhi: ISPCK, 2009

Italy

Allison, Gregg R. *Historical Theology.* Grand Rapids: Zondervan, 2011.

Benedict XV. *Spiritus Paraclitus* (Encyclical Letter on St. Jerome). Vatican Website. September 15,1920. http://www.vatican.va/holy_father/benedict_xv/encyclicals/documents/hf_ben-xv_enc_15091920_spiritus-paraclitus_en.html (accessed December 1, 2014).

Calvin, John. *Institutes of the Christian Religion.* Translated by Henry Beveridge. Grand Rapids: Wm. B. Eerdmans Publishing Company, 1989.

Catechism of the Catholic Church: With Modifications from the Editio Typica. New York: Doubleday, 1995.

De Chirico, Leonardo. "88. Is Scripture True Only in a 'Limited' Way? The Truth of the Bible According to the Pontifical Biblical Commission." Vatican Files. http://vaticanfiles.org/2014/08/88-is-scripture-true-only-in-a-limited-way-the-truth-of-the-bible-according-to-the-pontifical-biblical-commission/ (accessed November 6, 2014).

Feinberg, John. "Literary Forms and Inspiration." In *Cracking Old Testament Codes: A Guide to Interpreting the Literary Genres of the Old Testament.* Edited by D. Brent Sandy and Ronald L. Giese, Jr. Nashville: Broadman & Holman Publishers, 1995.

Feinberg, Paul D. "The Meaning of Inerrancy." In *Inerrancy*, Edited by Norman L. Geisler, 265-304. Grand Rapids: The Zondervan Corporation, 1980.

Ferguson, Sinclair. "Scripture and Tradition," In *Sola Scriptura! The Protestant Position on the Bible*, Edited by Don Kistler. Morgan, PA: Soli Deo Gloria Publications, 1995.

Frame, John M. The *Doctrine of the Word of God.* Phillipsburg, NJ: P&R Publishing, 2010.

Geisler, Norman. "Biblical Inerrancy: Inductive or Deductive Basis?" Defending Inerrancy. http://defendinginerrancy.com/inductive-deductive-inerrancy/ (accessed November 25, 2014)

———. "Inerrancy: Limited or Unlimited?" Defending Inerrancy. http://defendinginerrancy.com/inerrancy-limited-or-unlimited/ (accessed November 25, 2014).

———. "Limited Inerrancy: A Contradiction in Terms." Defending Inerrancy. http://defendinginerrancy.com/what-is-limited-inerrancy/ (accessed November 25, 2014).

Gerstner, John H. "The View of the Bible Held by the Church: Calvin and the Westminster Divines."*In Inerrancy*. Editedby Norman L. Geisler. Grand Rapids: The Zondervan Corporation, 1980.

John Paul II. "Address on the Interpretation of the Bible in the Church." April 23, 1993. In *The Interpretation of the Bible in the Church*. Pontifical Biblical Commission. Translated by Vatican. 7-21. Sherbrooke, Quebec: Editions Pauline, 1994.

Leo XIII. *Providentissimus Deus* (Encyclical Letter on the Study of Holy Scripture). Vatican Website. November 18, 1893. www.vatican.va/holy_father/leo_xiii/encyclicals/documents/hf_l-xiii_enc_18111893_providentissimus-deus_en.html (accessed November 6, 2014).

Marie, Andre. "Biblical Inerrancy." Catholicism.org. http://catholicism.org/biblical-inerrancy.html (accessed November 3, 2014).

Merrick, J., and Stephen M. Garrett, eds. *Five Views on Biblical Inerrancy*. Grand Rapids: Zondervan, 2013.

Montgomery, John Warwick. "The Approach of New Shape Roman Catholicism to Scriptural Inerrancy: A Case Study for Evangelicals." *Bulletin of the Evangelical Theological Society* 10, no. 4 (Fall 1967).

Nicole, Roger. "The Biblical Concept of Truth." In *Scripture and Truth*. Edited by D. A. Carson and John D. Woodbridge. Grand Rapids: Zondervan Publishing House, 1983.

Packer, James I. "Encountering Present-Day Views of Scripture." In *The Foundation of Biblical Authority*. Edited by James Montgomery Boice. Grand Rapids: Zondervan Publishing House, 1978.

Payne, J. Barton. "Higher Criticism and Biblical Inerrancy." In *Inerrancy*. Edited by Norman L. Geisler. Grand Rapids: The Zondervan Corporation, 1980.

Pius X. *Pascendi Dominici Gregis* (Encyclical Letter on the Doctrines of Modernists). Vatican Website. September 8, 1907. http://www.vatican.va/holy_father/pius_x/encyclicals/documents/hf_p-x_enc_19070908_pascendi-dominici-gregis_en.html (accessed December 1, 2014).

Pius XII. *Divino Afflante Spiritu* (Encyclical Letter on Promoting Biblical Studies, Commemorating the Fiftieth Anniversary of Providentissimus Deus). Vatican Website. September 30,1943. www.vatican.va/holy_father/pius_xii/encyclicals/documents/ hf_p-xii_enc_30091943_divino-afflante-spiritu_en.html (accessed November 6, 2014).

Pontifical Biblical Commission. *The Interpretation of the Bible in the Church.* Translated by John Kilgallen and Brendan Byrne. Sherbrooke, Quebec: Editions Pauline, 1994.

———. *The Inspiration and Truth of Sacred Scripture.* Translated by Thomas Esposito and Stephen Gregg. Collegeville, MN: Liturgical Press, 2014. iBooks.

Pontificia Commissione Biblica. *Ispirazione e Verità* della Sacra Scrittura. Città del Vaticano: Libreria Editrice Vaticana, 2014.

Preus, Robert D. "The View of the Bible Held by the Church: The Early Church Through Luther." In *Inerrancy*. Edited by Norman L. Geisler. Grand Rapids: The Zondervan Corporation, 1980.

Schroeder, H. J., trans. *Canons and Decrees of the Council of Trent.* Rockford, IL: Tan Books and Publishers, 1978.

Turretin, Francis. *Institutes of Elenctic Theology.* Volume 1. Translated by George Musgrave Giger. Edited by James T. Dennison, Jr. Phillipsburg, NJ: P & R Publishing, 1994.

Vatican II Council. *Dei Verbum* (Dogmatic Constitution on Divine Revelation). November 18, 1965. In *The Documents of Vatican II*, Vatican Website. http://www.vatican.va/archive/hist_councils/ ii_vatican_council/documents/vat-ii_const_19651118_dei-verbum_en.html (accessed November 6, 2014).

Webster, William. *The Church of Rome at the Bar of History.* Carlisle, PA: The Banner of Truth Trust, 1995.

Wells, David F. *Revolution in Rome.* London: Tyndale Press, 1973.

White, James R. *The Roman Catholic Controversy: Catholics & Protestants— Do the Differences Still Matter?* Minneapolis: Bethany House Publishers, 1996.

———. *Scripture Alone.* Bloomington, MN: Bethany House Publishers, 2004.

Woodbridge John D. *Biblical Authority: A Critique of the Rogers/McKim Proposal.* Grand Rapids: Zondervan, 1982.

Malawi

Boice, James Montgomery. *Does Inerrancy Matter?* Carol Stream, IL: Tyndale House Pub, 1980.

Clark, Gordon H. "The Evangelical Theological Society." *Journal of the Evangelical Society*, no. 9 (1966).

González, Justo L. *The Story of Christianity*. Volume 2. San Francisco: Harper & Row, 1985.

MacArthur, John. "Biblical Inerrancy and the Pulpit." *Expositor Magazine* (Oct. 2014).

————. *2 Timothy*. The MacArthur New Testament Commentary. Chicago: Moody, 1995.

————. *The MacArthur Study Bible*. Electronic edition. Nashville: Word Pub, 1997.

Merrick, J., and Stephen M. Garret, eds. *Five Views on Biblical Inerrancy*. Grand Rapids: Zondervan, 2013.

New American Standard Bible. Updated. LaHabra, CA: The Lockman Foundation, 1995.

Pierard, Richard V. *The Unequal Yoke*. Philadelphia: J. B. Lippincott, 1970.

Saayman, W. "Missionary or Missional? A Study in Terminology." http://hdl.handle.net/10500/7094 (accessed November, 2014).

Tengatenga, J. *The UMCA in Malawi*. Zomba, Malawi: Kachere Books, 2010.

Thomas, R. L. *Evangelical Hermeneutics: The New Verses the Old*. Grand Rapids: Kregel, 2002.

Mexico

Anderson, Allan. *Introduction to Pentecostalism: Global Charismatic Christianity*. Cambridge: Cambridge University Press, 2013.

Campos, Bernardo. *El Post Pentecostalism: Renovación de Liderazgo y Hermenéutica del Espíritu* (Post Pentecostalism: Leadership Renewal and Hermeneutic of the Spirit). CyberJournal for Pentecostal-Charismatic Research, 2003. http://www.pctii.org/cyberj/cyberj13/bernado.html (accessed November 22, 2014).

Chicago Statement on Biblical Hermeneutics. www.bible-researcher.com/chicago2.html, 1982 (accessed November 29, 2014).

Cox, Harvey. *Global Pentecostal and Charismatic Healing*. Oxford: Oxford University Press, 2011.

Frame, John. *Systematic Theology: An Introduction to Christian Belief*. Phillipsburg, NJ: P & R Publishing, 2013.

Grudem, Wayne. *Systematic Theology*. Grand Rapids: Zondervan, 1994.

Jones, David and Russell Woodbridge. *Health, Wealth, and Happiness*. Grand Rapids: Kregel, 2011.

Ledesma, Patricio. *Reseña del libro "El Reino de Poder"—Explorando las enseñanzas de Guillermo Maldonado* (Review of the book "The Kingdom of Power"—Exploring the teachings of Guillermo Maldonado). es.9marks.org/resena/resena-del-libro-el-reino-de-poder-explorando-las-ensenanzas-de-guillermo-maldonado/, 2014 (accessed November 28, 2014).

Luna, Cash. *En honor al Espiritu Santo: ¡No es un algo, es un alguien!* (In honor of the Holy Spirit: He is not a something, He is Someone!). Miami: Editorial Vida, 2010. Kindle e-book.

———. *Ministerios Cash Luna: Casa de Dios, tu casa* (Cash Luna Ministries: House of god, your house). http://www.cashluna.org/index.cfm/page/conocenos/view/Ministerios-Cash-Luna, 2014 (accessed November 22, 2014).

———. Declaración de Fe (Declaration of Faith), Cash Luna. http://cashluna.org/index.cfm/page/conocenos/show/202/Declaracion-de-Fe/ (accessed November 22, 2014).

MacArthur, John. *Strange Fire: the Danger of Offending the Holy Spirit with Counterfeit Worship*. Nashville: Thomas Nelson, 2013.

———. *The Master's Plan for the Church*. Chicago: Moody Publishers, 2008.

Maldonado, Guillermo. El Reino de Poder: Cómo Demostrarlo Aquí y Ahora (The Kingdom of Power: How to Demonstrate it Here and Now). New Kensington, PA: Whitaker House, 2013. Kindle e-book.

——— *El rey Jesus (King Jesus)*. http://www.elreyjesus.org/org/acerca-de-nosotros/nuestro/credo/ (accessed November 22, 2014).

Olvera, Pedro. *Credo: Perfil Doctrinal* (Creed: Doctrinal Profile), Iglesia Cristiana Independiente Pentecostés A.R. (Apizaco, Tlaxcala, Mexico), icipar.net/web/ (accessed November 22, 2014).

Peralta, Marco. Unpublished e-mails. October 16 and December 3, 2014. Used by permission of author.

Pew Forum on Religion and Public Life. *Spirit and Power: A 10-Country Survey of Pentecostals*. http://www.pewforum.org/uploadedfiles/Orphan_Migrated_Content/pentecostals-08.pdf. (October 2006) (accessed October 13, 2014).

TBN Enlace USA. *Wikipedia*. http://en.wikipedia.org/wiki/TBN_Enlace_USA (accessed October 18, 2014).

New Zealand

The Shepherd's Bible College Faculty. "A Biblical Philosophy of Ministry for Church Life" (Lecture Notes). 2013.

————. "Expository Preaching and Teaching" (Lecture Notes). 2013.

————. "Hermeneutics 1" (Lecture Notes). 2013.

Keown, Mark. *Is Laidlaw College 'Liberal'?* http://drmarkk.blogspot. co.nz/2013/07/is-laid-law-college-liberal.html (Accessed Nov. 2014).

"The Invitation: Hope for All." http://hopeproject.co.nz/e-book/ (Accessed Nov. 2014).

"Christianity in New Zealand." Wikipedia. http://en.wikipedia.org/wiki/ Christianity_in_New_Zealand (Accessed Nov. 2014).

Wise, Sally. "New Zealand Women and Church Leadership." *Reality Magazine* issue 66 (2004). http://www.reality.org.nz/article.php?ID=407. (Accessed Nov. 2014).

Philippines

Culver, Robert. *Systematic Theology*. Roth-shire: Mentor Imprint, 2005.

Davis, John J. *Moses and the Gods of Egypt*. Old Testament Studies. Grand Rapids: Baker Book House, 1983.

Geisler, Norman L. ed. *Inerrancy*. Grand Rapids: Zondervan Publishing House, 1980.

Grudem, Wayne. *Systematic Theology*. Grand Rapids: Zondervan Publishing House, 1994.

Harris, Murray J. "2 Corinthians." In *The Expositor's Bible Commentary*. Volume 10. Edited by Frank E. Gaebelein et al. Grand Rapids: Zondervan Publishing House, 1976.

Hasselgrave, David. "Syncretism: Mission and Missionary Induced?" In *Contextualization and Syncretism: Navigating Cultural Currents*. Edited by Gailyn Van Rheenen. Pasadena: William Carey Library, 2006

Hendriksen, William. *John*. New Testament Commentary. Grand Rapids: Baker Academic, 2007.

Henry, Rodney. *Filipino Spirit World: A Challenge to the Church*. Mandaluyong: OMF Literature, 1986.

Hiebert, Paul. *Anthropological Insights for Missionaries*. Grand Rapids: Baker Book House, 1985.

Keil, C.F. and Franz Delitzsch. *Commentary on the Old Testament*. Volume 1. Peabody: Hendrickson Publishers, 1996.

Kistemaker, Simon J. *2 Corinthians. New Testament Commentary*. Grand Rapids: Baker Academic, 1997.

MacArthur, John. *The MacArthur Bible Commentary*. Nashville: Thomas Nelson Publishers, 2005.

Maggay, Melba. *A Clash of Cultures: Early American Protestant Missions and Filipino Religious Consciousness*. Manila: Anvil, 2011.

Mohler, Albert. "When the Bible Speaks, God Speaks: the Classic Doctrine of Biblical Inerrancy." In *Five Views on Biblical Inerrancy*. Edited by J. Merrick, et al. Grand Rapids: Zondervan Publishing House, 2013. Kindle Electronic Edition.

Myers, Allen, ed. *The Eerdmans Bible Dictionary*. Grand Rapids: William B. Eerdmans Publishing Company, 1987.

Schumacher, John. "Syncretism in Philippine Catholicism." *Philippine Studies* 32, (1984).

Tenney, Merrill C. "John." In *The Expositor's Bible Commentary*. Edited by Frank E. Gaebelein, et al. Volume 9. Grand Rapids: Zondervan Publishing House, 1981.

Van Rheenen, Gailyn. "Syncretism and Contextualization: The Church on a Journey Defining Itself." In *Contextualization and Syncretism: Navigating Cultural Currents*. Edited by Gailyn Van Rheenen. Pasadena: William Carey Library, 2006.

Russia

Andrew, Stephen L. "Biblical Inerrancy." *Chafer Theological Seminary Journal* 8, no. 1 (January 2002).

Beale, Gregory K. *The Erosion of Inerrancy in Evangelicalism: Responding to New Challenges to Biblical Authority*. Wheaton: Crossway, 2008.

Bird, Michael F. "Inerrancy Is Not Necessary for Evangelicalism Outside the USA." In *Five Views on Biblical Inerrancy*. Edited by J. Merrick and Stephen M. Garrett. Grand Rapids: Zondervan, 2013.

Carson, D. A. "Recent Developments in the Doctrine of Scripture." *Hermeneutics, Authority, and Canon*. Edited by D. A. Carson and John D. Woodbridge. Eugene, OR: Wipf&Stock Publishers, 1986.

Erickson, Millard J. *Christian Theology*. Grand Rapids: Baker Books, 1986.

Fairbairn, Donald. *Eastern Orthodoxy Through Western Eyes*. Louisville: Westminster/John Knox Press, 2002.

Feinberg, Paul D. "The Meaning of Inerrancy." In *Inerrancy*. Edited by Norman L. Geisler. Grand Rapids: Zondervan Publishing House, 1980.

Frame, John M. *The Doctrine of the Word of God*. Phillipsburg, NJ: P&R Publishing, 2010.

Geisler, Norman L. *Systematic Theology*. 4 volumes. Minneapolis: Bethany House, 2002.

Geisler, Norman L., and William C. Roach. *Defending Inerrancy: Affirming the Accuracy of Scripture for a New Generation*. Grand Rapids: Baker Books, 2011.

Grudem, Wayne A. "Scripture's Self-Attestation and the Problem of Formulating a Doctrine of Scripture." In *Scripture and Truth*. Edited by D. A. Carson and John D. Woodbridge. Grand Rapids: Baker Book House, 1992.

————. *Systematic Theology: An Introduction to Biblical Doctrine*. Grand Rapids: Zondervan Publishing House, 1994.

Lewis, Gordon R., and Bruce A. Demarest. *Integrative Theology: Historical, Biblical, Systematic, Apologetic, Practical*. 3 volumes. Grand Rapids: Zondervan, 1996.

Marsden, George M. *Reforming Fundamentalism: Fuller Seminary and the New Evangelicalism*. Grand Rapids: Wm. B. Eerdmans Publishing Company, 1995.

McCune, Rolland. *A Systematic Theology of Biblical Christianity*. 3 volumes. Detroit: Detroit Baptist Theological Seminary, 2008.

Nassif, Bradley. "Are Eastern Orthodoxy and Evangelicalism Compatible? Yes." In *Three Views on Eastern Orthodoxy and Evangelicalism*. Edited by James Stamoolis. Grand Rapids: Zondervan, 2004.

Packer, James I. "Infallible Scripture and the Role of Hermeneutics." *Scripture and Truth*. Edited by D. A. Carson and John D. Woodbridge. Grand Rapids: Baker Book House, 1992.

Preus, Robert D. "The View of the Bible Held by the Church: The Early Church through Luther." In *Inerrancy*. Edited by Norman L. Geisler. Grand Rapids: Zondervan Publishing House, 1980.

Reymond, Robert L. *A New Systematic Theology of the Christian Faith*. 2nd edition. Nashville: Thomas Nelson, 1998.

Sexton, Jason. "How Far Beyond Chicago? Assessing Recent Attempts to Reframe the Inerrancy Debate." *Themelios* 34, no. 1 (2009).

Silva, Moises. *God, Language, and Scripture: Reading the Bible in the Light of General Linguistics*. Foundations of Contemporary Interpretation. Grand Rapids: Zondervan Publishing House, 1990.

Vanhoozer, Kevin J. "Response to Michael F. Bird." *Five Views on Biblical Inerrancy*. Edited by J. Merrick and Stephen M. Garrett. Grand Rapids: Zondervan, 2013.

Woodbridge, John D. *Biblical Authority: A Critique of the Rogers / McKim Proposal*. Grand Rapids: Zondervan Publishing House, 1982.

———. "Some Misconceptions of the Impact of the 'Enlightenment' on the Doctrine of Scripture." *Hermeneutics, Authority, and Canon*. Edited by D. A. Carson and John D. Woodbridge. Eugene, OR: Wipf&Stock Publishers, 1986.

Russian Works

Винс, Яков. *Наши баптистские принципы*. Харбин: Типо-Литография и Цинкография Л. М. Абрамовича, 1924.

Грачев, Юрий. *Как ты относишься к Библии?* Reprint. СПб.: Библия для всех, 2007.

Гуртаев, Александр. *Укрепление фундамента: Библейское основание учения о непогрешимости Писания*. СПб.: Библия для всех, 2014.

Данн, Джеймс Д. *Новый взгляд на Иисуса: Что упустил поиск исторического Иисуса* / Пер. с англ. М.: ББИ, 2009.

Десницкий, Андрей. Фундаментализм: выход или вызов для православной библеистики? http://www.bogoslov.ru/text/1240183 (accessed January 3, 2014).

Дубровский, Алесь. Фундаментализм как тормозящий фактор в развитии евангельских церквей постсоветского пространства. http://www.mbchurch.ru/publications/articles/15/6058/ (accessed November 2, 2014).

Евангельские христиане-баптисты в СССР. М.: Изд. ВСЕХБ, 1979.

Евангельские христиане баптисты. Сохранившие верность Евангелию. М.: Протестант, 1992.

Егоров, Евгений, и Алексей Прокопенко. "О безошибочности Писания: российский контекст." Альманах «Кафедра» 7 (May 2014).

Изложение евангельской веры, или вероучение евангельских христиан. Edited by Иван Проханов (1910). http://slavicbaptists.com/2012/02/10/prohanovconfession/ (accessed November 1, 2014).

Исповедание веры христиан-баптистов. Edited by В. Павлов (1906). http://slavicbaptists.com/2012/02/10/pavlovconfession/ (accessed November 1, 2014).

История евангельских христиан-баптистов в СССР. М.: Изд. ВСЕХБ, 1989.

Каргель, Иван. *Собрание сочинений*. Reprint. СПб.: Библия для всех, 1997.

Каретникова, Марина. *400 лет баптизма: История в картинках*. СПб.: Библия для всех, 2010.

Коломийцев, Алексей. *Библейская принципиальность в служении*. Ванкувер: Церковь «Слово Благодати», 2012.

Краткое вероучение христиан евангельского исповедания. Edited by П. Фризен (1903). http://slavicbaptists.com/2012/07/31/1903shortconfession/ (accessed November 1, 2014).

Краткое изложение вероучения евангельских христиан. Edited by И. Каргель (1913). http://slavicbaptists.com/2012/02/09/kargelconfession/ (accessed November 1, 2014).

Крыжановский, Ростислав. *Кто такие баптисты?* Ирпень: Духовное возрождение, 2012.

Пузынин, Андрей. *Традиция евангельских христиан: Изучение самоидентификации и богословия от момента ее зарождения до наших дней*. М.: ББИ, 2010.

Решетников, Юрий, и Сергей Санников. *Обзор истории евангельско-баптистского братства на Украине*. Одесса: Богомыслие, 2000.

Савинский, С. *История евангельских христиан-баптистов Украины, России, Белоруссии*. 2 volumes. СПб.: Библия для всех, 1999.

Серафим Слободской. *Закон Божий: руководство для семьи и школы*. 4th edition. Reprint. М.: Молодая гвардия, 1990.

Символ евангельской веры петербургских верующих (1897). http://slavicbaptists.com/2012/02/10/symbolegveng/ (accessed November 1, 2014).

Singapore/China

Aldrich, Roy L. "The Sign of Pompous Obscurity." *Bibliotheca Sacra* 128:509 (January 1971).

Allen, R. Michael. *Karl Barth's Church Dogmatics: An Introduction and Reader*. New York: T&T Clark, 2012.

Barth, Karl. *Church Dogmatics*. Translated by G. T. Thomson. Volume 1. Book 1. Edinburgh: T. & T. Clark, 1936.

———. *Church Dogmatics*. Translated by G. T. Thomson and Harold Knight. Volume 1. Book 2. New York: Charles Scriber's Sons, 1956.

Berkouwer, G. C. *Studies in Dogmatics: General Revelation*. Grand Rapids: W.B. Eerdmans Pub. Co., 1955.

Bolich, Gregory. "Barth as Friend." In *Karl Barth and Evangelicalism*. Downers Grove, IL: Intervarsity Press, 1980.

Bromiley, G. W. "Karl Barth's Doctrine of Inspiration." *Journal of the Transactions of the Victoria Institute* 87, 1955.

Brown, Colin. *Karl Barth and the Christian Message*. Chicago: Intervarsity, 1967.

Clark, Gordon H. *Karl Barth's Theological Method*, Philadelphia: The Presbyterian and Reformed Publishing Company, 1963.

DeVine, Mark. "Evangelicals and Karl Barth: Friends or Foes?" Annual meeting of the Evangelical Theological Society, Colorado Springs, 2001.

Enns, Paul P. *The Moody Handbook of Theology*. Chicago: Moody Press, 1989.

Helm, David. *Expositional Preaching: How We Speak God's Word Today*. Wheaton: Crossway Books, 2014.

Machen, J. Gresham. "Karl Barth and 'The Theology of Crisis.'" *Westminster Theological Journal* 53:2 (Fall 1991).

Morrison, John D. "Barth, Barthians, and Evangelicals: Reassessing the Question of the Relation of Holy Scripture and the Word of God." *Trinity Journal* 25:2 (Fall 2004).

Mueller, David L. *Karl Barth*. Waco, TX: Word Books, 1972.

———. "Karl Barth and the Heritage of the Reformation." *Review and Expositor* 86:1 (Winter 1989).

Muller, Richard A. "The Place and Importance of Karl Barth in the Twentieth Century: A Review Essay." *Westminster Theological Journal* 50:1 (Spring 1988).

Oakes, Kenneth. *Karl Barth on Theology and Philosophy*. Oxford: Oxford University Press, 2012.

Ramm, Bernard. *After Fundamentalism: The Future of Evangelical Theology*. San Francisco: Harper & Row, 1983.

Riviere, Willliam T. "The Philosophy Underlying Barth's Theology." *Bibliotheca Sacra* 91:362 (April 1934).

Runia, Klaas. *Karl Barth's Doctrine of Holy Scripture*. Grand Rapids: William B. Eerdmans Publishing Company, 1962.

Stoll, John H. "Contemporary Theology and the Bible." *Grace Journal* 3:1 (Winter 1962).

Tinder, Donald. "The Doctrine of the Trinity: Its Historical Development and Departures." *Emmaus Journal* 13 (Summer 2004).

Torrance, Thomas F. *Karl Barth: An Introduction to His Early Theology*. London: SCM Press, 1962.

Van Til, Cornelius. "Has Karl Barth Become Orthodox?" *Westminster Theological Journal* 16:2 (May 1954).

Weber, Otto. *Karl Barth's Church Dogmatics: An Introductory Report on Volumes I-III.* 4. Philadelphia: Westminster Press, 1953.

Wells, William W. "The Reveille that Awakened Karl Barth." *Journal of Evangelical Theological Society* 22:3 (September 1979).

Webster, John. *Karl Barth.* 2nd ed. London: Continuum, 2004.

Woodbridge, John D. "Biblical Authority: Towards an Evaluation of the Rogers and McKim Proposal." *Trinity Journal* 1:2 (Fall 1980).

South Africa

Hofney, J. W., and G. J. Pillay, eds. *A History of Christianity in South Africa.* Volume 1. Pretoria: HAUM Tertiary, 1994.

Kantzer, Kenneth S. "Evangelicals and the Doctrine of Inerrancy." In *The Foundation of Biblical Authority.* Edited by James Montgomery Boice. London & Glasgow: Pickering & Inglis, 1979.

Merrick, J., and Stephen Garret. "Introduction: On Debating Inerrancy." In *Five Views on Biblical Inerrancy.* Edited by J. Merrick, et. al. Grand Rapids: Zondervan, 2013.

O'Donovan, W. *Biblical Christianity in African Perspective.* Carlisle, PA: The Paternoster Press, 1996.

Timothy Training Institute. *The Church in African Context.* Johannesburg: Timothy Training Institute, 1997.

Spain

Abbott, Walter M., ed. *The Documents of Vatican II with Notes and Comments by Catholic, Protestant and Orthodox Authorities.* Translated by Joseph Gallagher. Boston: The America Press, 1996.

Adam, Karl. *The Spirit of Catholicism.* Revised edition. Translated by Justin McCann. Garden City, NY: Doubleday Image Books, 1954.

Arndt, William, Frederick W. Danker, and Walter Bauer. *A Greek-English Lexicon of the New Testament and Other Early Christian Literature.* Third edition. Chicago: University of Chicago Press, 2000.

Augustine of Hippo. *Letters of St. Augustine.* Volume 1. *In The Confessions and Letters of St. Augustine with a Sketch of His Life and Work: A Select Library of the Nicene and Post-Nicene Fathers of the Christian Church, First Series.* Edited by Philip Schaff. Translated by J. G. Cunningham. Buffalo: Christian Literature Company, 1886.

————. *Reply to Faustus the Manichaean*. Volume 4. In *The Nicene and Post-Nicene Fathers*. Edited by Philip Schaff. Grand Rapids: Wm. B. Eerdmans, 1976.

Bechard, Dean Philip, ed. *The Scripture Documents: An Anthology of Official Catholic Teachings*. Collegeville, MI: Liturgical Press, 2002.

Beck, W. David. "Agnosticism: Kant." In *Biblical Errancy: An Analysis of Its Philosophical Roots*. Edited by Norman L. Geisler. Eugene, OR: Wipf and Stock Publishers, 1981.

Berkouwer, G. C. *Holy Scripture*. Studies in Dogmatics. Edited by Jack Bartlett Rogers. Grand Rapids: W. B. Eerdmans Pub. Co., 1975.

Best, Steven, and Douglas Kellner. *The Postmodern Turn*. New York: The Guilford Press, 1997.

Blum, Edwin A. "The Apostles' View of Scripture." In *Inerrancy*. Edited by Norman L. Geisler, Grand Rapids: Zondervan Publishing House, 1980.

Bookman, Douglas. "The Scriptures and Biblical Counseling." In *Introduction to Biblical Counseling*. Edited by John F. MacArthur and Wayne A. Mack. Dallas: Word, 1994.

Borgmann, Albert. *Crossing the Postmodern Divide*. Chicago: Chicago Press, 1992.

Canham, Michael. "The Inerrancy of the Bible." Exalting Christ Pastor's Conference Notes, September 2014.

Costello, Charles Joseph. *St. Augustine's Doctrine on the Inspiration and Canonicity of Scripture*. Washington, D.C.: Catholic University of America, 1930.

Descartes, René. *Meditations on First Philosophy*. Sioux Falls, SD: NuVision Publications, 2007.

Donahue, John R. "Scripture: A Roman Catholic Perspective." R*eview and Expositor* 79, no. 2 (Spring 1982): 231–41.

Edgard, William. "No News Is Good News: Modernity, The Postmodern, and Apologetics." *Westminster Theological Journal* 52, no. 2 (1995)..

Enns, Peter. "Inerrancy, However Defined, Does not Describe What the Bible Does." In *Five Views on Biblical Inerrancy*. Edited by J. Merrick and Stephen M. Garrett. Grand Rapids: Zondervan, 2013.

Enwald, Marika. "Displacements of Deconstruction." Academic Dissertation, University of Tampere, 2004.

Feinberg, Paul D. "The Meaning of Inerrancy." In *Inerrancy*. Edited by Norman L. Geisler. Grand Rapids: Zondervan Publishing House, 1980.

Ferguson, Sinclair. "Scripture and Tradition: The Bible and Tradition in Roman Catholicism." In *Sola Scriptura! The Protestant Position on the Bible*. Edited by Don Kistler. Morgan, PA: Soli Deo Gloria Publications, 1995.

Geisler, Norman L. "Inductivism, Materialism, And Rationalism: Bacon, Hobbes, And Spinoza." In *Biblical Errancy: An Analysis of Its Philosophical Roots*. Edited by Norman L. Geisler. Eugene, OR: Wipf and Stock Publishers, 1981.

———. "Philosophical Presuppositions of Biblical Errancy." In *Inerrancy*. Edited by Norman L. Geisler. Grand Rapids: Zondervan Publishing House, 1980.

Geisler, Norman L, and William C. Roach. *Defending Inerrancy: Affirming the Accuracy of Scripture for a New Generation*. Grand Rapids: Baker Books, 2011. Kindle Electronic Edition.

Gerstner, John H. "The View of the Bible Held by the Church: Calvin and the Westminster Divines." In *Inerrancy*. Edited by Norman L. Geisler. Grand Rapids: Zondervan Publishing House, 1980.

Grau, José. *Catolicismo Romano: Origenes y Desarrollo*. Segunda edición de Concilios. Volume 2. Barcelona: Ediciones Evangélicas Europeas, 1965.

Greer, Robert C. *Mapping Postmodernism, a Survey of Christian Options*. Downers Grove: InterVarsity Press, 2003.

Grudem, Wayne. *Systematic Theology: An Introduction to Biblical Doctrine*. Grand Rapids: Zondervan, 2004.

Habermas, Gary R. "Skepticism: Hume." In *Biblical Errancy: An Analysis of Its Philosophical Roots*. Edited by Norman L. Geisler. Eugene, OR: Wipf and Stock Publishers, 1981.

Harris, R. Laird. "The Basis For Our Belief in Inerrancy." *Bulletin of the Evangelical Theological Society* 9, no. 1 (Winter 1966).

Harrisville, Roy A. "A Theology of Rediscovery." *Dialog* 2, no. 3, 1963.

Hart, D.G. "J. Gresham Machen, Inerrancy, and Creedless Christianity." *Themelios An International Journal for Pastors and Students of Theological and Religious Studies* 25, no. 3 (June 2000).

Henry, Carl F. H. *God, Revelation, and Authority: God Who Speaks and Shows*. Vol. IV. Wheaton, IL: Crossway Books, 1999.

Herbert of Cherbury, Edward Lord. *De Veritate*. Translated by Meyrick H. Carre. Bristol: J. W. Arrowsmith Ltd., 1937.

Hodge, Charles. *Systematic Theology*. Volume 1. New York: Scribner, Armstrong and Co., 1873.

Holt, Jim. "Is Paris Kidding?" *New York Times*, November 15, 1998. http://
www.nytimes.com/1998/11/15/books/is-paris-kidding.html?ref=-
bookreviews (accessed November 3, 2014).

Irenaeus of Lyons. "Against Heresies." In *The Ante-Nicene Fathers: The
Apostolic Fathers With Justin Martyr and Irenaeus*. Volume 1.
Edited by Alexander Roberts, James Donaldson and A. Cleveland
Coxe. Buffalo: Christian Literature Company, 1885.

Johnson, Harold. "The Research and Development of a Storing Model to
Address The Postmodern Worldview with the Biblical Worldview."
Doctoral Thesis, New Orleans Baptist Seminary, March 2000.

Kurian, George Thomas. *Nelson's New Christian Dictionary: The
Authoritative Resource on the Christian World*. Nashville, TN:
Thomas Nelson Publishers, 2001.

Leith, John H., ed. *Creeds of the Churches: A Reader in Christian Doctrine,
from the Bible to the Present*. Third edition. Louisville: John Knox
Press, 1982.

Lessing, Gotthold Ephraim. *Lessing's Theological Writings*. Selection
in translation with an Introductory Essay by Henry Chadwick.
Stanford: Stanford University, 1957.

Levie, Jean. *The Bible, Word of God in Words of Men*. Translated by S. H.
Treman. New York: P. J. Kenedy, 1961.

Likoudis, James, and K. D. Whitehead. *The Pope, the Council and the Mass*.
Revised edition. Steubenville, OH: Emmaus Road Pub., 2006.

Lindsell, Harold. "A Historian Looks At Inerrancy." *Bulletin of the Evangelical
Theological Society* 8, no. 1 (Winter 1965).

Luther, Martin. *Luther's Works*. American edition. Edited by Jaroslav Pelican.
Saint Louis: Concordia Publishing House, 1955ff.

Mack, Wayne A. "The Sufficiency of Scripture in Counseling." *The Master's
Seminary Journal* 9, no. 1 (Spring 1998).

MacKenzie, R. A. F. *Faith and History in the Old Testament*. New York:
Macmillan, 1963.

McKenzie, John L. *Myths and Realities: Studies in Biblical Theology*.
Milwaukee: Bruce Publishing Co., 1963.

Mohler, R. Albert. "When the Bible Speaks God Speaks: The Classic Doctrine
of Biblical Inerrancy." In *Five Views on Biblical Inerrancy*. Edited by
J. Merrick and Stephen M. Garrett. Grand Rapids: Zondervan, 2013.

Montgomery, John Warwick. "Biblical Inerrancy: What is at Stake?" In *God's
Inerrant Word: An International Symposium on the Trustworthiness*

of Scripture. Edited by John Warwick Montgomery. Minneapolis: Bethany House Publishers, 1974.

————. "Inspiration And Inerrancy: A New Departure." *Bulletin of the Evangelical Theological Society* 8, no. 2 (Spring 1965).

————. "The Approach of New Shape Roman Catholicism To Scriptural Inerrancy: A Case Study For Evangelicals." *Bulletin of the Evangelical Theological Society* 10, no. 4 (Fall 1967).

Nygren, E. Herbert. "Existentialism: Kierkegaard." In *Biblical Errancy: An Analysis of Its Philosophical Roots*. Edited by Norman L. Geisler. Eugene, OR: Wipf and Stock Publishers, 1981.

Oden, Thomas C. "The Death of Modernity." In *The Challenge of Postmodernism*. Edited by David S. Dockery. Wheaton: BridgePoint Books, 1995.

Pailin, David A. "Reason in relation to Scripture and Tradition." In *Scripture, Tradition, and Reason: A Study in the Criteria of Christian Doctrine: Essays in Honour of Richard P.C. Hanson*. Edited by Richard Bauckham and Benjamin Drewery. New York: T&T Clark, 1998.

Payne, J. Barton. "Apeitheo: Current Resistance To Biblical Inerrancy." *Bulletin of the Evangelical Theological Society* 10, no. 1 (Winter 1968).

Peters, Ted. "David Bohm, Postmodernism, and the Divine." *Zygon* 20, no. 2 (June 1985).

Phillips, Craig A. "Postmodernism." In *The Encyclopedia of Christianity*. Edited by Erwin Fahlbusch and Geoffrey William Bromiley. Volume 4. Grand Rapids: Wm. B. Eerdmans, 2005.

Preus, Robert D. "The View of the Bible Held by the Church: The Early Church Through Luther." In *Inerrancy*. Edited by Norman L. Geisler. Grand Rapids: Zondervan Publishing House, 1980.

Ramm, Bernard. *Protestant Biblical Interpretation: A Textbook of Hermeneutics*. Third Revised Edition. Grand Rapids: Baker Book House, 1970.

Reymond, Robert L. *A New Systematic Theology of the Christian Faith*. Nashville: Thomas Nelson, 1998.

Ryrie, Charles C. "Some Important Aspects of Biblical Inerrancy." *Bibliotheca Sacra* 136, no. 541 (January 1979).

Satta, Ronald F. "Inerrancy: The Prevailing Orthodox Opinion of the Nineteenth-Century Theological Elite." *Faith and Mission* 24, no. 1 (Fall 2006).

———. *The Sacred Text: Biblical Authority in Nineteenth-Century America*. Eugene, OR: Pickwick Publications, 2007.

Saucy, Robert L. "Difficulties With Inerrancy." *Bulletin of the Evangelical Theological Society* 9, no. 1 (Winter 1966).

Sexton, Jason S. "How Far Beyond Chicago? Assessing Recent Attempts to Reframe the Inerrancy Debate." *Themelios An International Journal for Students of Theological and Religious Studies* 34, no. 1 (April 2009).

Shrader, Rick C. "Postmodernism." *Journal of Ministry and Theology* 3, no. 1 (Spring 1999).

Sire, James W. *The Universe Next Door*. Downers Grove, IL: IVP Academic, 2004. Kindle Electronic Edition.

Sproul, R. C. *Can I Trust the Bible?* The Crucial Questions Series. Lake Mary, FL: Reformation Trust, 2009.

———. "The Case for Inerrancy: A Methodological Analysis." In *God's Inerrant Word: An International Symposium on the Trustworthiness of Scripture*. Edited by John Warwick Montgomery. Minneapolis: Bethany House Publishers, 1974.

Thomas Aquinas. *Summa Theologica*. Translated by Fathers of the English Dominican Province. London: Burns Oates & Washbourne, 1921.

Veith, Gene Edward. *Postmodern Times*. Wheaton: Crossway Books, 1994.

Warfield, B.B. *Revelation and Inspiration*. Grand Rapids: Baker Book House Company, 2000.

Webster, William. *Roman Catholic Tradition: Claims and Contradictions*. Battle Ground, WA: Christian Resources, 1994.

Williamson, Peter. *Catholic Principles for Interpreting Scripture: A Study of the Pontifical Biblical Commission's The Interpretation of the Bible in the Church*. Subsidia Biblica. Roma: Pontificio Istituto Biblico, 2001.

Ukraine

Aland, Kurt and Barbara. *The Text of the New Testament: an Introduction to the Critical Editions and to the Theory and Practice of Modern Textual Criticism*, 2 ed. Grand Rapids: Eerdmans, 1995.

Cabal, Ted, et al. *The Apologetics Study Bible: Real Questions, Straight Answers, Stronger Faith*. Nashville: Holman Bible Publishers, 2007.

Comfort, Philip Wesley and David P. Barrett. *The Text of the Earliest New Testament Greek Manuscripts*. Wheaton: Tyndale House, 2001.

Cooper, Kenneth R. "Why Believe the Bible?" *Journal of Dispensational Theology Volume 15*, no. 46 (2011).

Cross, F. L. and Elizabeth A. Livingstone. eds. *The Oxford Dictionary of the Christian Church*. Oxford: Oxford University Press, 2005.

Ehrman, Bart D. *Lost Christianities: Battles for Scripture and the Faiths We Never Knew*. New York: Oxford University Press, 2005.

———. *Misquoting Jesus: The Story Behind Who Changed the Bible and Why*. New York: Harper, 2005.

Frame, John M. *Salvation Belongs to the Lord: An Introduction to Systematic Theology*. Phillipsburg, NJ: P&R Publishing, 2006.

Grier, James M. "The Apologetical Value of the Self-witness of Scripture." *Grace Theological Journal* 1.1 (Spring 1980).

Holmes, Michael W. "Textual Criticism." In *Dictionary of Paul and His Letters*. Edited by Gerald F. Hawthorne, et al. Downers Grove, IL: InterVarsity Press, 1993.

Howe, Richard G. "The New Testament, Jesus Christ, and the Da Vinci Code." In *Reasons for Faith: Making a Case for the Christian Faith*. Edited by Norman Geisler and Chad Meister. Wheaton: Crossway Books, 2007.

Hurtado, L. W. "Codex: Codex Washingtonianus." *In The Anchor Yale Bible Dictionary*. Edited by David Noel Freedman. New York: Doubleday, 1992.

Komoszewski, Ed, Sawyer, M. James and Daniel B. Wallace. *Reinventing Jesus: What The Da Vinci Code and Other Novel Speculations Don't Tell You*. Grand Rapids: Kregel, 2006.

Merrick, J., and Stephen M. Garrett, eds. *Five Views on Biblical Inerrancy*. Grand Rapids: Zondervan, 2013.

Metzger, Bruce M. *A Textual Commentary on the Greek New Testament*, 2nd ed. New York: United Bible Societies, 1994.

Metzger, Bruce M., and Bart Ehrman. *The Text of the New Testament: Its Transmission, Corruption, and Restoration*, 4th ed. New York: Oxford University Press, 2005.

Wagner, Brian H. "New Testament Criticism: Helps and Hurts." *Journal of Dispensational Theology* 15, no. 46 (2011).

Wallace, Daniel B. "Inspiration, Preservation, and New Testament Textual Criticism." *Grace Theological Journal* 12 (1991).

———. "Textual Criticism of the New Testament." In *The Lexham Bible Dictionary*. Edited by John Barry and Lazarus Wentz. Bellingham, WA: Lexham Press, 2012.

White, James R. *Scripture Alone: Exploring the Bible's Accuracy, Authority and Authenticity*. Minneapolis: Bethany House, 2004.

————. "Textual Criticism And The Ministry Of Preaching." *The Reformed Baptist Theological Review* 2, no. 2 (2005).

————. *The King James Only Controversy*, 2nd ed. Minneapolis: Bethany House, 2009.

————. *What Every Christian Needs to Know about the Qur'an*. Minneapolis: Bethany House, 2013.

US – Russian Language

English Language Sources

Calvin, John. *Institutes of the Christian Religion*. Translated by Henry Beveridge. Volume 1. Grand Rapids: Eerdmans, 1964.

————. *Eastern Orthodox Christianity: Contemporary Reader*. Grand Rapids: Baker Books, 1995.

Fairbairn, Donald. *Eastern Orthodoxy through Western Eyes*. Louisville: Westminster John Knox Press, 2002.

Florovskiy, George. "The Function of Tradition in the Ancient Church." In *Eastern Orthodox Theology. A Contemporary Reader*. Edited by Daniel Clendenin. Grand Rapids: Baker Books, 1995.

Frame, John M. "God and Biblical Language: Transcendence and Immanence." In *God's Inerrant Word*. ed. by J.W. Montgomery. Minneapolis, Minnesota: Bethany Fellowship, 1974.

————, ed. *Inerrancy*. Grand Rapids: Zondervan, 1980.

Lloyd-Jones, D. Martyn. *Authority*. Carlisle, PA: The Banner of Truth Trust, 1997.

————. "The Adequacy of Human Language." In *Inerrancy*. Edited by Norman Geisler. Grand Rapids: Zondervan, 1980.

Van Til, Cornelius. *The Defense of the Faith*. Phillipsburg, NJ: Presbyterian and Reformed Publishing, 1955.

Russian Language Sources

Булгаков, Сергей. *Православие*. Москва: Издательство АСТ, 2003.

Гололоб, Г. «Предопределяет ли Бог зло?» Луч Евангелия 8:117 (Август, 2004).

Корнилов, Н.А., «Какого рода богословие нам нужно?» *Путь Богопознания. Богословско-публицистический журнал.* №6. Москва: Московская богословская семинария, 2000.

Кураев, Андрей, *Конфликт интерпретаций*, http://www.kuraev.ru/ konflict.html (1 Nov, 2004).

Старогородский, Сергей. *Православное Учение О Спасении.* http://www. pravbeseda.org/library/books/strag1_5.html (14 Nov. 2003).

US – Spanish Language

Coalición Apostólica de Colombia. "Escuela Profética," http://coaliciona-postolica.blog.com/files/2011/01/4-CÓMO-RESPONDER-A-LA-PROFECÍA-PERSONAL.pdf (accessed December 29, 2014).

http://www.pentecostalesdelnombre.com (accessed December 29, 2014).

http://www.iafcj.org (accessed December 29, 2014).

http://www.cashluna.org/templates20/print.cfm?id=347 (accessed December 29, 2014).

http://iglesiametodistaarroyito.blogspot.com/p/recursos.html (accessed December 29, 2014).

http://www.llamadafinal.com/ministerio/credo.html (accessed December 29, 2014).

McKenna, Josephine. "Pope Says Evolution, Big Bang Are Real." http:// www.usatoday.com/story/news/world/2014/10/28/pope-francis-evolution-big-bang/18053509/ (accessed December 29, 2014).

CONTRIBUTORS

Albania

Florenc Mene is a member of the IFES (Albania) leadership staff and theological educator at the Albanian Bible Institute. After graduating with an M.Div degree at Southeastern Europe Theological Seminary he went on to study in the Netherlands, graduating *Summa Cum Laude* with a Th.M degree in 2011. He is married to Alta and they have two small children, David and Ema.

Croatia

Miško Horvatek is serving as Dean of Theological Biblical Academy in Krapina, Croatia. He received a diploma in Theology at Evangelical and Bible Institute in Vienna, Austria, as well as a D.D. at Shepherds Theological Seminary in North Carolina and an M.Div from The Master's Seminary. Miško is married to Mira and they have four children and eighteen grandchildren.

Czech Republic

Anthony Vahala received his M.Div and Th.M degrees at Southeastern Baptist Theological Seminary. He currently serves as professor of Bible and Preaching at the Czech Bible Institute, and is a Ph.D. candidate at the University of New England, Armidale, Australia.

Lance Roberts received his M.Div and D.Min at The Master's Seminary, and has ministered in the Czech Republic since 2001. He currently serves as dean and professor of Bible and Preaching at the Czech Bible Institute.

Germany

Martin Manten, Dean of the European Bible Training Center in Zurich, received his M.Div from The Master's Seminary and serves as a pastor and church planter in Switzerland. Martin and his wife Gabi have four boys and two girls ranging from age 6 to 19.

Honduras

Carlos Montoya received his MABS from Dallas Theological Seminary and his M.Div from The Master's Seminary. He currently serves as president of Ministerios Evangélicos de las Américas in Siguatepeque, Honduras. He and his wife Lori have seven children, one son-in-law, and an adorable grandson.

India

Samuel Williams received his BA in Biblical Studies from The Master's College and M.Div from The Master's Seminary. He is the Dean of the Pastoral Training Seminary in Goa, India and teaches Preaching, Hebrew and Church History. Samuel and his wife Nicole live in Goa with their five children.

Italy

Massimo Mollica received his M.Div from The Master's Seminary in 2009 (Th.M in progress). He currently serves as an adjunct faculty member for the Italian Theological Academy while working on evangelism and church planting in Central Italy. Massimo and his wife Susanna have four children aged 7, 6, 4, and 4.

Malawi

Brian Biedebach has received his M.Div and D.Min degrees from The Master's Seminary and is scheduled to defend his Ph.D thesis in 2015 at the University of Stellenbosch in Cape Town, South Africa. Originally from Southern California, Brian has served as a missionary for twenty years, including eight years as a pastor in Johannesburg, South Africa and nine years in Malawi. Brian is currently pastoring the International Bible Fellowship Church in Lilongwe. He trains pastors at African Bible College as well as the Central African Preaching Academy.

Gideon Manda has more than ten years of pastoral experience in Blantyre, Malawi. His undergraduate studies were completed in South Africa. In May of 2015, Gideon is planning to graduate with an M.Div from African Bible College in Lilongwe, Malawi. Gideon also serves on the faculty of the Central African Preaching Academy.

Mexico

Jim Dowdy is a graduate of Prairie Bible Institute with a diploma in Bible and Missions ('75). He currently serves as a missionary-professor for the Word of Grace Seminary in Mexico City, Mexico. Jim and his wife Carolyn have two children and five grandchildren.

New Zealand

This article was co-authored by the faculty of The Shepherd's Bible College (TSBC), a TMAI training center in New Zealand. The faculty authors include: Russell Hohneck, Phil Henderson, Matthew Johnston, Tony Nuñez and Greg Stephenson. TSBC is committed to equipping God's people for every good work.

Philippines

Allan Luciano received his M.Div at The Master's Seminary. He currently serves as an instructor for The Expositor's Academy in Manila, Philippines. Allan and his wife Sandi have three children aged 4, 3, and 11 months.

Russia

Alexander Gurtaev received his M.Div from Samara Center for Biblical Training in Samara, Russia ('10) and Th.M from The Master's Seminary ('12). He currently serves as the Director and an instructor at Samara Center for Biblical Training. Alexander and his wife Irina have four small children ages 9, 7, 3, and 1.

Singapore/China

Roger Ng, pastor of Grace Bible Fellowship and president of Grace Bible Seminary, received his M.Div degree from The Master's Seminary and is currently working on his D.Min degree. Roger has been teaching in China for the past ten years. Roger and his wife have three children aged 21, 19 and 17.

John Zheng, assistant pastor of Grace Bible Fellowship and professor of Grace Bible Seminary, received his M.Div and Th.M degree from The Master's Seminary. Born in China and raised in New York, John has been involved in the teaching ministry in East Asia for the past three years. John and his wife have two children ages 3 and 1.

Andrew Choo, pastor of Zion Chinese Church and professor of Grace Bible Seminary, received his M.Div degree from The Master's Seminary. Andrew has been pastoring various churches in the U.S. and East Asia. Andrew and his wife have two girls ages 9 and 7.

South Africa

Nathan Odede is a 2013 Christ Seminary graduate from Kenya. He is currently pursuing postgraduate theological studies at North-West University in South Africa. Nathan also works for the seminary as a part-time assistant administrator and lecturer.

David Beakley received his M.Div at The Master's Seminary in 2002. He graduated from North-West University of South

Africa (formerly University of Potchefstroom) with a Ph.D in Old Testament Studies. He is currently the Academic Dean of Christ Seminary (a TMAI Training Institute in South Africa) and pastor of Christ Baptist Church in Polokwane, South Africa.

Spain

Ruben Videira received his M.Div and Th.M degrees at The Master's Seminary. He currently serves at the Berea Seminary and Evangelical Church of Leon in Spain. Ruben and his wife Jenn have one child and one on the way.

Ukraine

Mykola Leliovskiy received his MABS from The Master's College and is currently pursuing a Th.M degree from the European Bible Training Center in Berlin, Germany. He currently serves as an adjunct professor of Bible exposition at Irpin Biblical Seminary in Ukraine.

United States – Russian Speaking

Alexey Kolomiytsev received his M.Div and Th.M degrees at The Master's Seminary. Since 2002 he has served as Pastor-Teacher at Word of Grace Bible Church in Battle Ground, WA. Alexey and his wife Tanya are enjoying thirty years of marriage, praising the Lord for the privilege to serve Him.

United States - Spanish Speaking

Josiah Grauman received his M.Div. from The Master's Seminary, where he is currently studying in the D.Min program. After serving for five years as a chaplain at LA County Hospital, he and his wife Crystal were sent out as missionaries to Mexico City. Josiah currently serves as the director of the Instituto de Expositores in Los Angeles and he and Crystal have three children.

About TMAI

The Master's Academy International

TMAI IS A MISSIONS ORGANIZATION THAT STRENGTHENS THE EVANGELICAL CHURCH AROUND THE WORLD BY TRAINING QUALIFIED LEADERS TO PLANT AND SHEPHERD LOCAL CHURCHES.

TMAI is training men in their own countries to be expositors of God's Word, "...who will be able to teach others also" (2 Timothy 2:2). We invite you to partner with us in this strategic movement and maximize your missions investment!

HOW TO PARTNER WITH TMAI	**SIGN UP FOR OUR EMAIL NEWSLETER** Go to www.tmai.org.	**RECEIVE OUR TRAINING CENTER SPOTLIGHT MAILING** Mailed to your mail box every month.

WWW.TMAI.ORG
WWW.FACEBOOK.COM/TMAI.ORG
WWW.TWITTER.COM/TMAI_ORG

Training Church Leaders
Worldwide

01 ALBANIA
02 CALIFORNIA
   Spanish Language
03 CROATIA
04 CZECH REPUBLIC
05 GERMANY/SWITZERLAND
06 HONDURAS
07 INDIA
08 ITALY
09 MALAWI
10 MEXICO
11 NEW ZEALAND
12 PHILIPPINES
13 RUSSIA
14 SPAIN
15 SINGAPORE
16 SOUTH AFRICA
17 UKRAINE
18 WASHINGTON
   Russian Language

The Master's Academy
INTERNATIONAL

PRAY FOR OUR SCHOOLS

Pray for the faculty and students at our TMAI locations.

HOST A WEEKEND TMAI MISSION CONFERENCE

TMAI offers a one-day missions conference covering topics on the theology of missions, academic training and needs in the mission field, including an exclusive mission update with your missions board.

GIVE TO TMAI

Financially support the training of pastors and church leaders.

I stand with my back shoulder leaning on a wall
and with my possession I want to combine together
the same landscape spaces with the one far out
the horizon;
everything seems to be fused of the other
and I think all to an entangled
the small land
and I begin to understand the
compassion for them

time has not changed the measure of the
human souls...

and the accumulated knowledge of humans
is not sensually to erase this
the questions search of each one
in itself

incarnate drives
enthrophic hopes
and not really understanding
what is the total possibility of faults
we have
we are,
eyes,
but have to explain that live is each the only the
age of God can enthropheds make to
to feel compassion...

this is not myth of tears and laughts or ever of all
others expressing their trails threads live as the community of departure